12

Designing Effective Wizards: A Multidisciplinary Approach

Daina Pupons Wickham
Dr. Debra L. Mayhew
Teresa Stoll
Kenneth June Toley III
Shannon Rouiller

ISBN 0-13-092377-X

9 7

90000

D1534452

Prentice Hall PTR, Upper Saddle River, NJ 07458
www.phptr.com

s Cataloging-in-Publication Data

approach / Daina Pupons Wickham ... [et al.].

1. Computer software--Development. I. Wickham, Daina Pupons.

QA76.76.D47 D476 2001
005.1--dc21

2001036525

Production Supervisor: Wil Mara
Acquisitions Editors: Mike Meehan/Mark Taub
Editorial Assistant: Linda Ramagnano
Marketing Manager: Debby van Dijk
Buyer: Maura Zaldivar
Cover Designer: Anthony Gemmellaro
Page Composition: Eileen Clark

© 2002 Prentice Hall PTR
Published by Prentice-Hall, Inc.
Upper Saddle River, NJ 07458

The publisher offers discounts on this book when ordered in bulk quantities. For more information contact: Corporate Sales Department, Prentice Hall PTR, One Lake Street, Upper Saddle River, NJ 07458. Phone: 800-382-3419; FAX: 201-236-7141; E-mail: corpsales@prenhall.com

Printed in the United States of America

10 9 8 7 6 5 4 3 2 1

ISBN 0-13-092377-X

Pearson Education LTD.
Pearson Education Australia PTY, Limited
Pearson Education Singapore, Pte. Ltd
Pearson Education North Asia Ltd
Pearson Education Canada, Ltd.
Pearson Educación de Mexico, S.A. de C.V.
Pearson Education—Japan
Pearson Education Malaysia, Pte. Ltd
Pearson Education, Upper Saddle River, New Jersey

TRADEMARKS

Contents

Welcome!

Many books on user interface design focus on a single aspect of design, such as how to create graphics for an interface or how to evaluate designs. For large software projects, this makes sense because you will most likely have different people assigned to specific design roles and activities. However, for smaller design projects, such as wizards, you are unlikely to have as many people, but you still require all the skills of a multidisciplinary team.

Designing Effective Wizards is a guide to help readers design, evaluate, and construct wizards for software products. It outlines processes and provides guidelines and methods to help experienced and inexperienced designers and developers approach the challenge of building a wizard given the broad range of specialized skills required. Many of the issues and guidelines discussed in this book can be applied to all software design projects.

What's different about this book?

This book takes a multidisciplinary approach to software wizard design. The authors are a multidisciplinary team consisting of human factors specialists, a visual designer, and a technical writer. We have several years of experience developing products and wizards for worldwide audiences, for complex products, and across multiple platforms. Based on our experiences, we have identified the guidelines and methods that we feel are key to effective wizard design. We provide practical examples, lots of graphics, and checklists. We hope that you find our approach useful, comprehensive, and easy to follow.

Is this book for you?

If you are a human factors engineer, visual designer, software developer, or technical writer, or if you want to understand what each field does—yes, this book is for you. If you are about to create a wizard, then this book will be of direct interest to you. However, even if you are not creating a wizard in the near future, wizard design is a good case study for other types of software projects.

We think this book will be useful if you are a:

- Human factors specialist
- Visual designer
- Software developer
- Manager
- Student
- Software tester, usability evaluator
- Training specialist
- Technical writer
- Project manager

How to use this book

This book consists of three main sections. The first section describes the general process for designing wizards—forming a team, estimating your available resources, gathering requirements, and designing and evaluating your wizards. The second section provides guidelines and issues for specific aspects of wizards—general design, navigation, visual design, error prevention, on-line help, multiple platforms, and so on. The third section provides a case study to show you how to apply the guidelines to design a fictional wizard. You can read the book from beginning to end or simply hone in on the chapters of interest, such as the chapter on visual design.

As you read this book, consider your role on the design team. Target the focus of your reading to the chapters that apply to your tasks first, then to the team as a whole. Each chapter contains a topic introduction, a section explaining why the topic is important, a section that lists the questions to answer before you begin, the main sections related to the chapter topic, and a summary of guidelines discussed in the chapter. Table x–1 lists the major topics of this book and their corresponding chapters.

Table x–1   Major topics of the book with corresponding chapters

Process for designing wizards	
How to build your team, evaluate whether you should create a wizard, and plan your project	Chapter 1, "Kicking off the project"
How to gather user and task requirements	Chapter 2, "Gathering requirements"
How to use the iterative design process to design an effective wizard	Chapter 3, "Applying the iterative design process"
How to conduct usability evaluations of your wizard	Chapter 4, "Evaluating wizard designs"
Guidelines and issues for specific aspects of wizards	
Guidelines and issues for design, including general layout, page areas, controls, visual design, navigation, and linking wizards	Chapter 5, "General wizard design"
	Chapter 6, "Navigation"
	Chapter 7, "Visual design"
	Chapter 8, "Launchpads and linking wizards"
Guidelines and issues for interacting with users via wizard feedback and messages, error prevention, and on-line help	Chapter 9, "Interactive feedback"
	Chapter 10, "Error prevention and recovery"
	Chapter 11, "On-line help"
Guidelines and issues to accommodate specific users, including expert and novice users, users with special needs, worldwide audiences, and users on various platforms	Chapter 12, "Experts and novices"
	Chapter 13, "Accessibility"
	Chapter 14, "Worldwide audiences"
	Chapter 15, "Multiple platforms"
Case study	
Fictional wizard designed using guidelines in this book	Chapter 16, "Case study: Installation wizard"

The appendixes provide sample documents that you can use to simplify the process of gathering requirements and conducting usability evaluations of your wizard:

- Worksheet of questions for gathering requirements
- Usability design checklist
- Sample materials for usability testing, such as a participant screener and a post-evaluation questionnaire

The interactive CD-ROM contains samples to help you explore concepts of color, layout,typography, navigation, and launchpads for wizards. It also contains the screens from the case study wizard.

The authors and editor

Daina Pupons Wickham has a Masters degree in Industrial Engineering with an emphasis on Human Factors. She is a Human Factors Specialist at IBM's Silicon Valley Lab in San Jose, CA. Daina has spent over 1000 hours conducting usability tests for products ranging from games to educational software to banking Web sites to databases. She has taught classes for graduate and undergraduate students. Daina has authored and co-authored papers presented at various professional conferences, including the Human Factors and Ergonomics Society, and ACM's Special Interest Group on Computer Human Interaction. In addition, Daina has several patents filed for her launchpad and wizard designs.

Dr. Debra L. Mayhew has a Ph.D. in Ergonomics from North Carolina State University. She is a Human Factors Specialist at IBM's Silicon Valley Laboratory in San Jose, CA and has designed, coded, and tested wizards for five years and general software products for 19 years. Over the years, Debra has administered usability tests to hundreds of users. Debra has several patents filed for launchpad and wizard designs. She has authored papers on gathering user definitions and task requirements, usability design processes, and speech recognition systems. Recently, Debra led a multidisciplinary team to create a set of consistency guidelines for wizards used across IBM data management products.

Teresa Stoll is an Interface Visual Designer at IBM's Silicon Valley Laboratory in San Jose, CA. She is a member of IBM's Visual Design Board of Directors, and oversees the visual design of IBM's award-winning DB2 workstation database product. Teresa holds a Bachelors degree in Graphics Communication from Universidad Autonoma Metropolitana-Atzcapotzalco. She has five years of experience in interface visual design, and has a colorful resume, which includes seven years in the film industry and eight years in corporate identity and editorial design and multimedia. Teresa has co-authored papers and filed patents on launchpad designs.

Kenneth June Toley III has a Bachelor of Science degree in Technical Writing from Carnegie Mellon University. Ken is a Technical Writer at IBM's Silicon Valley Laboratory in San Jose, CA. He has designed and tested on-line help systems and Web pages, and assisted in wizard and dialog interface design for various products, ranging from databases to distance learning software. In addition, Ken has designed and coded multimedia tools.

Shannon Rouiller has a Bachelor of Science degree in Mathematics from California Polytechnic State University, San Luis Obispo. Shannon has over 14 years of experience writing and editing technical information, including books, on-line help, wizards, and product interfaces for worldwide products. Shannon is a Technical Editor at IBM's Silicon Valley Laboratory, where she also worked on the team to create wizard guidelines for IBM data management products. Shannon has published articles on on-line help and is a co-author of the award-winning *Developing Quality Technical Information*, Prentice Hall, 1998.

Acknowledgments

Writing a book is not an easy task, and we would like to thank the many people who contributed along the way. Without their help, this book could not have been completed.

We are forever grateful to Kristi Ramey for the many hours she spent creating a detailed and thorough index and for building our book. We could not have completed the book without her!

We thank Deborah Slayton for taking the time to create some of the graphics for our book and for reviewing several chapters. She is a lifesaver!

Many thanks to Dr. Lee Anne Kowalski for coming up with the original idea for this book and for providing several examples; Gary Faircloth for setting up our software tools and for his contributions early in the planning phases; Leonid Korostelev for the examples of globalized graphics; Dr. Thomas Sharp for the multiplatform graphics; and Gord Davison and Kevin McBride for their mockups of several wizard designs and wizard prototypes.

Reviewers were an essential part of developing this book, giving us many useful and insightful comments on our drafts. Our special thanks to Donald Cox, Naomi Friedlander, Fred Hornbruch, Leila Johannesen, Susan E. Kahler, Dr. Lee Anne Kowalski, Jasna Krmpotic, Moira McFadden Lanyi, Dr. Lynn Percival, Eric Radzinski, Ayanna Sawyer, and Deborah Slayton.

We are grateful to the following people for their help with last-minute checking: Barbara Isa, Moira McFadden Lanyi, Stacy Newman, Kathleen Nojima, Carl Petty, and Eric Radzinski.

Along with the writing, editing, and reviewing of the book, there were many business tasks. We thank Barbara Isa for being our "Write-Now" representative, helping us through the legal process, being our liaison to Prentice Hall, helping us with planning and scheduling, and providing food at late-night work sessions. We also extend our thanks to members of IBM Silicon Valley Lab's IP Law team: Susan Dahm and Richard Alvarez for negotiating the legal contract between IBM and Prentice Hall for us, Ingrid Foerster for reviewing the book from a legal standpoint, and Jean Talbot for putting together the confidentiality agreements for our non-IBM reviewers.

For their encouragement and support of our efforts, and for their review of the book, we would like to thank our management team at IBM, Silicon Valley Laboratory: Lori Fisher, Bob Jones, Eileen Kopp, Norma Fries, and Frank Eldredge.

Finally, we thank Mike Meehan at Prentice Hall Professional Technical Reference for his guidance in preparing, writing, and selling the book. We also thank Lisa Iarkowski and Wil Mara at Prentice Hall for helping us with our templates and formatting questions.

Lastly, we thank our families, friends, and pets for their understanding when we worked evenings, weekends, and vacations on this project.

If we missed or slighted someone in these acknowledgments, we did not mean to.

Daina Pupons Wickham

Debra L. Mayhew

Shannon Rouiller

Teresa Stoll

Kenneth June Toley III

Chapter 1

Kicking off the project

▲ Why plan your project?
▲ Is a wizard appropriate for the task?
▲ Team skills
▲ Resources and planning
▲ Summary

D esigning and building an effective wizard involves many different tasks and skills, which are explained in detail in this book. Before you begin work on your wizard, you need to make sure that your idea will work well as a wizard, and then you need to build a team of people with the skills needed for the various aspects of wizard design. You also need to schedule the various activities involved. Good wizard designs begin with strong development teams and effective project management.

This chapter provides you with a guide to the essential factors of a wizard development project to help ensure that your project stays exciting and concludes successfully.

Why plan your project?

A common mistake many teams make when beginning a new and exciting project is to underestimate the skills and resources required to complete the project. For example, a wizard may seem easier to program than a dialog with a similar function because the wizard has fewer choices per page. However, wizards are quite difficult to program because the code must keep track of what path the user takes and update the content of future pages.

The process of project planning identifies tasks that must be completed, completion dates for each task, and who is responsible for each task. The benefits of project planning include:

- **You can allow for tasks to be done simultaneously or in the appropriate order.** Project planning identifies tasks that team members must complete. Task dependencies are identified and tasks can be arranged accordingly.

- **You can ensure that necessary resources are available.** Project planning identifies completion dates for each task and requires you to assign team members and equipment to each task. Project planning also shows the impact to a project if a person is removed from the team or if equipment is not available.

- **You can assess progress and risks to keep the project on schedule.** Project planning identifies checkpoints to assess whether the project is proceeding on schedule. If your team is running late, you can identify areas where time needs to be "made up."

- **You can estimate costs for future projects.** If you create a project plan and track its success, you can use this data to estimate the time and cost of future projects more accurately.

Is a wizard appropriate for the task?

Wizards were originally developed to help novice users through a task. In recent years, wizards have been utilized in a wider range of situations and for a more diverse target audience. During our internal usability sessions, expert users stated that they often like to use wizards. However, because wizards require a significant amount of resources to design, test, and implement, you must identify whether a task is a good candidate for a wizard. Table 1–1 includes a series of questions to help you determine the appropriateness of a wizard as an aid to helping users complete a task.

Table 1–1   Questions to ask to determine if a task is a good candidate for a wizard

Characteristics	Related questions	Reason for asking
Task frequency	How frequently do users complete the task? Do the users complete the task only a single time, daily, weekly, or other?	Rarely completed tasks are good candidates for wizards because users will probably not gain expertise in them.
Task importance	How important is the task? Do the users consider the task critical? Is it optional?	Both optional and critical tasks can be good candidates for wizards. In general, it is more useful to support critical tasks well.
Task difficulty	Do users feel that the task is difficult or easy? If the task is difficult, can it be made significantly easier in a wizard? Are other interventions, such as a product re-architecture or tutorial, needed?	If the task is too easy, it may not warrant the resources needed to create a wizard. Alternatively, the task may be too difficult to be improved by a wizard. Other interventions may be needed.

Chapter 2, "Gathering requirements," describes task analyses, which are methods to help you collect this information from your target audience. However, your team should have some idea of the answers to these questions before you begin your project.

Team skills

Once you determine that it makes sense to create a wizard, you need to put together a team to design and implement the wizard. Various disciplines come together to produce a successful software design and deploy that software to the user.

To build an effective wizard, your team needs the following members or members with the following skills:

- **Human factors engineer.** The human factors engineer helps define the operation of the wizard and how the user will interact with it. The human factors engineer is involved with the design of the user interface, audience analysis, audience definition, user testing, and assessment of the wizard's usability. The human factors engineer can also participate in the wizard's visual design, documentation, packaging, and measuring the performance of the code.

- **Programmer.** The role of the programmer on your team is to develop and test the code that will make your wizard function in the intended user environments. The programmer must build the interface of your wizard, write the code that handles user interaction, and handle any software architecture issues. The programmer is responsible for providing adequate feedback mechanisms to the user when errors occur, developing solutions to platform portability problems, and ensuring accessibility.

- **Project manager.** The project manager is responsible for acquiring, assessing, and managing the use of project resources. The project manager defines the phases of the product life cycle, determines the start and completion dates for each piece of the project, and writes the plan of execution for the project. During the life of the project, the project manager adjusts the plan of execution to ensure that the primary deliverables of the project are completed by the deadlines.

- **Technical writer.** The technical writer is responsible for all of the text that the user will read from the interface of the wizard. This includes on-page instructions and explanations, error messages, and summary information. If your wizard requires any additional documentation such as help, installation instructions, books, and so on, the technical writer is responsible for producing those documents and designing their structure and basic layout. The technical writer, perhaps in conjunction with a technical editor, implements text style and writing guidelines and maintains the consistency of the language throughout the wizard content. The technical writer is often also involved with translation planning or coordination.

- **Visual designer.** The visual designer is responsible for defining the visual look and feel of the wizard. The visual designer is involved with the design of the user interface and ensures visual consistency on each page of the wizard. The visual designer develops the graphics required for the wizard, and incorporates visual design guidelines and corporate branding for the wizard and any materials the wizard is packaged with, including documentation.

Although it is not critical that you have one or more individuals fulfilling each of these roles in any official or exclusive capacity, it is critical that the basic range of skills defined by each of these roles is represented on your team.

Resources and planning

You need to know up-front if the wizard your team designs can actually be constructed and tested with the resources your team has available. A major part of project management is acquiring, assessing, and managing resources.

Resources include the number of team members and their skill levels, funding for project development, tools or equipment, and the time available for project completion. Resource management is the most critical factor in the success of the project.

Before any work begins, the project manager should develop a flexible plan of execution that clearly identifies key phases of the project development and factors that affect the success of the project. The project manager must determine which pieces of the project have dependencies on one another, and therefore, when each piece must be started and completed during the various parts of the project cycle. Table 1–2 illustrates a sample project plan that you can use to fill in the start dates and end dates for your wizard project. Be aware that several of your tasks will have overlapping dates.

Table 1–2   Sample project plan

Task	Person responsible	Start date	End date
Specify wizard scope			
Create high-level design			
Usability test high-level design			
Create specification documents for wizard high-level design			
Review high-level design specification documents			
Create low-level design			
Create high-level design of on-line help			

Table 1–2   Sample project plan (continued)

Task	Person responsible	Start date	End date
Usability test low-level design			
Create interactive design			
Usability test interactive prototype			
Create low-level design of on-line help			
Create specification documents for wizard low-level design and on-line help			
Review specification documents for wizard low-level design and on-line help			
Usability test help content			
Complete wizard code			
Test wizard for bugs in code			
Usability test working wizard code			
Write and implement on-line help			
Translate wizard text and on-line help text			
Test wizard and on-line help translations for usability and accuracy			
Test wizard and on-line help for accessibility			
Release wizard beta code			
Wizard is completed!			

Table 1–3 provides a set of questions whose answers will help the project manager to build the team and develop the schedule for the project.

Table 1–3   Questions to develop the project plan

Characteristics	Related questions	Reason for asking
Schedule or delivery dates	When is your final wizard due? What are the dates for each phase of the wizard design, implementation, and testing?	You can take this information and work backwards to identify start and end dates for all of your milestones.
Budget for the team, user testing, and system testing	How much money is available to pay the wizard team? How much money can be devoted to usability testing?	A large budget will allow you to hire more skilled personnel or a large staff to distribute work to. Usability testing can be very expensive because it can involve not only monetary compensation to the subjects, but travel costs, time, and money to obtain or deploy testing tools, and time or other resources to build testing scenarios that fit the user audience.
Number of people on the wizard team	How many people do you have on your team?	In general, a large team will be able to do more in a limited amount of time than a small team. However, larger teams require the use of more sophisticated project management techniques, and it is easier to waste resources with larger teams that are not well-managed.
Team member availability	How much effort can each team member spend on the wizard? What priority will each team member place on his or her responsibilities to the wizard's construction? Do any team members need to split their time between multiple projects, and are those projects related to the wizard?	Project managers must account for scheduling difficulties with team members who have to juggle several projects. Some "padding" or extra completion time for deliverables may need to be added or exchanged at various checkpoints in the product cycle.

Table 1–3   Questions to develop the project plan (continued)

Characteristics	Related questions	Reason for asking
Skill of the wizard team	What skills do the members of the team have? Does your team have experience with programming, testing, writing, visual design, usability, software design, translation, and so on? What level of experience do they have? Might there be an imbalance of required skills on the team; for example, lots of design and usability testing skills but little or no programming skill?	You may need to hire experts to work on the team. You may want to consider sending some team members to classes or buying educational literature or software to build up the team's skill levels for the needs of the project.
Access to equipment	Does your team have access to the hardware you need to conduct cross-platform testing? Are there any limitations to their access?	You must test your wizard design on all platforms and configurations that you support. Problems detected on foreign platforms during testing are best corrected when team members can troubleshoot and develop solutions on the platforms on which the problems are found.

After work on the project begins and estimates drift to solid figures, the project manager may need to move completion dates, adjust funding focus, or even adjust the responsibilities of individual team members to meet project deadlines. Careful planning before your team begins working and steady monitoring of progress will facilitate the success of your project and avoid expensive mistakes later in the project cycle.

Summary

Good wizard designs are the result of strong development teams and thorough project management. To build an effective wizard, you must first determine if the task is a good candidate for a wizard. If yes, build a multidisciplinary team with the following roles represented: human factors engineer, programmer, project manager, technical writer, and visual designer. Ideally, skills will overlap among the team members and your team will be able to build your wizard as designed with the available resources.

Resource assessment and planning are essential to your project's success. Before any work begins, the project manager should develop a flexible plan of execution that clearly identifies key phases of the project development and factors that can affect the success of the project.

Gathering requirements

- ▲ Why gather requirements?
- ▲ Wizard design requirements
- ▲ User definition—Who will be using your wizard?
- ▲ Product definition—What will the wizard do?
- ▲ Task analysis—What will the user be using the wizard for?
- ▲ Work environment—Where, when, and how will the users be using the wizard?
- ▲ Competitive evaluation—Who else is creating a similar product or wizard?
- ▲ Summary

B efore you begin designing wizard pages, you need to understand exactly what you are going to be designing. Although this step may seem obvious, too many designers begin by sketching or prototyping designs for their wizard pages. Unfortunately, an unclear scope will result in a lot of time, money, and effort spent in rework.

As software development cycles become shorter, you may be tempted to begin designing immediately. You may feel as though there is not enough time to gather requirements. However, the more time you spend in the requirements phase of the process, the more solid your design will be. A solid design requires fewer changes later in the development cycle.

This chapter will help you to identify your wizard design requirements in several categories: users, product, tasks, work environment, and competition. This chapter provides a series of questions to help the entire team understand the scope of the design. The questions are grouped under different categories to help the design team think about the issues. You do not need to complete a separate set of activities to collect information for each category of wizard design requirements. In fact, answers to many of the questions in each section will impact others and can be collected in the same series of user activities. This chapter also introduces techniques that you can use to gain the answers to the questions. The technique descriptions in this chapter are meant to help you think about how to collect the information you need. More information on each of these techniques can be found in other books if needed.

Why gather requirements?

Gathering requirements is a key step in the wizard development process because it provides you with valuable information that all team members can use to better understand the wizard design goals and restrictions. Benefits of gathering requirements include:

- **Gathering requirements helps to reduce development costs.** The earlier a problem is discovered in the design cycle, the cheaper it is to fix. The later a problem is discovered, the more it costs to change the software code, rewrite the on-line help, and change the manuals. Gathering requirements at the start of a design cycle helps you to catch problems early in the cycle.

- **Gathering requirements helps to ensure that all shareholders agree on the scope of the design.** You should identify and record as many assumptions as possible to prevent potential misunderstandings. All shareholders—team members, clients, and managers—should agree on the design goals.

- **Gathering requirements helps to define the design constraints**. You need to recognize design constraints early in the cycle to guarantee that the final design can be implemented.

Wizard design requirements

Your wizard design requirements fall into these five categories: users, product, tasks, work environment, and competition. Each of these categories functions as a source of information that you can use to set the scope and function of your wizard. Additionally, categories may overlap. Questions and techniques that are valid for one category may also be valid for others. Figure 2–1 shows the relationship among the different categories of wizard design requirements. The users are in the center. They have certain expectations of the wizard based on their experiences with the tasks they perform, the work environment in which they perform these tasks, their understand-

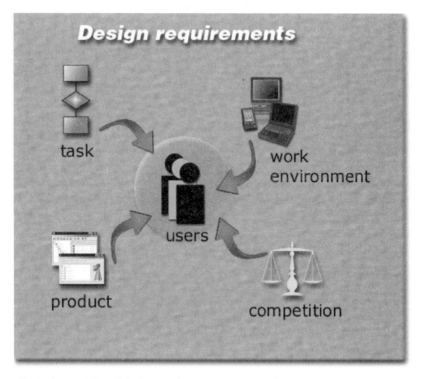

Figure 2–1   *Wizard design requirements span several categories: users, product, task, work environment, and competition.*

ing of the role of the wizard, the software tools they use to perform the tasks, and the offerings that exist on the market. You must manage these expectations to ensure that you have a wizard design that is useful and easy to use.

User definition—Who will be using your wizard?

The user definition helps you to understand exactly who the target audience is. A design cannot truly be for "everyone;" it must be optimized for a set of users. For example, wording on a Web site designed for children will be quite different than that used on a site designed for scientists.

A user definition helps you to specify a detailed set of characteristics that describe your target audience, those for whom you will optimize your design. The user definition is the basis for design decisions and tradeoffs. A user definition should contain information about the target audience's:

- Inherent characteristics
- Experience and education
- Social and cultural characteristics

This section discusses each of these aspects in more detail and describes a technique you can use to collect the information you need to define your target audience.

Inherent characteristics

Your target audience has several inherent characteristics that may impact the wizard you ultimately design. Inherent characteristics are aspects about your user that the user cannot change—for example, age and gender. Table 2–1 lists questions that are related to these characteristics.

Table 2–1   Questions to ask about your target audience's inherent characteristics

Characteristics	Related questions	Reason for asking
Age range	Will the product be used by children, adults, or both? Are elderly adults a target audience?	The age range will impact the graphic style and vocabulary used. Furthermore, if elderly adults are a target audience, special consideration must be given to issues such as font size.

Table 2–1   Questions to ask about your target audience's inherent characteristics (continued)

Characteristics	Related questions	Reason for asking
Gender	Will the product be used by women, men, or both? What proportion of the target audience are women?	As with age range, gender may impact graphic style and vocabulary.
Special needs/ disabilities	Does the target audience include users with mental, visual, auditory, or other physical or cognitive disabilities?	If yes, you must ensure that the design is usable by users with these needs. Accessibility is covered in detail in Chapter 13, "Accessibility."

Experience and education

A second aspect or dimension of your target audience is their experience and education. Users differ in their level of understanding of the task domain, computers, and so on. Your assumptions of the target audience's experience and education will dictate the appropriate tone, vocabulary, and other aspects of your wizard. However, unlike inherent characteristics, your target audience can actively change its experience and education. Table 2–2 lists several questions that can help you to quantify your target audience's education and experience.

Table 2–2   Questions to ask about your target audience's experience and education

Characteristics	Related questions	Reason for asking
Educational level	Has the target audience completed college, high school, a specific professional degree? What is its reading level?	Different tone, metaphors, and vocabulary are appropriate for different levels of education.
Job title and job description	What are your target audience's job titles? What are their job descriptions?	Job titles and descriptions may help you to understand how your target audience thinks about the tasks that you are supporting. For example, a database administrator in charge of strategic direction will probably be looking for very different information than a database administrator in charge of day-to-day operations.

Table 2–2   *Questions to ask about your target audience's experience and education (continued)*

Characteristics	Related questions	Reason for asking
Experience with computers	How much experience does your audience have with computers in general?	Many "intuitive" features of computers and software are actually learned. For example, you can probably safely assume that users with a lot of computer experience have learned that a right mouse click on an object will reveal a pop-up menu of action choices. Other potentially "hidden" software features include mnemonics and the existence of shortcut keys for menu actions.
Experience with the Internet	How much experience does your audience have with the Internet in general? What browsers do they use? What types of Internet applications or Web sites are they familiar with?	As with all software, Web sites usually behave in a specific way. Experienced users of the Internet have learned the common mechanisms to successfully use the Web. For example, Web users learn that underlined phrases provide links to other pages. Users also learn how **Back** and **Next** buttons work in Web sites that have frames versus those that don't have frames.
Experience with the tasks that your wizard will support	How well does the target audience understand the task domain that is supported by your wizard?	Experts in the domain will expect different vocabulary than novices. Furthermore, experts will expect a different level and type of help than novices. Experts will require help that allows them to map their knowledge to the software, but novices may need conceptual help about the domain.
Experience with previous releases of your product	How familiar is your target audience with previous releases of your product?	Users learn how to do tasks and actions in the context of particular software. For example, they learn that certain menu choices contain the actions they commonly perform or learn the order of inputs in a wizard. Changing these features can be a source of frustration for existing users.

Table 2–2   Questions to ask about your target audience's experience and education (continued)

Characteristics	Related questions	Reason for asking
Experience with other software that supports the task	Does your target audience have experience with products created by your competitors? How much experience? Is there a particular product that most of your target audience is familiar with?	Each software product enforces a particular way of thinking about the domain that it supports. If your target audience has experience with another product, you may want your wizard to help the user map actions or concepts from the previous product to yours.
Experience with other software products	Does your target audience have experience with specific software products such as Lotus Notes or Microsoft Word?	If you know that your audience uses certain products regularly, you may choose controls or icons that are used in these products to decrease the learning needed for your wizard. For example, Lotus Notes uses "twisty" controls that expand to show content or lists. If your target audience is experienced with Lotus Notes, you could use this control within your wizard without fearing that users may not understand how to use it.
Experience with specific operating systems	Does your target audience use Macintosh, UNIX, Microsoft Windows, or another operating system?	Users of different operating systems expect software to behave in different ways. You need to know user expectations so that you can match them in your wizard design.

Social and cultural characteristics

The final characteristics that you should identify in your user definition are the social and cultural characteristics of your target audience. Social and cultural characteristics might impact your final wizard design, especially in terms of its look and feel. Cultural background impacts what users consider appropriate, how they interpret different symbols and colors, and what they find appealing. For example, in general, Japanese users prefer a more minimalist look and feel while U.S. audiences prefer graphics that are more lifelike, similar to the detail and quality of a photograph. These topics are covered in greater detail in Chapter 14, "Worldwide audiences." Table 2–3 lists several questions that can help you gather information about your target audience's social and cultural characteristics.

Table 2–3   Questions to ask about your target audience's social and cultural characteristics

Characteristics	Related questions	Reason for asking
Ethnicity	What ethnic groups does your target audience belong to?	The most obvious impact of an ethnic group to a wizard design is in the wizard graphics. The wizard graphics should be designed to represent your target audience, especially if the graphics contain any images of people. For example, the audience illustrated in a wizard to help African American business owners sign up for a newsgroup should not contain pictures of only Anglo-Saxon people.
Languages spoken	Does your target audience speak English? What language is their primary language? Do they speak multiple languages?	If your users speak a variety of languages, you will need to design your wizard to support these languages. See Chapter 14, "Worldwide audiences," for hints on supporting multiple languages.
Geographic location (United States, New York State, Italy, and so on)	Are most of your users from the United States? What countries or regions are they from?	Users from different cultures or regions may have different expectations and ascribe different meanings to colors, metaphors, words, and so on. See Chapter 14, "Worldwide audiences," for information on supporting people from different cultures.

A technique for creating user definitions—User surveys

One technique for gathering target audience characteristics to create a user definition is a user survey. Use marketing research as the basis for defining the target audience, and supplement this information with user surveys or questionnaires. For example, your marketing department might have determined what geographical areas will be targeted, but might not have determined the range of experience with computers and specific platforms. A few tips to help you get started are:

- Begin your survey by telling respondents how the data from the survey will be used and when the results must be returned (if appropriate). Be sure to let them know that their responses will be confidential. A one- or two-sentence description should be enough.

- Keep all answers confidential. Never associate a particular respondent with his or her specific answers, simply report averages. Do not sell your data to others.

- Keep your survey short and to the point. Ask only questions that you care about and only questions whose answers will impact your design.

- Make each question easy for the user to answer and easy for you to analyze. Multiple-choice questions are often preferable to open-ended questions. For example, suppose that you want to know how long respondents have been at their current job. If you do not provide any choices, respondents may provide answers such as 8 months, 2 weeks, 3.2 years, and so on. This data will take longer to analyze because you will need to convert all data to the same unit. In addition, you may not care about this level of granularity. You may simply want to know how many people have less than one year of experience, between one and five years of experience, and more than five years of experience. For this situation, it is best to provide the three categories of answers directly on the survey.

- Allow users to select more than one choice in cases where a single answer may not apply. For example, suppose that you want to ask users about their geographic location. You might think that this question can have only one answer per respondent; however, some respondents may live in one geographic location for part of the year and another for the remainder of the year.

- If you are not able to predict all possible answers, leave a space for an open-ended choice called "Other (please describe)." For example, you may know the majority of job titles for the members of your target audience. However, it is unlikely that you can predict all of them, so you should leave an open-ended choice for the respondents whose specific job titles are not listed.

- If possible, use an objective (numerical) measure rather than a subjective (feelings-based) one. For example, suppose that you care about the expertise of your target audience. If you ask respondents to rate their expertise, the results may be meaningless. Respondents may lie or they may have no idea how they compare to others. A better approach would be to find specific tasks that indicate expertise and ask users if or how often they do these tasks.

- Do not ask questions that the respondent might consider insulting or personal.

- Thank respondents for their time and participation. Always include a simple thank you at the end of your survey.

- Be aware that in general, surveys have a very low response rate. If you send out surveys, expect about 10% of them to be returned.

Because background interviews and surveys are not very time-consuming, you might find it useful and effective to combine gathering target audience descriptions with gathering other requirements. For example, you might ask participants in your task analysis, a technique discussed later in this chapter, to fill out the background questionnaire. For more information on questionnaires and surveys, see Chapter 4, "Evaluating wizard designs," *Real World Research: A resource for social scientists and practitioner researchers* by Colin Robson, *Survey Research Methods* by Earl Babbie, and *Questionnaire Design, Interviewing, and Attitude Measurement* by Abraham Oppenheim.

Product definition—What will the wizard do?

The product definition defines the scope and purpose of the product that will be built. It describes what role the wizard will play in the overall product offering. Because you cannot create a wizard that does *everything*, the product definition helps you to specify what exactly the wizard will do. The product definition should contain information about:

- The purpose and scope of the wizard
- The tools used to create the final wizard

This section discusses these product facets in more detail and describes a technique you can use to gather product requirements.

Purpose and scope of the wizard

The main goal of the product definition is to clarify the purpose and scope of your wizard. The purpose and scope are determined by identifying:

- The roles that your wizard will play with respect to other products and wizards
- How the wizard will be marketed
- What the user will need to know before using the wizard

Table 2–4 lists several questions that can help you to start formalizing the purpose and scope of your wizard. Most of these questions will be addressed up-front by the design team. However, the design team's assumptions should be validated by user feedback.

Table 2–4   Questions to ask about the purpose and scope of your wizard

Characteristics	Related questions	Reason for asking
Application purpose	What is the application used for? How does the application work?	You need to understand what the purpose, scope, and behavior of your application is before you can clearly define the role of any wizards that belong in it.

Table 2–4   Questions to ask about the purpose and scope of your wizard (continued)

Characteristics	Related questions	Reason for asking
Wizard's role	What is the role of the wizard? Is the wizard the entire application, or is it simply part of an application? Are there other ways for users to complete the tasks supported by the wizard?	This information helps you to determine design tradeoffs for functional complexity of the wizard. If alternatives to the wizard are present in the product, then you might be able to simplify the wizard function to make it easier to use. However, if the wizard is the entire product, it will need to contain full functionality.
Software version	Is the wizard a new product or is it a new version of an existing wizard or product?	If the wizard is part of an existing product, then the wizard design should be consistent with the current product in terms of look and feel, interface controls used, and guidelines followed. If the wizard is an updated version of a previous wizard, it should be consistent with the previous wizard. If the wizard is the entire product and it is new, then you have a lot of flexibility in terms of look and feel, controls used, and guidelines followed.
Integration with other products	Will the wizard integrate with other products or wizards? For example, if your wizard is an airline reservation wizard, will it integrate with a hotel reservation or car rental wizard?	If the wizard is integrating with other products, then the wizard design should be consistent with those products in terms of look and feel, interface controls used, and guidelines followed.
Tone	What is the tone that you want your wizard to demonstrate or communicate?	The answer to this question impacts the font, colors, layout, terminology, and so on used in your wizard design. A software wizard that is designed for a bank will most likely be more formal and professional than one designed to help children create on-line postcards.
Measures of success	How will you measure the success of your wizard design? Time to complete the task? Percentage of tasks completed without errors? User ratings of product look and feel?	The measures need to be decided before the design process begins. Use these measures to evaluate your design throughout its iterations.

Table 2–4   Questions to ask about the purpose and scope of your wizard (continued)

Characteristics	Related questions	Reason for asking
User tasks supported by the application	What tasks does the user use the application for?	You need to understand the tasks supported by your product. You might need to perform a task analysis to ensure that the way users think about the scope of your application and the tasks it supports match your assumptions. If not, your wizard will not be very useful.
Prerequisite knowledge	What will the user need to know to use the wizard? What prerequisite knowledge does the target audience need in terms of computers, the task domain, and your software product? Can your wizard provide that information? If so, how?	This information helps you to develop the on-line help and supporting documentation for your wizard.
Translation plans	Will the wizard and help be translated into multiple languages?	This choice should be made early in the design process based on the characteristics of the target audience. It is easier to design for multiple languages if you plan ahead so that you don't need to retrofit code and visual design later.
Software prerequisites	Will the user need to own other software products to be able to use your wizard? For example, if the wizard is on the Web, will a certain level browser be required?	This information helps you to determine the scope of your wizard design, if any products need to be packaged with your wizard, and what you need to test to ensure your wizard is compatible. It also helps you to make assumptions about your users' skills.

Technology and tools used to create the final wizard

A second aspect of your product definition involves the more technical aspects of your wizard. The technology that underlies your wizard and the tools that will be used to create it can have a big impact on your wizard's design. Table 2–5 lists several questions to help you start thinking about the design constraints created by the tools that you use.

Table 2–5   Questions to ask about the technology and tools used to create your wizard

Characteristics	Related questions	Reason for asking
Structural and architectural issues	What structural or architectural issues may impact the wizard design?	You need to understand how your product works to be able to design a wizard on top of it. You need to understand in what order the product expects information as well as any architectural issues that may prevent certain checks or actions to be done.
Supported operating systems	Will your product run on Windows NT, UNIX, Linux, or something else?	Each operating system will have a different set of interface controls, colors, look-and-feel guidelines, and so on. See Chapter 15, "Multiple platforms," for more information.
Coding language	What language will it be coded in?	The language that you use to code your wizard may impact your final design. Each language has its own strengths and weaknesses. For example, Java results in a final product that is sharable across different platforms. However, Java's portability is partially a result of using the lowest common denominator of user interface controls—only those controls that are available on all platforms are supported. You may need to write the Java code yourself if you want to use common Windows NT controls. Java may also be slower than other languages.

A technique for gathering product requirements—Focus groups

As with your target audience definition, use marketing research to form the basis of your product definition. Another source of information that is particularly relevant in the context of wizard design is usability feedback. Usability tests may have uncovered the need to provide additional task support, such as wizards, in the application. In some cases, however, you may need to supplement the usability tests and market research data to understand the scope of your product definition.

One technique that you can use to flesh out your product definition is the focus group. You can use a focus group to validate your assumptions about the target audience and to collect feedback on your proposed product definition. For example, your team may have decided that your wizard needs to

23

run only on the Windows NT operating system. Participants in your focus group may tell you that this is not acceptable because most of them have plans to migrate to Linux. Another example may be that you defined your wizard task too narrowly. You might be designing a wizard to help users create presentation slides. A focus group might suggest a feature that was not in your original wizard design, such as allowing users to share their presentation formats.

The most basic focus group consists of a moderator who manages the discussion, several participants, and several open-ended discussion questions. Basically, you invite a group of participants to discuss key issues. Part of the advantage of the focus group technique is that it is a group technique. Members of the group may piggyback off of each other's ideas and may discuss tradeoffs that would not arise if the participants were interviewed separately. Use these tips when you run a focus group:

- If you expect participants to be using specialized vocabulary and acronyms, choose a moderator that understands your product domain.

- Limit the size of your group. More than 10 people are often difficult to moderate, and you may miss important comments.

- Ensure that everyone participates. You want to make sure that all good ideas are heard and not simply the ideas of one dominating person.

- Record the session. Either videotape the session or have someone transcribe participants' comments.

- Use open-ended questions that invite brainstorming and discussion. For example, ask participants what their ideal product would consist of. Then later, ask them to rate or prioritize their top requirements.

- Consider giving all participants a few moments to jot down their individual answers to your questions before you begin the group discussion. This technique helps to ensure that everyone will have something to say once the conversation starts.

- Summarize at the end of the session. Make sure that you correctly interpreted the group's input and consensus, if any. Ideally, your session results will contain data about functional priorities.

- As with questionnaires, inform participants of the goals of the session before beginning and thank them for their participation at the end. Do not sell their data to others.

For more information on focus groups, see *Focus Groups: A Practical Guide for Applied Research* by Richard A. Krueger and Mary Anne Casey.

Task analysis—What will the user be using the wizard for?

Once you understand who your users are and have a preliminary idea of the scope of your wizard, you should complete a task analysis to understand the tasks that users are completing. As mentioned in Chapter 1, "Kicking off the project," you should have data about each task's frequency, importance, and difficulty. If you did not collect this data earlier, collect it during the task analysis. A task analysis is basically a description of how your target audience completes the task that your wizard will support.

Use a task analysis as the basis for your wizard design as well as for activities such as predicting errors that users may make. A task analysis can uncover mistaken assumptions in your product or wizard scope and help you adjust the scope early in the design cycle. The task analysis can also uncover where users may have problems that a wizard can help them overcome. A task analysis should provide information about:

- The underlying structure of the task
- The aspects of the task that can be simplified

The following sections discuss each of these topics in more detail and describe a technique to collect information about the tasks that your wizard will support.

Underlying structure of the task

To create an effective wizard design, you must understand both how the software supports the task and how the user thinks about the task. The task analysis helps you to define how your target audience thinks about the task. Your users may think of the actual task as larger than, as smaller than, or as the same as the task supported by your wizard. Table 2–6 lists several questions to help you think about the task from the user's point of view. These questions help you to identify the "building blocks" of the tasks that users complete.

Table 2–6   Questions to ask about the underlying structure of the task

Characteristics	Related questions	Reason for asking
User tasks	What tasks do the users complete as part of their job? What do they consider the end-to-end set of tasks?	You need to identify all tasks that a user does regardless of what your wizard will support. By identifying all tasks, you can get a better understanding of the space in which your wizard belongs.

Table 2–6   Questions to ask about the underlying structure of the task (continued)

Characteristics	Related questions	Reason for asking
Supported tasks	What tasks will the wizard support?	A single product or a single wizard cannot support all user tasks. You must determine which subset of tasks will be supported. For example, you may choose the most important, the most difficult, the most frequent, or the most infrequent tasks.
Number of required steps	How many steps are required to complete the entire task?	Wizards can support only a limited number of steps before they become unusable. If the number of steps is greater than ten, you may want to create multiple wizards rather than one.
Groupings of steps	Do the steps fall into natural groupings (subtasks)?	Your wizard should span a single task. Each page of the wizard should be a single and important subtask or step.
Constancy of steps	Is the number of steps constant or can additional steps be added based on user entries?	Some tasks vary in complexity based on individual user situations. For example, a tax return for someone who itemizes deductions requires extra calculations compared to a tax return for a person who does not itemize. In cases like this, you will need to change the number of wizard steps based on user entries.
Commit points	Does the task have multiple commit points?	A commit point refers to a point in the process where code must be run before the future steps or tasks can be completed. Your wizard should have a single commit point, which occurs when the user clicks the **Finish** button. If this is not possible, you need to be sure that adjacent pages impact the same commit point. For more information, see Chapter 9, "Interactive feedback."

Table 2–6   Questions to ask about the underlying structure of the task (continued)

Characteristics	Related questions	Reason for asking
Detailed user actions	How do users complete the tasks? What are the detailed actions that users take to complete the tasks? What information do users need to complete the tasks? In what order do users need this information? For example, if the users need to input measurements, what units do they use—inches, feet, meters, or others?	These details will help you determine the order of wizard pages as well as the controls and text used on each page.
Constancy of step order	Is the order of the steps static or might it depend on user entries?	Sometimes the order of steps can change based on user entries. For example, a wizard that helps users to buy airline tickets may consist of two different paths. The users follow one set of steps if they know the exact dates that they want to travel and a different set of steps if they know the maximum price they are willing to pay.
Dependencies among steps	Must the user perform several steps in a sequential order? Can steps be repeated before proceeding to the next step?	Some tasks involve some looping or repetition within themselves. Other tasks have strict dependencies. These dependencies can impact medium-level design decisions, such as whether or not your wizard will launch secondary dialogs, as well as low-level design decisions, such as enabling and disabling buttons.
Target users for each subtask	Does the same target user complete all of the subtasks?	Ensure that the same user completes all of the subtasks within your wizard. A wizard that seems very useful and usable in theory can be completely unusable if different target users typically complete the subtasks in the actual work environment.

Aspects of the task that can be simplified

One interesting result of a task analysis is that it should identify opportunities for simplifying the task. If you can't or don't want to reduce the complexity of a task, then a wizard is not an appropriate solution. Table 2–7 lists a series of questions to help approach simplifying a user task.

Table 2–7   Questions to ask to determine if there are aspects of the task that can be simplified

Characteristics	Related questions	Reason for asking
Ability to predict defaults	Can you predict default entries or values for wizard steps or will user entries be needed to complete the steps?	Default selections help simplify the task. Sometimes you can predict default entries; sometimes you can't. For example, it is difficult to predict default departure and destination cities in a wizard that helps users book airline reservations.
Desired defaults	If you can predict default entries, what values will most users want? What percentage of the target audience will agree with these defaults?	If less than half of your target audience will agree with your defaults, it might be better to not provide any.
Automation possibilities	Can aspects of the task be automated?	Automating aspects of the task is one effective way to simplify tasks. After identifying steps, step back and brainstorm about ways to eliminate the need for each step. For example, an installation wizard might be able to examine current computer settings to ensure that all software prerequisites are installed. This code would aid users by eliminating the tedious and error-prone process of reading the software documentation to uncover prerequisite products, finding the products on the computer, and checking each product's version to ensure that it is acceptable.
Errors	What errors might the users make?	You need to predict and identify the errors that users will make so that you can try to prevent these errors by design. See Chapter 10, "Error prevention and recovery," for a more detailed discussion of predicting errors.
Error prevention	How can errors be prevented?	You can use specific strategies to decrease, if not eliminate, user errors altogether. For example, the choice of interface control can impact the types of user errors. If users are expected to be poor typists, then you could use a pull-down menu as an alternative to a text entry field to prevent errors due to mistyping. See Chapter 10, "Error prevention and recovery," for a more detailed discussion of preventing errors.

A technique for gathering task requirements—Task analysis

The standard technique for gathering information about tasks is called a task analysis. Task analyses differ along two key dimensions: the type of task data collected (cognitive tasks, visible tasks, and so on) and the method used to collect the task data (observation, survey, and so on.). Traditional task analyses were developed to help gain an understanding of labor-intensive jobs, such as assembly work. However they can also be applied to software tasks. For example, the results of a task analysis for the task of "Opening a file from inside a word processing program" might be:

1. Go to the **File** menu and click on it.

2. Choose the **Open** menu option.

3. Select the file that you want to open.

4. Click the **OK** button.

Cognitive task analyses were developed to help designers better understand the cognitive demands of certain tasks. They can include visible actions, but their focus is on cognitive activities such as perception, comparison, and decision-making. A cognitive task analysis can be particularly useful in the design of a wizard, because it can identify where the original task is difficult for the user. The results of a cognitive task analysis for the task of "Opening a file from inside a word processing program" might be:

1. Remember where the **Open File** menu action is.

2. Go to the **File** menu and click on it.

3. Choose the **Open** menu option.

4. Remember where the file you want to open is located.

5. Navigate through the directory structure to locate the file.

6. Select the file that you want to open.

7. Click the **OK** button.

8. Look at the contents of the file to ensure that it is the one you meant to open.

The traditional way of conducting a task analysis is to videotape the participant as he or she is completing the task. If possible, observe the user completing the task. Your results will be more accurate. Afterward, the participant is asked to watch the tape and describe what is going on. Another method is to ask the participant to describe how the task is done without actually completing the task. With either method, the researcher may ask several questions or probe the participant for more information to ensure that the task requirements are truly understood. A few tips to help you plan and conduct a task analysis are:

- If you do not know what tasks are being done by your target audience, begin the task analysis by having the participants generate a list of tasks that they do.

- If you have some idea of the tasks that your target audience completes, begin the task analysis by showing participants a list of the tasks that you know about. You can then ask participants to validate your list by adding tasks that you are missing or removing tasks that they do not do.

- Consider asking participants to group the list of tasks into similar "piles" and naming these piles. This grouping can help you understand how your target users think about the tasks, which can impact how you group and separate tasks within and among wizards.

- After you have a general sense of what the main tasks are, gather details by either watching the users complete the tasks or by having users describe what they need to do to complete the tasks.

- If you ask participants to describe what they need to do to complete a task, provide a sample description to ensure that users describe the task at a level that you feel is useful. For example, you would probably prefer a description such as "type the name of the file" rather than "type the first letter of the word, type the second letter of the word, and so on."

- Have users rate or describe the tasks along characteristics that you care about. Some questions may be: How important is the task?, How frequently do you do the task?, How difficult is the task?, Do beginners complete this task at the company where you work?, How well does the current product support the task?, and so on. To prevent participants from rating all tasks as equal, enforce some limits on their ratings. For example, you may ask participants to list their top five tasks in terms of importance rather than having them rate each task as very important, important, and so on.

- Summarize what you learned and ask participants to verify your interpretation. If possible, tell them what you will do with the information you collected.

For more information on task analysis, see *User and Task Analysis for Interface Design* by JoAnn Hackos and Janice Redish.

Work environment—Where, when, and how will the users be using the wizard?

You need to understand the users' work environment to understand where and in what context your wizard will be used. Two key aspects of the users' work environment are the hardware and software that will be used to access the wizard. However, the users' work environment also consists of aspects such as the physical environment and the people with whom the users interact. These details are closely related to how the users complete their tasks and therefore may also be uncovered during the task analysis. Information about the users' work environment includes:

- Physical environment
- Tools used to access the wizard
- Social or workflow-related issues

The following sections discuss each of these aspects of the work environment in more detail and describe a technique to collect information about your users' work environment.

Physical environment

The first series of questions relates to the physical environment in which users will be completing your wizard. You may be tempted to assume that all of your users will be completing your wizard in an office environment. However, in today's highly mobile work environment, this assumption should be explored with your target audience and agreed upon by the entire design team. Table 2–8 includes a series of questions to help identify where the user will be completing your wizard.

Table 2–8   Questions to ask to identify where the user will be completing your wizard

Characteristics	**Related questions**	**Reason for asking**
General use	Where will the user use the wizard: at home, in the office, other?	Even if your wizard is for a business application, your target audience might not limit its use to the office. Small business owners might work from home. Other users might work remotely, either from home or when traveling on business. Your assumptions about where the user is using your wizard can impact wizard performance and usability.

Table 2–8   Questions to ask to identify where the user will be completing your wizard (continued)

Characteristics	Related questions	Reason for asking
Use during travel	Will users use the wizard while traveling, from hotels, or on the road?	If users are traveling, they will be using the wizard from unfamiliar locations, potentially with variable equipment or Internet connections. This variability may impact the wizard's performance and design tradeoffs. You may also need to provide information to help users understand how to get to your wizard from a remote location and how to troubleshoot the problems they encounter.
Ambient light	Will anyone use the wizard outside? Is ambient light an issue?	Wizard images and fonts can be degraded by the amount of light and glare that users will encounter. If you expect that the wizard may be used outside or in a wide range of lighting conditions, be sure that your graphics account for this variability.
Noise	Is noise a concern in the environment where your target audience will use your wizard?	If your target audience will be using the wizard in a noisy environment such as a factory or shopping mall, limit the number of auditory cues provided by the wizard. For example, present warnings or errors in on-screen textual messages rather than in "beeps."

Tools used to access the wizard

A second aspect of your users' work environment consists of the tools they use to access your wizard. Not all of your users will be using high-end computers with large monitors and incredibly fast Internet connections. A design that is usable with top-of-the-line equipment may be extremely unusable and slow when the equipment is older. Table 2–9 lists a series of questions to ask about the tools and equipment that your target audience will use to access your wizard.

Table 2–9   Questions to ask to identify what tools will be used to access your wizard

Characteristics	Related questions	Reason for asking
Hardware	Will the user be using a TV, laptop, computer, palm device, special device (kiosk, car navigation system), or other device to display and interact with your wizard?	As mobile technologies improve, the number of options to access and use software increases. You need to make a decision about what technologies to design for because each can have different screen sizes, system software, available colors, and so on.

Table 2–9   Questions to ask to identify what tools will be used to access your wizard (continued)

Characteristics	Related questions	Reason for asking
Connection speed	If the wizard is on the Web, what is the lowest speed connection that users can have?	Not all high-end users will always be using high-speed connections. High-end users are likely to travel or use their laptops or palm devices in areas where connections are sub-optimal. Your wizard graphics and functions must be designed to function effectively for all connection speeds that your target audience may experience.
One-handed use	If the user is accessing the wizard from a portable device, should the design assume one-handed use?	Users might not always have both hands free. If the supported task requires the user to examine objects and then input settings into the wizard, you probably want to ensure that the wizard can be completed with one hand. Avoid two-handed key combinations (such as Ctrl+Alt+Del).
Assistive technologies	Will the users be using any specialized keyboards, screen readers, or other assistive technologies to access your wizard?	If users will access your wizard through an assistive technology, ensure that your wizard is properly interpreted by the technology. See Chapter 13, "Accessibility," for more information.
Monitor size	What monitor (or screen) size can be assumed?	Laptops tend to have smaller monitors than "traditional" computers. Palm devices have even less available screen real estate. The maximum available screen size impacts the dimensions and layout of your wizard.
Display settings	What display settings do most of your target users utilize for resolution and number of colors?	The display settings will impact both the design of your graphics and the general layout of the wizard pages.
Computer speed and memory	What computer speed and memory can be assumed?	Performance, or the speed with which the wizard loads, redraws itself, and so on, is a concern. An interface that is slow might be unusable, especially if the user feels hindered by the response time of the wizard. If your target audience's computers are low-end in terms of processing speed, be careful with aspects such as the size of your graphics and the efficiency of your wizard code.
Storage space	How much storage space will the users have on their computers?	If users have a lot of storage space, they can install larger products and more options. However, users with limited storage space may be unable to use wizards with large graphics and animation. They may also not be able to install on-line manuals or on-line help.

Social or workflow-related issues

The final series of questions about your users' environment consists of social and workflow-related issues. For example, a wizard design that assumes that the user will be able to complete the wizard without interruption might be unrealistic. Table 2–10 lists questions about the social interactions and workflow that surround the use of your wizard.

Table 2–10   Questions to ask to identify where the user will be completing your wizard

Characteristics	Related questions	Reason for asking
Access to software	How will users get the actual software? Do users have CD-ROM drives, diskette drives, or both? Should the wizard be downloadable? What mechanisms will you provide to allow your target audience to get the wizard?	You must provide mechanisms to allow your users to get to your wizard. The mechanisms that you provide impact the file size limitations. For example, if the wizard is provided on a diskette or is downloadable, then the files sizes should be small.
Training and support	Will the users receive any training or support on your product, the wizard, or both?	Sometimes software sales include service or training agreements. These agreements might alter the level of help that you need to provide with your wizard. For example, you might opt to include your wizard in any training programs that are provided. Alternatively, you might want to check that any task training that is provided is consistent with the task model that your wizard assumes.
Dedicated computers	Do users share their computers, or does each user have a dedicated machine?	If you are designing a wizard that will be used on a shared computer or from multiple computers, then you might need to include security features such as user IDs and passwords.
Interruptability	Will the user be able to devote full attention to the wizard or will he or she be doing other tasks at the same time? How likely is it that the user will be interrupted while completing the wizard?	Many users have jobs that are often interrupted, by meetings, emergencies, other tasks, and so on. You might want to allow the users to save the wizard state or to save partially completed wizards and allow them to re-enter the wizard at a later time. You will also need to make it easy for the users to understand where they were before.

A technique for gathering work environment-related requirements— Observational study

Although you can use other techniques to gather work environment information, the best way to understand your users' work environment is to actually go there and watch users as they work. This type of study is called an observational study because you are observing the target users as they go about their daily work. Observational studies are useful because your participants might not be able to accurately remember if they are able to devote full attention to your wizard or might not know how to get information about their computer speed, memory, display settings, and so on. When you perform an observational study:

- Be sure that it is legal for you to go and observe the users in their work environment. Some software company license agreements forbid competitors from observing their products in use.

- Have a clear set of goals. The unpredictability of a real work environment often results in the "accidental" learning of interesting information. However, this unpredictability also makes it easy to get off track from the goal of your study. Be sure that you leave the study with information that you can use for your wizard, in addition to any additional accidental learning that takes place.

- Try to be as unobtrusive as possible. You'd like the people that you are observing to act as naturally as possible. Occasionally, you'll need to ask the users to explain what they are doing, but you do not want to be constantly asking the users to talk aloud.

- If a number of users are using your product at the same company, try to get a sense of the range of working conditions. For example, go to multiple offices to see if the noise level changes, watch workers of various levels of expertise use the product, check if Web connection speeds vary throughout the day, and so on.

- If possible, take videotapes or photos of the work environment. This type of data will help other team members get a true sense of the work environment. Be sure to ask ahead of time if it would be possible for you to take videotapes or photos.

- Summarize what you learn and ask participants to verify your interpretation. If possible, tell them what you will do as a result of this information.

- Because observational studies are expensive, consider combining them with other techniques or expanding their scope to allow you to collect data about product requirements or tasks during the same session.

For more information on observational studies and work environment analyses, see *Contextual design: defining customer-centered systems* by Hugh Beyer and Karen Holtzblatt.

Competitive evaluation—Who else is creating a similar product or wizard?

Be sure to judge the competitiveness of your wizard before you create it. This is most important if your wizard is the entire product, but can also be valuable if your wizard is simply a part of a product. The only way to do this is to compare your wizard or product definition with wizards or products of other companies. You may also choose to compare your wizard against the competition later in the design cycle. That type of competitive evaluation is discussed in Chapter 4, "Evaluating wizard designs."

Aspects and features of competitive products or wizards

Table 2–11 lists questions to determine how your product or wizard fares against the competition. Use any areas where your wizard falls short of the competition as requirements to your wizard design.

Table 2–11   Questions to ask to evaluate the competition

Characteristics	Related questions	Reason for asking
Competitor	Who is my competition? What similar products already exist in the marketplace?	Every wizard will have some competition. If no similar products exist, you can look at other products that have wizards regardless of the tasks they support.
Scope	What is the scope of the competitor's offering? What tasks does your competitor's wizard support? What functions does it provide? What platforms does it support?	You need to understand the scope of your competitors' offerings to determine if the comparison is a fair one.
Competitor's strengths	What does your competitor's wizard do well? What are the strengths of your competitor's wizard: ease of use, visual appearance, scalability, speed of completion, integration with other products, or other?	Any areas where your wizard falls short of the competition should become requirements for your wizard. You can also use these areas as measures of success for your wizard.

Table 2–11   Questions to ask to evaluate the competition (continued)

Characteristics	Related questions	Reason for asking
Competitor's weaknesses	What does your competitor's wizard do poorly? What are the weaknesses of your competitor's wizard: ease of use, visual appearance, scalability, speed of completion, integration with other products, or other?	These weaknesses help you identify areas in which you can win market share.
Comparison	How do you fare against the competitor?	Gauge your wizard against those offered by your competitors. Focus on the aspects that your target audience considers important. You might identify multiple competitors, each of whom is strong on at least one of these aspects, and use these competitors as goals or benchmarks for your final design.
Cost	How much does the competitor's product cost?	Almost every target audience cares about cost. If your product is inferior to your competition and costs more, you are unlikely to succeed.

A technique for evaluating the competition—Competitive analysis

The ideal way to evaluate the competition is to have participants that represent your target audience complete the tasks with your wizard design and with the competitor's. However, you must gain some information about the competitor *before* you begin designing. You can use a competitive analysis to collect this type of information. Use these ideas when you perform a competitive analysis *before* you design your wizard:

- Begin by collecting information about all your competitors and their products. You don't necessarily have to buy the competitor's product. You may be able to obtain all the information you need from their Web sites, marketing brochures or advertisements, or demonstration copies of their software.

- Validate that you have the correct competitor. Be sure that your target audience still feels that the competitor you list is truly the most important competitor.

- When comparing your product to a competitor's, match the method of delivery and degree of realism. For example, if you want the participants to rate how desirable the competitor's product is based on a marketing brochure, then you should create a marketing brochure for your product also.

- Avoid showing your participants a more realistic version of the competitor's product before you do any direct comparisons. You don't want your participants' ratings to be influenced by this additional information that does not yet exist for your product. For example, if your competitor's product has professional graphics and your product simply has sketches, either increase the quality of your graphics or create equivalent sketches for the competitor's wizard.

- Ask participants to rate both how well the competitor does something and how important that feature is. For example, your participants might feel that the competitor's product is very good at creating graphs. However, they might never create graphs at work or never want to create graphs. You do not want to spend time and effort designing a feature into your product that no one will use. Ideally, focus on designing features that the competitor does poorly and your target audience thinks are very useful.

- Be sure to rate the competitor's product and your proposed product along multiple dimensions, not just one. For example, compare the ease-of-use *and* visual appearance of both wizards.

- Explicitly ask your participants about design tradeoffs. For example, if you could create a product that was faster than the competitor's or one that integrated with other products, which would they prefer?

- Ask participants about purchasing decisions. For example, ask them how much they would pay for your product and the competitor's product, or ask them how likely they would be to purchase each product.

For more information on product evaluation methods, see Chapter 4, "Evaluating wizard designs."

Summary

Before beginning to design your wizard, be sure to clearly define your wizard's requirements. These requirements span several categories: users, product, tasks, work environment, and competition. Use the questions in this chapter to help the entire team collect information about these requirements. The answers to these questions will drive your wizard's structure, look and feel, and information design. The questions in this chapter are repeated in subsequent chapters of this book where appropriate.

Chapter 3

Applying the iterative design process

▲ Why follow the iterative design process?

▲ Questions to ask before beginning

▲ Overview of the iterative design process

▲ High-level design iterations

▲ Low-level design iterations

▲ Interactive prototype iterations

▲ Working product iterations

▲ Summary of guidelines discussed in this chapter

Once you gather all the requirements necessary to design your wizard, it is tempting to start coding your wizard right away. However, we have found that a successful wizard design requires 80% preparation and 20% implementation. Before you start coding, you need to follow an iterative design process, which involves early and continuous design, test, and redesign with representative users. The output of this process is a design that meets your users' needs and is then ready to be coded.

This chapter describes the iterative design *process* and provides practical guidelines for implementing this process. Detailed guidelines for usability *evaluation* are described in Chapter 4, "Evaluating wizard designs." Detailed guidelines for wizard *design* are described in Chapters 6 through 15.

Why follow the iterative design process?

An iterative design process is needed to ensure that your wizard design is useful and usable. Benefits of an iterative design process include:

- **Usability problems are more likely to be found and resolved.** The iterative process places emphasis on design and evaluation early in the development cycle. This process increases the probability that the most important usability problems will be resolved because it is easier to redesign a prototype than it is to change code. Changing code requires a lot more detail and time with the additional burden of code testing for compile errors, navigational errors, and so on.

- **Problems are more likely to be identified early in the design cycle.** Usability testing well in advance of actually coding your wizard ensures fewer usability problems later in the development cycle, less rework, and ultimately, a shorter and faster development cycle.

- **The iterative design process ensures the wizard design meets users' needs**. Early and continuous involvement with users ensures that the wizard design meets their needs.

Questions to ask before beginning

You need to understand the task and subtasks of your wizard, your schedule, your goals, and your target audience before you begin the iterative design process. Chapter 1, "Kicking off the project," and Chapter 2, "Gathering requirements," should provide the information you need to answer the following questions:

- **What task will the wizard support?** Each wizard should represent only one task. This information will help you determine how many wizards you will develop.

- **How many steps are required to complete the entire task? Do the steps fall into natural groupings (subtasks)?** Each page should contain one subtask or a grouping of subtasks.

- **What are your target audience's job titles and their job descriptions?** This information will help you design your wizard and will help you determine what kind of test participants to employ to evaluate your wizard.

- **What are the schedule and delivery dates for the wizard?** This information will help determine how many design iterations are possible.

- **How will you measure the success of your wizard design?** This information will help determine when the iterative design process is complete.

- **How many people do you have on your design team?** This information will help you determine the types of and the number of usability evaluations you can conduct.

Overview of the iterative design process

The iterative design process consists of:

1. Developing an initial wizard design

2. Conducting usability evaluations on the design with representative users

3. Modifying the design based on usability feedback

4. Evaluating again to ensure your modifications are usable

Repeat this process as many times as possible during the development of your wizard, or until your design has met some criteria of acceptability, such as "90% of participants complete the task without making any errors." Figure 3–1 shows the flow of activities in the iterative design process.

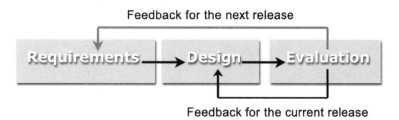

Figure 3–1   The iterative design process.

The figure shows that user and task requirements are the basis for your wizard design. You then conduct usability evaluations of the design with representative users. As the figure shows, you use feedback from usability evaluations to modify the design. The design is evaluated again to ensure the modifications are usable. Sometimes, you cannot incorporate feedback from usability evaluations into your design. For example, your development tools might not support the inclusion of a new design idea, or you might not have enough development resources to add additional functionality. In these cases, you can document the usability feedback and save it as requirements for future releases. Generally, you will want to incorporate all usability feedback, however.

Start the iterative design process as early as possible in the development cycle of your wizard to allow time to perform multiple design iterations. Rarely will you find all problems in one usability evaluation, so it is important to conduct as many iterations as possible. Even if you find problems, design changes can introduce new problems, and you will want to uncover these errors and fix them.

For your first iteration, you can start with simple sketches of your high-level design. Subsequent design iterations can move from screen captures of wizard pages, prototypes, and finally to a working product.

The following sections describe the iterative design process in more detail using a tax wizard as an example. Note that the process is very flexible and the number of iterations depend on the length of your development cycle, availability of test participants, and personnel resources. The iterations and steps outlined in each section are merely suggestions. You can combine, eliminate, or modify the steps and iterations presented in this chapter.

High-level design iterations

The first step in the iterative design process is to develop the high-level design concept for your wizard. Based on your understanding of the users and their tasks, you need to determine what task your wizard will perform, which subtasks will be included, and what information will be required on each wizard page.

This section explains the steps to create your high-level design and the guidelines for testing it.

High-level design steps

Follow these steps to create your high-level design:

1. Understand the technical aspects of the process or task that your wizard will perform. Because your wizard is providing an easy-to-use interface to some process or task, make sure you fully understand that process before designing your wizard. Talk to experts in the field and read technical manuals on the subject. If a non-wizard method exists to perform the task (even if it involves entering commands), make sure to familiarize yourself with that method. Ensure that your wizard covers only one task.

2. Create a flow diagram of your wizard. This diagram should be based on your task analysis. This diagram could be in the form of paper and pencil, a chalkboard, or a whiteboard. The diagram should list each page of the wizard, and in what order the steps (pages) will occur.

   Ensure that each page of the wizard covers one subtask or grouping of subtasks. For example, in a tax wizard, each page could include groupings of subtasks such as personal information, deductions, and interest income. Figure 3–2 shows an example of a flow diagram of the tax wizard, which shows the number of pages and what grouping of information will be included on each page.

3. Discuss the high-level design among the wizard team members to gather feedback. Update the design if necessary.

4. Discuss the high-level design with experts in the task or process. Update the design if necessary.

5. Develop the high-level design. Sketch out what information will be requested on each page of the wizard. Use "low-fidelity" methods to develop your design. Fidelity refers to the realism of your prototype. Low-fidelity methods include paper and pencil sketches, whiteboard sketches, and Post-it® notes where each wizard page is represented by one Post-it note. You can even have users develop the high-level design themselves with paper, pencil, scissors, and tape. It is not necessary to

Tax Wizard Flow

Personal   Dependents   Income   Taxes/Credits   Deductions   Payments   Summary

Figure 3–2   *Flow diagram of a high-level wizard concept.*

determine what controls you will use and what the layout of these controls will be. For example, on the Personal Information page of the tax wizard, you might want to request information on filing status. Figure 3–3 shows an example of an initial sketch of the Deductions page of the tax wizard.

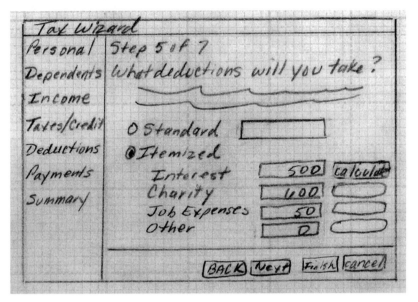

Figure 3–3   *Example of a high-level sketch of a wizard page.*

High-level design tests

Follow these guidelines for testing high-level designs:

- Bring in users as early in the design cycle as you can to evaluate the design direction.

- Test your design. There are a number of usability evaluation methods, but at this point in the design of your wizard, a heuristic review or design exploration is most appropriate. See Chapter 4, "Evaluating wizard designs," for more details on when and how to conduct these evaluations.

- Evaluate the flow of your wizard and its terminology. Try to identify missing functions and unnecessary functions. You will not be able to evaluate timing, feel, interaction among controls, and error recovery at this point in the design process.

- Keep an open mind and ear to users' feedback. Don't become attached to your first design; the wizard design will change with each iteration.

- *Do a lot of this type of testing!* It's cheaper and faster to evaluate and change paper and pencil designs than it is to do the same to code. Additionally, users won't think the design is real and will be more likely to suggest changes.

- Keep track of usability problems and issues as you iterate your design.

- If you update your design based on usability evaluation feedback, test again.

- Move to low-level design and testing when you are confident that your design direction meets your users' needs.

Low-level design iterations

After you conduct several iterations on your high-level design, you can begin to provide more details for the wizard pages. The low-level design consists of a detailed design for each wizard page. This is a good time to increase the fidelity of your prototype and increase the scope of usability testing.

This section explains the steps to create your low-level design and the guidelines for testing it.

Low-level design steps

Follow these general steps to create your low-level design:

1. Determine what information the user will be prompted for on each page of the wizard.

2. Determine what controls will be used to prompt the user for that information. For example, on the Personal page of the tax wizard, you might want to request information on filing status. Because you can select only one status—single, married filing a joint return, married filing separate returns, head of household, or qualifying widow(er) with dependent children—use radio buttons or a drop-down.

3. Create an initial layout for the controls on each page.

4. Choose initial labels for the controls on the wizard pages.

5. Write textual descriptions for each page. These descriptions are one or two sentences that describe the scope and goal of the page. For example, the textual description of the Personal page of your tax wizard might be something like "Please enter your mailing address and filing status."

6. Determine if the completion of each wizard page is dependent on completion of previous pages (sequential wizard) or if the user can complete the wizard pages in any order (non-sequential wizard).

7. Determine where, in the flow, the **Finish** button can be enabled based on what information is necessary to complete the wizard.

8. Create pictures of each screen or limited functioning prototypes of the low-level design. You can use any number of graphics programs available today such as Jasc PaintShop Pro, Adobe Photoshop, Macromedia Director, and Microsoft Visual Basic. Alternatively, you can continue with paper and pencil, whiteboard, and other lower-fidelity prototypes. Figure 3–4 shows an example of one page of a tax wizard. Notice that the types of controls have been determined and a task description is included.

9. As with the initial design and wizard flow iteration, discuss the low-level page design among the wizard team members and with experts in the domain. Update the design if necessary.

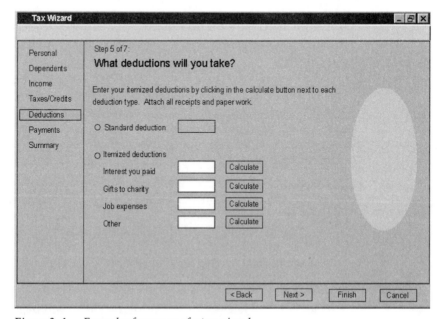

Figure 3–4   *Example of one page of a tax wizard.*

Low-level design tests

Follow these guidelines for low-level page design testing:

- Test your designs. The usability evaluation methods that are appropriate for testing low-level designs are the same for those used to evaluate the initial design: heuristic review or design exploration. See Chapter 4, "Evaluating wizard designs," for more details.

- Test the appropriateness of your controls, default values, and selections in lists and drop-down lists. You will not be able to evaluate interactions between pages, timing, feel, interaction among controls, and error recovery at this point in the design process.

- Sit with the test participants to "turn the pages" as they progress through each wizard page.

- Act as an on-line help source. For example, if the test participant does not understand how to complete a wizard page or what value is required for a particular control, provide assistance. Then, document where help was needed and whether your help actually helped. Use this information as input to context-sensitive help and text descriptions on the wizard pages.

- Pretend you are the computer. If the user makes an incorrect selection or input, give a verbal error message.

- Keep track of usability problems and issues as you iterate your design.

- If you update your design based on usability evaluation feedback, test again.

- Move to interactive designs when you are confident that your low-level design is usable.

Interactive prototype iterations

After you've conducted several iterations on your low-level design using paper and pencil sketches or pictures of the wizard screens, develop interactive prototypes to evaluate interactions between wizard pages and controls and to gather feedback on error situations.

This section explains the steps to create your interactive prototype design and the guidelines for testing it.

Interactive prototype design steps

Follow these steps to create your interactive prototype design:

1. Determine what actions or processes are associated with the buttons on each wizard page. For example, when the user clicks the **Next** button on the Dependents page, not only is the next page of the wizard displayed, but also the number of exemptions is transferred to the Deductions page. Documenting this type of information in a table can be very useful. Table 3–1 is an example of a table with interactions between wizard pages.

Table 3–1   Example of button actions for pages of the tax wizard

Wizard page	Button name	Action
Dependents page	Next	Display Income page of wizard; enter value on Personal Deductions page.
Dependents page	Back	Display Personal Information page, but save entries on this page.
Dependents page	Cancel	Close wizard; prompt user to save values.
Income page	Next	Add totals of wages, interest, and so on. Enter value on Personal Information page.
Income page	Back	Display Dependents page; save input.
Income page	Cancel	Close wizard; prompt user to save values.

2. Determine which defaults might be available to users and for which controls. Include this information in a table of control information. Table 3–2 is an example of how to document information for controls on each wizard page. Create one table for each page of the tax wizard.

Table 3–2   Example control information for the Income page of the tax wizard

Control name	Mandatory?	Default values	Valid values	Description
Wages, salaries, tips entry field	Yes	None	Any decimal value	Enter total wages from W-2 form.
Taxable interest entry field	No	None	Any decimal value	Enter interest from Schedule B, if appropriate.
Capital gains check box	Yes	Yes (unchecked)	Checked or unchecked	Check if Schedule D is required.

3. Determine what interactions exist between controls on a wizard page. For example, if a user has no taxable interest on the Income page of the tax wizard, the controls necessary to calculate that interest will be disabled (grayed out). Or, if the user does not complete the necessary information to complete a page of the tax wizard, the **Next** button is grayed out. Create a table of interactions between controls. Table 3–3 is an example of a table showing interactions between controls. Create one table for each page of the wizard.

Table 3–3   Example of interactions between controls on the Payments page of a tax wizard

Name of control	State	Interactions
Refund radio button	Payment larger than tax owed	Enable **Refund** entry field.
		Disable **Amount you owe** field.
		Enable **Amount to be applied to next year's estimated tax** field.
Refund radio button	Payment smaller than tax owed	Disable **Refund** entry field.
		Enable **Amount you owe** field.
		Disable **Amount to be applied to next year's estimated tax** field.

4. Create limited functioning prototypes or high-fidelity prototypes of the detailed design. You can use any number of prototyping software programs available today such as Macromedia Director, Microsoft Visual Basic, Semantic Visual Café, and Microsoft Visual C++.

5. If possible, use graphics that will be used in the actual wizard to gather feedback on the "look and feel" of the wizard.

6. Build in some interactivity between wizard pages. For example, make sure that when the user clicks the **Next** button, the next page of the wizard is displayed. You do not have to build in every possible branch from the wizard page, but at least enable the main flow between pages.

7. If possible, determine where errors might occur in your wizard and develop all necessary error dialogs.

8. Include default values wherever possible. For example, if possible, default any address information to last year's.

9. Use "scaffolding" where your wizard is not functional. For example, include dummy data in lists and list boxes. You can also imbed bitmaps or images for pages you have not prototyped. You can also include non-functional controls and ask the test participant to comment on how they would use that control.

Figure 3–5 shows an example of a wizard page from a high-fidelity prototype.

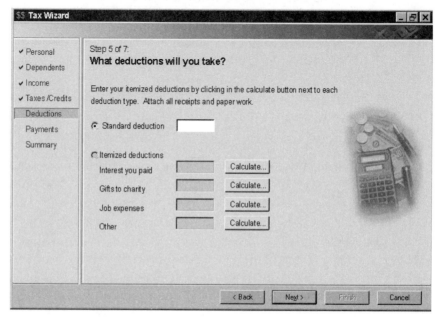

Figure 3–5   *Example of a wizard page from a high-fidelity tax wizard prototype.*

Interactive prototype design tests

Follow these guidelines for interactive prototype design testing:

- Test your designs with representative users. The usability evaluation method that is appropriate for interactive prototype design tests is design evaluation. See Chapter 4, "Evaluating wizard designs," for more details.

- Develop scenarios to specifically test error conditions to determine how helpful your error dialogs are.

- Sit with test participants during testing to ensure that they do not click on functions that may crash the prototype.

- As with testing of detailed page designs, act as an on-line help source. Again, document where help was needed and whether your help actually helped. Use this information as input to context-sensitive help and text descriptions on the wizard pages.

- Act as the computer for functions that are not prototyped. For example, if the user enters incorrect information, provide a verbal error message.

- Gather information on error conditions and interactions between pages and controls. You can also test your default values.

- Set up your scenarios so that users stick to the flow that has been prototyped.

- Keep track of usability problems and issues as you iterate your design.

- If you update your design based on usability evaluation feedback, test again. Increase the fidelity of your prototype each time you test.

- Move to working product iterations when you feel that your interactive prototype designs are usable.

Working product iterations

After you conduct several iterations on high-fidelity prototypes and you feel your design is usable, code your wizard. At this point, many design and testing iterations have taken place. Because users have been involved every step of the way, you can be pretty sure that the wizard you are coding is usable and meets their needs. However, once code is in place, you still need to involve users in evaluation.

This section explains the steps to create your working product design and the guidelines for testing it.

Working product design iteration

Follow these steps to code your design:

1. Wait to code your wizard until you have conducted as many iterations as possible and are assured that your wizard meets your users' needs.

2. Implement the wizard to follow the tested designs or prototypes as closely as possible.

3. Document any deviations from the intended design. Deviations might occur if there are differences between the prototyping tool and the coding language in terms of what can be implemented.

Working product design tests

Follow these guidelines for coded design testing:

- Test your designs with representative users. The usability evaluation methods that are appropriate for code design tests are design evaluation and design validation. See Chapter 4, "Evaluating wizard designs," for more details.

- Test all aspects of your wizard, including all error conditions, and additional "fit and finish" aspects such as tab order, mnemonics, accelerator keys, graphics, and layout.

- Evaluate context-sensitive help (if available), labels for all controls, and all text descriptions on your wizard pages.

- If your wizard is being translated into other languages, conduct usability evaluations on the translated versions of your wizard. Use test participants who are fluent in the language you are evaluating.

- If your wizard is part of an application, test your wizard with the application.

- Develop scenarios that ensure any deviations from the intended design are evaluated to ensure they are usable.

- Test in a usability test lab and, if possible, in a real-world setting where users are actually using the wizard to perform their jobs.

- Do not interact with your test participants once they begin the usability evaluation. You want your test situation to mirror the real world as closely as possible, and you would not be available to help or guide users who buy your wizard.

- Gather information on what paths the user takes through the wizard.

- If there is time in the development cycle, update your design based on usability evaluation feedback. Test again if possible.

Summary of guidelines discussed in this chapter

- ❏ Start the iterative design process early.

- ❏ Evaluate your designs with representative users.

- ❏ Conduct as many iterations on the high-level design as possible. This is the most important phase of your wizard design because it lays the foundation for remaining iterations.

- ❏ After each iteration, redesign the wizard based on the results of the design tests.

- ❏ Increase the fidelity, or realism, of your design with each iteration.

- ❏ Increase the scope of testing as your design becomes more firm.

- ❏ Evaluate the terminology, flow, and missing and unnecessary functionality during high-level design tests.

- ❏ Evaluate the appropriateness of controls, default values, and selections in lists and drop-down lists during low-level design tests.

- ❏ Evaluate interactions between wizard pages and controls, and gather information on error conditions during interactive prototype tests.

- ❏ Do not begin coding your wizard until you are sure your design is usable.

- ❏ Evaluate the working product to ensure that any deviations from the design are usable.

- ❏ Evaluate error conditions, context-sensitive help, and "fit and finish" aspects of the wizard such as tab order, layout, graphics, and mnemonics during working product evaluations.

Chapter 4

Evaluating wizard designs

▲ Why evaluate wizard designs?

▲ Questions to ask before beginning

▲ Usability evaluation techniques

▲ Tasks to prepare for usability evaluations

▲ Guidelines for conducting usability evaluations

▲ Follow-up tasks for after the usability evaluation

▲ Summary of guidelines discussed in this chapter

A key step in the iterative design process is evaluating your wizard design for usability problems. This step is repeated for each iteration of the design process. The only way to successfully evaluate your design is to perform usability evaluations. See Chapter 3 "Applying the iterative design process," for more details on the iterative design process.

This chapter explains the following usability evaluation techniques: heuristic evaluations, design explorations, design evaluations, competitive benchmarks, and beta or post-release evaluations. This chapter also provides advice for preparing for a usability evaluation, conducting a usability evaluation, and following up after a usability evaluation.

Why evaluate wizard designs?

Effective usability testing is key to developing a quality wizard. Benefits of usability evaluations are:

- **Usability evaluations ensure your wizard meets the requirements of your target users.** By iteratively testing your wizard with representative users and tasks, you can ensure your wizard will help the users perform their tasks more easily.

- **Usability evaluations identify any usability problems so you can fix them before your wizard ships to the general public.** The iterative design process ensures that usability problems are uncovered, fixed, and re-evaluated by continually designing, evaluating, and redesigning throughout the wizard design cycle. See Chapter 3, "Applying the iterative design process," for more details.

- **Usability evaluations ensure your wizard compares favorably with its competition.** Competitive benchmarking is a method for comparing working wizard code to its closest competitor, where users perform similar tasks on both products. You can compare performance measures and ratings to see if your wizard "stacks up."

- **Usability evaluations can help uncover bugs.** If you are testing working wizard code, usability evaluations can help uncover code bugs that should be fixed prior to making your wizard available to the general public.

- **Usability evaluations help uncover any overlooked requirements.** During usability testing, missing functions or subtasks not covered in the wizard will become apparent.

Questions to ask before beginning

The type of usability evaluation that you perform is dictated by several factors. Ask yourself these questions before conducting a usability evaluation:

- **Who will be using your wizard and what are their characteristics**? Characteristics include job title, experience with wizards, experience with your product, and experience with different operating systems. You should employ test participants that match the intended user population.

- **What is the purpose and scope of your wizard**? You need to ask test participants if the wizard did indeed meet these goals.

- **How will you measure the success of your wizard design?** You will want to make sure these measures are collected in your evaluations.

- **Will there be any types of on-line help that will need to be evaluated**? If yes, you need to include the use of on-line help in your scenarios.

- **What operating systems will be supported?** You should conduct evaluations on all supported platforms.

- **What task and subtasks will the wizard support**? Your scenarios should be based on these tasks.

- **What errors might the users make?** You may want to include scenarios that force users to make errors to ensure they can recover from them.

Usability evaluation techniques

There are many evaluation techniques you can employ; the specific technique you choose is dictated by several factors. This section provides a brief overview of various evaluation techniques and some practical guidelines for conducting evaluations.

Table 4–1 presents an overview of each usability evaluation technique. Notice that early in the design cycle, you test low-fidelity (or low-realism) designs, while later in the cycle, you test designs that are closer in appearance and behavior to the final product. For more information about the performance and subjective measures mentioned in Table 4–1, see "Collect both performance and subjective measures" on page 77.

Table 4–1   Selecting an evaluation technique

Evaluation technique	When in cycle	Fidelity of design	Test participants	Measures
Heuristic evaluation	Early	Low—Paper prototypes, pictures of screens, chalk talks, or limited prototypes	Internal and external; should have knowledge of wizard domain	List of heuristics, such as consistency and use of defaults.
Design exploration	Early	Low—Paper prototypes, pictures of screens, or limited prototypes	Internal and external; focus on internal	Usually subjective measures such as comments and satisfaction ratings. Performance measures can include number and type of errors and task success.
Design evaluation	Middle to Late	Medium to high—High-fidelity interactive prototypes or working product code	External or customers	Performance measures, such as number and type of errors, task time, task success, and number of help usages. Subjective measures such as satisfaction ratings, comments, and comparison ratings with previous release.
Competitive benchmark	Late	High—Working wizard code and closest competitor wizard	External	Same performance and subjective measures as in design evaluation. Compare measures between two products during data analysis. Rating of preference between two products and strong and weak points of competitor.
Beta or post-release evaluations	Just prior to, or after product is released	High—Working wizard code	Customers	Subjective measures, such as ratings of overall satisfaction with wizard-specific components. Comparison of satisfaction with previous releases of product, and what customers liked and what could be improved about the wizard.

The method for each of these techniques is discussed in more detail in this section.

Heuristic evaluation

A heuristic evaluation involves a small set of evaluators examining a user interface and using a checklist to judge the wizard's usability against recognized usability principles.

It is best to conduct heuristic evaluations early in the design cycle using paper prototypes or pictures of wizard pages. These evaluations are used to uncover the most obvious usability problems before conducting more time-consuming and expensive usability evaluations with high-fidelity prototypes or working product code. It would be a shame to "waste" valuable test participants on a design that is not as clean as can be. However, heuristic evaluations can also be conducted on more high-fidelity prototypes or working product code.

Methods

If at all possible, use more than one evaluator because a single evaluator will rarely find all usability problems in an interface. It is also best to choose evaluators who have human factors and domain knowledge. You can have the various evaluators play different roles to try and uncover different types of problems. For example, roles could include novice and expert users.

Be sure to conduct other types of evaluations during the iterative design cycle. Although heuristic evaluations are useful, they cannot replace usability feedback from representative users.

Measures

You can come up with your own heuristics or use several published checklists. See *Usability Engineering* by Jakob Nielsen, and *Usability Inspection Methods* by Jakob Nielsen and Robert L. Mack, for heuristic checklists. Keep the number of checklist items to a manageable number, around 10. Examples of common heuristics include error prevention, consistency, use of defaults, and visibility of system status or feedback. See Appendix B, "Sample design checklist," for an example of a consistency checklist.

You can apply severity ratings to each heuristic to help allocate resources to fix the most serious problems and to use as an indicator of where additional usability testing might be needed. No matter what rating scale you employ, make sure all evaluators understand what each rating represents.

Design exploration

Design explorations are used to explore, or evaluate, the high-level design or direction of your wizard or product. This type of evaluation is also best used to gather feedback on missing functionality and terminology, and to compare various design alternatives. For example, for an installation wizard, you might want to compare several designs to select components.

Design explorations are usually conducted early in the design cycle using either paper prototypes, pictures of your wizard pages, or low-fidelity software prototypes. This will allow you to develop, evaluate, change, and evaluate your design again quickly without the time investment necessary for higher fidelity software prototypes.

Methods

Methods for conducting design explorations can vary somewhat and include:

- **Design walkthrough**. You demonstrate the prototype to one or more participants using task scenarios. Test participants provide comments and ratings of satisfaction with the user interface. This method is useful for gathering initial feedback on functionality from a large group of participants.

- **Users create the user interface**. You provide participants with an overview of the function of the wizard and then provide them with paper templates of a blank wizard page along with cutouts of controls. You also give them some tape or glue, additional paper, and pens or pencils to create new controls. Participants then paste cutouts of controls onto a wizard page in an order or layout that makes sense to them. This approach is useful for gathering feedback on what function the participants want and how they would organize it.

- **Traditional usability test.** Test participants perform tasks using paper or low- to medium-fidelity prototypes and follow scenarios. There may be a fair amount of interaction between test administrators and participants after each scenario to gather additional feedback on the function or interface.

Measures

Measures are usually more subjective in nature and consist of test participant comments and satisfaction ratings or preference ratings. Depending on the fidelity of your prototype, measures can also include performance measures such as number and type of errors and successful task completion.

Design evaluation

Design evaluations gather information on detailed or low-level designs once the high-level design issues are resolved through heuristic evaluations or design explorations. The purpose of the design evaluation is to evaluate the detailed design, which is the navigation, order and flow of controls within a wizard page, and error handling. Error handling refers to how the wizard will help the user recover from an error such as not having enough hard disk space during installation.

You usually conduct design evaluations in the middle and continue into the later part of the development cycle. They are usually conducted on high-fidelity interactive prototypes and should also be conducted on working product code.

Design evaluations also give you a chance to gather feedback on how your wizard interacts with the overall product.

If you are testing late in the development cycle, design evaluations can be used as a final validation before your wizard is ready for the marketplace. Testing late in the development cycle can help you:

- **Ensure that code to be released matches the intended design.** Frequently, there is a misinterpretation of design specifications or design tradeoffs, which are made because of limitations of code. You, as a test administrator, will be in a position to evaluate whether the code matches the design. Your test participants cannot determine this.

- **Evaluate late-breaking customer requirements**. User requirements that were included in your wizard design late in the development cycle should be evaluated prior to releasing your wizard. This will help ensure that these changes to your wizard design are usable.

Methods
You observe and record performance measures and test participant comments while they perform wizard tasks. There is very little communication between test administrators and participants other than to ask the participant questions between scenarios.

At the completion of a design evaluation, participants complete a post-evaluation questionnaire to provide ratings of satisfaction. See Appendix G, "Sample post-evaluation questionnaire," for an example questionnaire.

If your wizard product code has known bugs, you can write your task scenarios to ensure test participants avoid these pitfalls.

Measures

Because design evaluations are more formal usability evaluations, you can collect both performance and subjective measures. Performance measures include number and type of errors, number of help usages, task completion time, and successful task completion. Subjective measures include ratings of overall satisfaction, ratings of ease of use of particular aspects of the wizard, and test participant comments. If you are comparing a wizard and non-wizard method, you could include ratings of preference or compare ratings on both methods.

Additionally, if a previous release of the product exists, you could collect ratings comparing the current release with the previous release.

Competitive benchmark

Competitive benchmarks are "head-to-head" comparisons between your wizard and its closest competitor. These evaluations are conducted on fairly stable code. User assistance such as on-line help, books, and pop-up help should be in place and can be compared. This technique can be used to test your wizard if it's part of an overall application, but the amount of time and resources involved in these evaluations may not warrant their use on testing a small wizard.

Note that Chapter 2, "Gathering requirements," describes competitive evaluations that are conducted to gather requirements for the current release. In that case, the competitor's product is either evaluated in isolation or it is compared against the high-level design of your wizard or product.

Competitive benchmarks are usually conducted late in the development cycle with stable or final working product code to ensure a valid comparison. The majority of the usability problems or suggestions are used as input to the next release of your wizard because it is generally too late in the development cycle to make changes to code.

Methods

Participants can perform tasks on one product or both products. If participants perform tasks using both products, you will have to employ methods to ensure that order effects are minimized either by counterbalancing or randomly assigning product order to participants. See "If comparing two or more designs, reduce order effects," on page 78 for more details on minimizing order effects. If participants perform tasks using only one product, you will need to at least double the number of participants in your benchmark evaluations.

Write scenarios that represent tasks that can be performed on both products. There should be very little communication between you and the participants. At the completion of the design validation, participants complete a post-evaluation questionnaire to provide ratings of satisfaction. See Appendix F, "Sample scenarios for an installation wizard" and Appendix G, "Sample post-evaluation questionnaire," for examples of a scenario and post-evaluation questionnaire, respectively.

It is also useful to evaluate the competitiveness of your books, on-line help, installation, and packaging as part of competitive benchmarking.

Because participants are performing tasks on two products, competitive benchmarks take longer in terms of overall test time than other usability evaluations.

Measures
Competitive benchmarks involve the evaluation of working product code; therefore, you can collect reliable performance measures. Performance measures include number and type of errors, number of help usages, task completion time, and successful task completion for both products. During data analysis, you can compare both products using these measures.

Subjective measures include ratings of overall satisfaction, ratings of ease of use of particular aspects of the wizard, and comments for both products. Additionally, you should include a rating of preference between the two products and ask test participants to provide a list of strengths and weaknesses of the competitor and your wizard.

Beta or post-release evaluations

You evaluate the product after it is released to gather feedback on overall customer satisfaction with your wizard in an actual customer environment. As with competitive benchmarking, this technique requires a large amount of time and resources and may not be warranted unless your wizard is the entire application.

The goals of these evaluations are:

- To gather requirements for the next release of your product to ensure that your product is competitive with other products in the marketplace.

- To give you an idea of where your product will stand in the marketplace.

- To help you prioritize requirements for the next release; for example, you may want to place a higher priority on items that will help make your product more competitive.

These evaluations can take place during beta tests (early versions of your product code) or after the final product is released. If the evaluation takes place during a beta test, there may be time to fix severe usability problems. If the evaluation takes place after the product is completed, any usability problems found will have to be fixed and shipped in "fixpacks," or resolved in the next release of the product. Generally, the results of these evaluations are used as input to the next release.

Methods

Methods for conducting evaluations during beta programs or after the product is completed can vary somewhat and include:

- **Mail-in surveys.** Fax or mail surveys to beta customers or customers who purchase your wizard. You can also include a survey in your product packaging. You can collect only subjective measures with mail-in surveys.

  The advantage of mail-in surveys is that they are a relatively quick and cheap method for collecting feedback. The disadvantage is the typical low response rate for surveys, which is typically around 10%. If you have a small customer base, the number of responses could be quite small. However, it is easier to gather feedback from beta customers because you are probably in closer contact with these customers than those who purchase your product. Incentives can increase the response rate somewhat, but then you need to mail the incentive to the users with all the associated time and cost.

- **Phone surveys.** Call customers or beta customers, ask them questions over the phone, and record their responses. You can collect only subjective measures with this method.

  Phone surveys are commonly used to follow up on poor ratings in a mail-in survey to get more detail on why the customer gave negative feedback. Be sure to call the customer first and arrange another time to call them regarding the survey; customers are at work and are typically busy.

  The advantages to phone surveys are:

  - Phone surveys are relatively easy and less time-consuming than other methods, but more time-consuming than mail-in surveys.

  - Response rates are higher than mail-in surveys because if you get a customer to agree to an interview, you can get your data.

  The disadvantage of phone surveys is that it is sometimes difficult to reach customers. If you do not reach the customer directly, leave a message with a toll-free phone number. However, if you do not get a response to your phone message, then it probably won't help to bother the customer again.

- **Web surveys.** Place a feedback survey on your company's Web site and ask customers to complete it. Again, with this method, only subjective measures can be collected.

  The advantage to Web surveys is that they are a relatively quick and cheap method for collecting feedback.

  The disadvantages to Web surveys are:

  - There is typically a low response rate for surveys, which may be lower in this case because you are dependent upon users visiting your Web site, and then actually finding and completing your survey.

  - If you have a small customer base, the number of responses could be quite small. Incentives can increase the response rate somewhat, but then you need to mail the incentive to the users with all the associated time and cost.

- **Customer focus sessions.** Invite a group of customers to your site and ask the group, as a whole, a set of structured questions. This method usually involves the use of groupware software that allows each customer to enter comments or ratings on a computer and view others' responses. The software also provides summary data of the group's ratings and comments.

  The advantages to customer focus sessions are:

  - You can gather a lot of detail on questions.

  - You can facilitate group discussion among customers (which can lead to interesting requirements or solutions to problems).

  - You can gather information on future requirements.

  The disadvantages to customer focus sessions are:

  - You need a large amount of time to plan and execute these types of sessions.

  - You have to pay for customers' travel expenses.

- **Customer site visits: Interviewing users.** Interview a select group of customers using a set of predefined questions. Only subjective measures can be collected using this method.

  The advantage to interviewing users is the ability to collect detailed information on interview responses. The disadvantages to interviewing users are:

  - Customer site visits are very time-consuming due to the planning, coordination, and travel involved.

  - You need to travel to more than one location to ensure that you get a variety of customer feedback.

- **Customer site visits: Observing users while they work.** Observe your product in use in an actual work environment. You can collect both performance and subjective measures. Task completion time is the least valid performance measure because distractions may occur as part of a normal workday or the user may be performing multiple tasks concurrently.

  The advantage of observing users while they work is that any data collected is more valid because it's part of a real environment. The disadvantages to observing users while they work are:

  - Customer site visits are very time-consuming due to the planning, coordination, and travel involved.

  - You need to travel to more than one location to ensure that you get a variety of customer feedback.

  - Distractions occur as part of the user's normal job.

- **Product problem records**. Monitor your product's problem records. Most companies have some type of formal process for recording problems that customers encounter. You can review these problem records, categorize them into functional groups such as installation, usability, or documentation (books and on-line help), and determine the severity of the problems (based on frequency with which the problem was reported, whether the user could complete the task, the amount and type of data lost, or sheer annoyance). Remember to keep customer or company names confidential.

  The advantage to monitoring problem records is that this method is not costly because no travel is involved. The disadvantages to monitoring product problem records are:

  - You may need to employ another method to contact the customer for more detail.

  - It is time-consuming to read each report, categorize, and provide severity ratings.

  - You must rely on service personnel to provide detailed and accurate accounts of the users' problems.

Measures

The measures collected during these evaluations are a function of the type of evaluation. In general, most of the evaluations involve the use of a survey, so subjective measures tend to be the most common. These include ratings of overall ease of use or ease of use of particular aspects of the wizard, and of other factors such as satisfaction with the function, performance, reliability, installation, maintenance, books and on-line help, and overall satisfaction with the product.

Measures can also include a comparison of satisfaction with previous releases of the product, and what the customers liked and what could be improved about the wizard. You can also include ratings of individual components or aspects of your wizard.

If your evaluation warrants the collection of performance data, possible performance measures include number and type of errors, number of help usages, task completion time, and successful task completion.

Tasks to prepare for usability evaluations

To prepare for your usability evaluations, you need to:

- Determine what to test.
- Recruit and schedule test participants.
- Prepare documents and questionnaires.
- Create prototypes.
- Determine what measures to collect.
- Conduct pilot tests.

These tasks are discussed in this section.

Determine what to test

In a business environment with short development cycles, you will be under some time constraints either in terms of development schedules or the amount of time a test participant can spend on your usability evaluation. You may not have the luxury of recruiting 30 test participants. As a result, you will *never* be able to test everything. Be sure to prioritize your open design issues and test only those you feel are most important or those of which you are least certain.

Recruit and schedule test participants

From your user and task analysis, you know what types of skills and experiences your test participants must possess. But how do you recruit users? This section discusses the following guidelines for recruiting and scheduling test participants:

- Aim for practical versus statistical significance.
- Develop a cover letter.

- Determine the best places to recruit.

- Develop a participant screener to identify participants that represent your customer set.

- Employ internal test participants when you are evaluating design concepts that could apply to any user interface.

- Offer incentives to participate in your usability evaluation.

- Accommodate test participants' schedules.

Aim for practical versus statistical significance

If you've ever taken a course in statistics or experimental design, you know that you need many test participants to ensure that results are not due to chance alone. But what if your intended user population is composed of extremely skilled users such as database administrators? These users probably have jobs, are very busy, are highly paid, and are rare in the general population. You may be able to enlist only four or five users of this type. Valid results are still possible even with small sample sizes.

If your goal is to diagnose usability problems, we have found that trends in usability results will start to appear after three to four users. And if four out of your five test participants make an error on the same page of your wizard, you can be pretty sure you have a problem.

Develop a cover letter

Before you gather test participants, you need a cover letter that explains, at a high level, the purpose of the usability evaluation. This includes a description of what will be tested (such as software, Web tools, or hardware), the date, the time, the location, and the approximate duration of the usability test. You should also indicate what type of honorarium, if any, you will provide, and if you will pay for travel, hotel, and rental car if travel is involved.

Determine the best places to recruit

Possible sources include existing customers, customers of related products, beta customers, recruiting agencies, your company's Web site, newspapers and ads, technical conferences, and user group meetings. Once you've worked with a test participant, keep that person's information in a database for future use, with permission, of course.

Develop a participant screener to identify participants that represent your customer set

Once you know the skills and experiences necessary for your usability evaluation, you will need to construct a screener questionnaire to ensure your test participants match the intended user population. Appendix C, "Sample screener questionnaire," provides an example of a participant screener.

Employ test participants that most closely represent the types of users identified in your user analysis. Using representative users helps ensure that the feedback you gather on your wizard is generalizable to those who will actually use your wizard.

If your product is multi-platform, try to find test participants with experiences on various platforms. This is especially important if your wizard has been coded in Java, where a single wizard interface is created that is expected to meet the usability needs of users on the various platforms. Unfortunately, user interfaces on different platforms have different behaviors. Test users with experience on each target platform to be sure your wizard meets their expectations.

Employ internal test participants when you are evaluating design concepts that could apply to any user interface

Internal test participants work for your company and may have the same skill set as your intended user audience. External test participants do not work for your company and purchase your product for money.

Internal participants can be used if they will use your wizard as part of their job. Internal test participants are especially useful for pilot testing. External participants are better when you are evaluating the product as a whole—function, task flow, terminology, defaults, and so on.

Offer incentives to participate in your usability evaluation

Try to provide some type of incentive such as paying for the test participants' travel, dinner, hotel, or airline tickets. If the test participants are not traveling, you can pay them for their time or provide non-monetary incentives, such as coffee mugs, t-shirts, and e-coupons. We've found that something as simple as a t-shirt is very much appreciated. Other nontangible incentives include the chance to see future releases of a product and provide feedback.

Accommodate test participants' schedules

Plan to conduct your evaluations in the evenings or on weekends to accommodate test participants. Make sure you provide food and beverages.

Prepare documents and questionnaires

Depending on the type of usability session you conduct, you might need to prepare all or some of these documents:

- Confidentiality agreement
- Participant agreement

- Participant instructions
- Scenarios
- Background questionnaire
- Post-evaluation questionnaire

This section explains each of these documents and provides guidelines for preparing your questionnaires.

Confidentiality agreement

A confidentiality agreement is a legal contract between your company and usability test participants who will be representing their company. The agreement specifies exactly what will be disclosed to the test participants and that the test participant is bound to keep this information confidential until the product is released. You should work with your company lawyers to draft such an agreement.

If you are evaluating designs that are new, you may want to protect your ideas by requiring your test participants to complete a confidentiality agreement. This agreement is especially important if you are employing external test participants.

Confidentiality agreements take a long time to draft and approve by both companies, so make sure you allow extra time in your testing schedules.

Participant agreement

The participant agreement provides an overview of the purpose of the usability evaluation, explains whether the evaluation will be videotaped or audiotaped, states that the test participant agrees to keep the session and design in confidence, and provides payment information.

The participant agreement also informs the users that they are free to *not* participate for any reason and that they can stop participating at any time. Participants must know that their participation is voluntary. Finally, the participant agreement should indicate that test participants' names will not be used in any reports. See Appendix D, "Sample usability participant agreement," for a sample of a participant agreement.

Participant instructions

Participant instructions usually include an overview of the usability evaluation, what the test participant will be doing, and any background information on the product above and beyond what will be spelled out in the scenarios.

Additionally, the instructions should explain or describe the prototype or code if necessary. For example, if you are testing with alpha- or beta-level code (early working code), you might warn the test participants of potential code bugs and inform them that these problems will be fixed before the product is sold. See Appendix E, "Sample participant instructions," for a sample participant instruction form.

Scenarios

Scenarios are scripts or tasks that the test participant follows while using your wizard. Scenarios mirror tasks the user would perform in the real world. Having participants follow scenarios helps ensure that your usability test results are more valid and generalizable to real-world applications.

Use scenarios to lead users through tasks or subtasks on which you want to focus. For example, if you feel that one aspect of the wizard task is difficult, structure your task scenario so that users encounter the wizard page that addresses this aspect. Scenarios can also reduce the number of features you need to test by focusing the user down certain paths.

Scenarios also provide control over the evaluation so that everyone is following the same script. This additional control makes it easier to compare results across test participants. Appendix F, "Sample scenarios for an installation wizard," provides samples of usability test scenarios.

Background questionnaire

Background questionnaires gather additional information on the test participants' product experience, their platform experience, or any other information you need to gather as part of the usability evaluation. This information is in addition to the information you gathered from the participant screener. Questions should match the important jobs and tasks you gathered in your requirements analysis.

These questionnaires can also be used to help explain the results of a particular test participant in your usability evaluation. For example, if eight out of ten test participants complete all tasks successfully, but two do not, their background questionnaire responses might tell you that they have the least experience with wizards or the task.

This questionnaire can be saved and used for participant recruitment for future tests with the consent of the participant.

Post-evaluation questionnaire

Post-evaluation questionnaires allow you to capture subjective evaluations of your wizard design. You administer these questionnaires at the completion of the usability evaluation, but you can also present them after each task or scenario.

Generally, a post-evaluation questionnaire should focus on ratings of satisfaction with the overall product or wizard, ratings of specific components or aspects of your wizard, what could be improved, and what the test participants liked about the wizard design.

If you are comparing your wizard to a competitive product, include a question asking the test participants to state a preference between the two products. Appendix G, "Sample post-evaluation questionnaire," shows a sample questionnaire.

Guidelines for creating questionnaires

Some practical guidelines for questionnaire design include:

- **Keep it short.** Try to keep the length of your questionnaire to a minimum (Gillham, 2000). We've found that the longer the questionnaire, the less reliable the responses are toward the end of the questionnaire.

  We've also found a positive correlation between blank responses and increased questionnaire length. For every question you add to your questionnaire, ask what you will use the data for. If you don't know, then do not include the question.

- **Use descriptions as well as numerical scale points.** For example, in a rating scale of satisfaction from 1 to 5, add descriptions such as "very satisfied," "somewhat satisfied," "neutral," "somewhat dissatisfied," and "very dissatisfied." Descriptions provide the advantage of reminding participants of the meaning of the scale steps and ensure that all participants interpret the scale in the same way (Nunnally, 1978).

- **Avoid "double barrel" questions.** If you include two or more dimensions in one question, you will not be able to determine what influenced the rating: the first dimension, the second dimension, or some combination of both. For example, the question, "How would you rate your satisfaction with the usability of the navigation and layout of Wizard X?" is asking the user to rate two dimensions: navigation and layout. What if the user was very satisfied with the navigation, but neutral with regard to the layout?

- **Include standard company questions.** Your company may require you to collect standard data or metrics. Be aware of any corporate metrics or measures that are required for your product, and include those in your questionnaire.

- **Ask questions that support the goal of the wizard.** If the goal of your wizard is to simplify a task where another method exists for completing the task, include a question that asks participants to compare the non-wizard method with the wizard method.

- **Ensure the team reviews the questionnaire.** Make sure the entire wizard team reviews your questionnaire to ensure that each member is satisfied that data of interest is collected. Be careful, however; additional reviewers usually mean additional questions.

Create prototypes

Prototypes are a visual means to instantiate your design. The fidelity, or realism, of your prototype can range from paper prototypes to interactive prototypes to working wizard code for your usability evaluation. The type you choose is a function of where you are in the development cycle and the types of resources you have available.

This section lists advantages and disadvantages of the various types of prototypes. Chapter 3, "Applying the iterative design process," discusses them in the context of iterative design and usability evaluations.

Paper prototypes

Paper prototypes consist of hand-drawn designs and pictures or printouts of your wizard pages. Paper prototypes are an important method of gathering feedback on your wizard design. If you are short on time and resources, focus on paper prototypes.

The advantages of paper prototypes are:

- You can quickly demonstrate high-level designs.
- They are easily modified to allow for many iterations early in the design cycle.
- You can gather feedback on graphics, terminology, and overall look.

The disadvantage of paper prototypes is that you cannot gather feedback on navigation, interactions between controls and wizard pages, error recovery, and system performance.

Interactive prototypes

Interactive prototypes are developed using some type of software tool, for example, Visual Basic. You can include navigation between wizard pages, error handling, interaction between controls, and perhaps early drafts of control-level help.

The advantages of interactive prototypes are:

- You can gather feedback on navigation, interaction among controls and pages, and error conditions.

75

- You can gather feedback on first drafts of control-level help.
- They can be modified to allow multiple iterations.
- You can test pieces of the total product rather than the entire product.

The disadvantages of interactive prototypes are:

- You could develop designs that cannot be coded because your prototype software has more capability than the language in which your final wizard will be coded.
- Interactive prototypes take more time to develop than paper prototypes.
- Interactive prototypes require some programming skill.
- The increased time investment may create some hesitancy to change the prototype based on user feedback.

Working wizard code

Using wizard code for usability evaluations involves testing the wizard in a form where it is almost complete. The code should be fairly stable at this point. The advantages to using working wizard code are:

- You are testing what will be released.
- You can be certain that the design you are testing can be implemented because you are working with the same language.
- Because the testing of working product code takes place later in the design cycle, you have the potential to test the entire product.
- Working-product-code testing can help flush out code bugs before the product is released.

The disadvantages of testing with working product code are:

- Testing is usually restricted to the end of the development cycle, when the code is ready. Changes based on usability testing can therefore be expensive to implement in terms of time and resource.
- Because the wizard looks so "final," test participants might be hesitant to make suggestions.
- Because the wizard is expensive to change, there is a tendency to not want to make changes based on usability feedback.

Determine what measures to collect

Deciding on what measures to collect will help you determine if your wizard is usable and if it meets your users' needs.

Two basic terms appear in all books related to the topic of experimental design and analysis: independent variables and dependent variables:

- *Independent variables* refer to what you are evaluating. For example, if you were testing two wizard design types, Design A and Design B, your independent variable would be "Design type" with two conditions, Design A and Design B.

- *Dependent variables*, or measures, refer to how you measure the success of your independent variables, or in this example, the usability of your two wizard designs.

This section discusses these practical guidelines for collecting measures to evaluate your independent variables, or wizard designs:

- Collect and present practical measures.
- Collect measures that demonstrate your impact on the product.
- Collect both performance and subjective measures.
- If comparing two or more designs, reduce order effects.

Collect and present practical measures
It may be tempting to collect many types of measures, but unless you use the data to pinpoint problems or make design decisions, you may be wasting your time and that of the test participant. We have found that the information that is needed most for evaluating designs is:

- What problems exist
- How to fix the problems
- How important it is to resolve those problems before your wizard ships as part of the product

Collect measures that demonstrate your impact on the product
For example, if you design a wizard that will allow users to perform a task they used to perform via a command line, you might want to gather data that shows the wizard method to be less error-prone, to be faster, and to have better ratings of satisfaction than the non-wizard method.

Collect both performance and subjective measures
The types of measures collected in your usability evaluation are a function of the phase of the development cycle, the type of evaluation you are conducting, and what types of things you are testing. See "Usability evaluation techniques" on page 59 for more details. The categories of measures are:

- **Performance measures (sometimes called objective or quantitative measures).** These include the amount of time to complete the task, number of errors, types of errors, percent successful task completion, and number of uses of on-line help.

Make sure all team members involved in conducting the usability evaluations (sometimes called test administrators) agree on the definition of the performance measures so that scoring across test administrators is consistent. For example, is forgetting to fill in an optional entry field an error? What qualifies as an unsuccessful task completion? An unsuccessful task completion might be that the user has attempted to complete the task three times, has looked at all the available on-line help or books, and simply does not know how to proceed. At this point, the test administrator needs to step in to tell the user how to complete the task or subtask; therefore, the task is scored as unsuccessful.

- **Subjective measures (sometimes called qualitative measures)**. These include ratings of satisfaction, ease of use, and comments. If you are comparing your wizard to that of a competitor, include a rating that asks participants to compare the two designs in terms of overall satisfaction, preference, and so on.

You need to collect both types of data because we have found that performance and subjective data sometimes do not correlate. That is, sometimes test participants can make a number of errors while performing a task and yet their ratings of satisfaction are high.

The reverse can also be true. Collecting both types of information provides you with valuable information about what problems the user is having (performance data) and how the user feels about these problems (subjective data). This data is valuable for helping you to prioritize usability problems. For example, you might place a higher priority on those aspects of your wizard that are rated most poorly.

If comparing two or more designs, reduce order effects

Order effects refer to results that occur based on the order in which your wizard design alternatives are presented to the test participants. For example, if your test participants are comparing two wizard designs, Designs A and B, and each test participant works with Design A first, measures on Design B may be more positive simply because the participant has had time to adjust to the experimental conditions, the task domain, and overall design issues.

The converse is true as well; for example, performance on Design B may be more negative due to the fact that users first learned to perform the task using Design A. Two common methods exist to reduce these effects:

- **Counterbalancing.** Place equal numbers of test participants in each possible combination of conditions. Using the example above, you would place an equal number of test participants in the Design A—Design B order as in the Design B—Design A order. This is the most statistically valid method to use to reduce order effects.

  Note: Statistical analyses exist to test for order effects if you have enough test participants. See *Introduction to Design and Analysis: A Student's Handbook* by Geoffrey Keppel and William H. Saufley, Jr, and *Design and Analysis: A Researcher's Handbook* by Geoffrey Keppel, for a description of these analyses and discussions of other topics related to measures.

- **Randomization**. Present design alternatives to the test participants in random order. Randomization assumes that the effects of any one order of presentation of designs are cancelled by the other order. Use this method only when the number of possible combinations of conditions is small. You will also want to make sure you have enough test participants so that not all receive the same order.

Conduct pilot tests

Conduct a pilot test, or dry run, of your usability evaluation to flush out any problems with your scenarios, questionnaires, prototypes, code, and methods prior to running your actual usability test. By eliminating problems, you ensure that the feedback you collect during your test is not influenced by problems with your test. For example, if your scenarios are not accurate, test participants might make errors or take more time to complete the wizard.

Pilot testing is especially critical before you bring in customers or highly skilled test participants who are being paid for their time.

Guidelines for conducting usability evaluations

This section discusses these guidelines for conducting your usability evaluations:

- Invite the entire team to participate quietly.
- Videotape the session as backup.
- Encourage "talking aloud."
- Don't assist the test participant.
- Consider testing multiple test participants at once.
- Consider performing remote usability testing.

79

Invite the entire team to participate quietly

This includes developers, visual designers, writers, and usability professionals. You can also include managers and high-level managers. Watching a test participant struggle to perform a task helps managers to understand why the additional work of making usability improvements is needed.

Videotape the session as backup

Videotaping is a good way to provide a record of the session in case you missed a comment or data. If you videotape a participant, make sure that the video release waiver in the participant agreement form is signed.

You can also use the videotapes to make highlight tapes of key points in the usability test to illustrate changes that need to be made. However, we've found that we rarely go back and watch these videotapes and that good note-taking or good data collection software is the most efficient method of gathering data. We recommend that videotaping not be the only data collection method used because reviewing the tapes is very time-consuming.

Encourage "talking aloud"

Talking aloud is a common usability test method where the test participants tell you what is going through their heads as they perform tasks with the wizard. You can gather valuable data you would otherwise not be able to collect, for example, what problems they are having, what other selections or controls they might have expected to see, or why they made a particular choice.

Some participants are better than others at talking aloud, but you can prompt the users to continue to talk aloud. For example, if your test participant is staring at the computer screen right in the middle of the task, you can simply prompt, "Remember to talk aloud."

Don't assist the test participant

Although it may be tempting (after all, you designed the wizard, so it should be obvious how to use the wizard, right?), do not provide advice, tips, or help unless the participant has tried a couple of times, and has tried using help or some type of assistance, but still does not know how to continue. Helping participants can contaminate your measures and you may never understand where the problems are or how users really want to use your wizard. Remember that you won't be there to help users to use your wizard after they've purchased it.

Consider testing multiple test participants at once

If two test participants are present at the same time, you can choose to test them separately or together. There are advantages and disadvantages to both.

- **One test participant at a time.** The advantage to testing one test participant at a time is that this method provides you with more data, which reduces the number of additional test participants you must run.

The disadvantages to testing one participant at a time are:

- You need two or more test administrators.

- You may need to coordinate the agenda if more than one wizard is being evaluated.

- **Multiple test participants.** Running test participants together is most practical if the participants represent the same company. Each test participant can trade off performing tasks to ensure maximum participation by each.

The advantages to running multiple test participants at once are:

- The discussion that takes place between multiple participants can sometimes provide you with data you would not ordinarily be able to collect, such as a "company viewpoint" of your wizard or collaborative data.

- Testing multiple participants at once requires only one test administrator and one agenda.

The disadvantage is that you are losing additional data points by combining participants into one test.

Consider performing remote usability testing

Test participants or actual customers are not always located near your place of business and cannot always travel. Additionally, your company may not have the monetary resources to fund test participant travel. In this case, you should consider remote usability testing. We have found remote testing to be a successful means of collecting feedback on a product.

Remote usability testing involves the use of software that allows you to store the prototype or code on your machine, but also allows the users to execute the wizard and work with it on their machine. You can see exactly what the users are doing on their screens. Software products are available to help you conduct remote testing. You may need the TCP/IP address at the remote end of the session to establish a connection. You will also need a separate telephone line at each end of the session for a speakerphone so you can communicate verbally.

The advantages to remote testing are:

- If your team has remote members, they can participate at their site as well.

- Remote testing helps keep costs and travel time to a minimum.

The disadvantages to remote testing are:

- Performance is slower than on-site testing. It takes time for the "remote" screen to update after the user moves the mouse or opens a window.

- Time zone differences are a factor. You may need to conduct your usability evaluation in the early hours of the morning in the U.S. if your test participants are located in Europe, for example.

Follow these practical tips for conducting remote usability tests:

- Send instructions, scenarios, and questionnaires ahead of time so that participants can print them out and have them available during the session. These can also be stored locally on your computer and displayed at the remote site. However, printouts will eliminate the need for participants to switch from the instructions to the prototype.

- If you have a camera and the capability to display video images with your remote testing software, use it. We've found that test participants appreciate being able to see the people they are working with.

- Provide a test administrator at both ends of the session to facilitate the test by handing out scenarios and post-questionnaires, and providing coffee or dinner for the participants.

Follow-up tasks for after the usability evaluation

When you finish conducting your usability evaluation, you need to thank your participants, write a summary report, and implement design changes based on your results. This section describes each of these activities.

Follow up with thank you notes

After the usability testing is complete, always follow up with thank you notes to extend your appreciation for the participants' time and great feedback. If possible, tell the participants what you will do with their input. You can use e-mail (which we use most of the time) or a more formal letter.

Write a summary report

After you conduct your usability evaluation, you need to summarize the results in a way that will help improve the user interface of your wizard. Every company has a different set of practices and processes, but this section discusses guidelines that work well for us:

- Keep the summary short.
- Provide an executive summary.
- Include a description of your test participants.
- Do not use test participants' names in summary reports.
- Provide a list of usability problems and their severities.

Keep the summary short
In short development cycles, the last thing the development team needs is a long, complicated summary of the usability test results. If you need to provide details, include those in an appendix.

Provide an executive summary
For those who want to know the bottom-line results of your usability test, always provide a one- or two-paragraph high-level summary of your results followed by practical details for resolving usability problems.

Include a description of your test participants
This description should include enough information for the development team to feel comfortable with the validity of the usability test results. The description includes the number of participants, the length of time of their participation, the dates of their participation, job titles and duties, whether they are internal or external participants, and if external, what company, if any, they represent.

Additionally, provide a summary of any relevant skills or experience; for example, experience with operating systems, number of years of database experience, and experience with previous products or competitive products.

Do not use test participants' names in summary reports
This guideline is considered basic courtesy to protect the anonymity of the test participants. Test participants must feel comfortable providing feedback without fear of having their name attached to specific results or comments.

Provide a list of usability problems and their severities
You can group usability problems by wizard and by page of your wizard to help organize the problems.

Severity ratings should be simple, such as "high," "medium," or "low." Other rating systems include numerical ratings of "1," "2," and "3." No matter what type of rating scale you use, make sure that the readers of your report understand what these severities mean in behavioral terms.

Nielsen (1994) states that the severity of a problem is a combination of three factors:

- **Frequency with which a problem occurs.** How often will the problem occur?

- **Impact of the problem.** Can users recover from the error?

- **Persistence of the problem.** Is it a one-time problem, or will users encounter this problem many times?

Nielsen also adds that you need to assess the market impact of the problem because certain problems can affect the perception of your product and its sales.

We use the following scale in our summary reports, which is based on the ability to complete the task, error recovery, and loss of data:

- **Severity 1 (High).** Users could not complete the task or subtask. The users could not recover from errors. Errors resulted in loss of significant amounts of data or important data.

- **Severity 2 (Medium).** Users completed the task or subtask, but with great difficulty or a number of errors. Users could recover from errors, but had difficulty. Errors resulted in loss of some data.

- **Severity 3 (Low).** Users completed the task and may not have encountered any errors in doing so, but found the interface inconsistent or somewhat confusing. Severity 3 errors tend to be more of an annoyance or make the wizard or product look less professional (that is, "fit and finish" problems). These types of problems do not generally result in lower user satisfaction by themselves, but large numbers of Severity 3 problems can certainly lower user satisfaction.

Implement design changes based on your results

The results of your data analysis should provide a list of usability problems and associated severity ratings. Of course, the most severe usability problems should be resolved, but don't forget the less severe usability problems. Remember that many Severity 3 problems can equal a Severity 1 problem!

Summary of guidelines discussed in this chapter

❏ Conduct heuristic evaluations early in the design cycle to uncover obvious usability problems early. Use paper or limited functioning prototypes.

❏ Conduct design explorations early in the design cycle to evaluate the high-level design or direction of your wizard, missing functionality, and terminology. Use paper or limited functioning prototypes.

❏ Conduct design evaluations middle to late in the design cycle to evaluate detailed wizard design such as navigation, order and flow of controls, and error handling. Use interactive prototypes.

❏ Conduct competitive benchmarks late in the development cycle to compare your complete wizard design and associated product with the closest competitor. Use working wizard code.

❏ Conduct evaluations after the product is released to gather requirements for the next release of your wizard and to determine how your wizard will do in the marketplace.

❏ Aim for practical versus statistical significance.

❏ When recruiting users, develop a cover letter and a participant screener, and explore all possible sources for finding representative users.

❏ Test with users that most closely resemble your actual customer set.

❏ Before you test your first participant, create several documents, including: confidentiality agreements, participant instructions, scenarios, background questionnaires, and post-evaluation questionnaires.

❏ Collect both performance and subjective measures.

❏ Control order effects using counterbalancing or randomization.

❏ Always pilot-test your methods, materials, and procedures.

❏ Invite the entire wizard design team to participate quietly.

❏ Encourage "talking aloud" to understand what the test participant is thinking.

❏ Do not assist the test participant.

❏ Use remote usability testing methods when your test participant is not local and traveling is not feasible.

❏ Follow up all evaluations with thank you notes.

❏ Follow these guidelines for summarizing the results: Keep the summary short, provide an executive summary, include a description of your test participants, do not use test participants' names in your report, and include a list of usability problems and associated severities.

❏ Don't fix just the most severe usability problems.

Chapter 5

General wizard design

▲ Why create wizard design guidelines?
▲ Questions to ask before beginning
▲ General wizard guidelines
▲ Page-specific wizard design guidelines
▲ Guidelines for launching dialogs from wizards
▲ Guidelines for wizards on the Web
▲ Summary of guidelines discussed in this chapter

W hen you begin designing your wizard, start by thinking about some general design issues, for example, which buttons to provide, what the layout will look like, what the text will say, and what text and controls will be placed on the first page of your wizard.

This chapter provides guidelines and examples for designing usable wizards. This chapter covers:

- General wizard guidelines
- Page-specific design guidelines
- Guidelines for launching dialogs from wizards
- Guidelines for wizards on the Web

Why create wizard design guidelines?

General design guidelines provide a basic structure for the overall wizard. Benefits of wizard design guidelines include:

- **Guidelines ensure a consistent design of the pages within your wizard.** Consistent design of wizard pages will make your wizard easier to use because controls are placed in the same location and behave similarly from page to page.

- **Guidelines ensure a consistent design for all wizards in your application or product.** Consistent wizard design across applications in your company help to ensure a common user experience.

- **Guidelines ensure that your design is consistent with industry standards for usable wizards.** Following industry standards will help make your wizard more competitive in the marketplace.

Questions to ask before beginning

- **How much experience do the users have with the tasks your wizard will perform?** If your users are experts, a different vocabulary and a different level of help will be needed than if the users are novices.

- **What will the user need to know to use the wizard? Are there software prerequisites**? Any prerequisite information or required software should be listed on the first page of the wizard.

- **Will the wizard be translated into multiple languages**? If your wizard will be translated, you will need to allow extra white space on your wizard pages to accommodate the longer text strings some languages require.

- **What are the subtasks, or steps, the wizard will support?** The subtasks supported by the wizard will determine the number of pages the wizard contains.

General wizard guidelines

This section presents some general guidelines to help you design usable wizards. Rather than summarize the many user interface guidelines used by the industry, this section focuses on guidelines that are of particular importance to the design of wizards. These guidelines are presented in three categories: overall goals of the design, writing style guidelines, and page count guidelines.

Overall goals of the design

Follow these general guidelines for the overall goals of your wizard design:

- **Hide the complexity of the underlying task**. Do not force users to understand the internal design of the system to complete a task. For example, a user should be able to create a database without having to understand the internal design of the system catalog tables.

- **Ask the user simple questions**. The wizard can calculate advanced results "under the covers."

- **Include as many defaults as possible so users don't need to enter all information for task completion**. Display defaults and allow users to change them if desired. Defaults may be most helpful for novice users who may be uncertain of where to find required information.

- **Reduce the number of entry fields by replacing them with choices in list boxes or radio buttons**. Your users will have a much easier time recognizing a correct selection than recalling the same information from memory.

- **Maintain task cohesiveness**. Do not require the user to leave the wizard to complete a task. If a related task must be performed, you can launch another dialog or pop-up window so the user can complete the task.

- **Provide a clear indication of mandatory fields**. That is, indicate which fields are required to be completed by the user. This can be done in a number of ways such as highlighting the text prompt next to the control, providing an asterisk (or some other type of symbolic notation) next to the field, providing color around the mandatory field (for example, outline in red), or providing smartfields. See Chapter 10, "Error prevention and recovery," for more details.

- **Keep the user in control**. For example, do not advance pages automatically.

Writing style

Although the design of the wizard pages aids in usability, the actual text on each page must be clear to users because it contributes to the ease of use of your wizard. Follow these general writing style guidelines for the text in your wizard pages:

- **Keep your writing style simple, clear, and concise**. Don't clutter your pages with extraneous or unnecessarily technical terms.

- **Minimize the number of words on your wizard pages**. We have found that users tend not to read text within a wizard. They assume the wizard will guide them through task completion very quickly and with no errors.

- **Use a conversational writing style**. Use words like "you" and "your."

- **Avoid passive voice and future tense**. Passive voice and future tense typically leave the actor unspecified and the time or cause of the outcome doubtful. For example, suppose the user reads the following sentence: "The action will occur according to the specific options." The user might wonder: Who sets the action in motion and how? When will the action occur? Who specified the options and where exactly? At this point in the wizard, do I have a chance to double-check the options that are specified before the action starts?

- **Use active voice where appropriate.** For example, "Specify the name of the printer you want to set up." This construction makes it clear who is doing what.

- **Work with a writer or editor (or both) to create or update the text that you use on your wizard pages and the text of your messages.** Writers and editors can help you with terminology issues, translation issues, sentence clarity, and tone and style.

- **Do not leave your user guessing what to do next**. Specify options where necessary, as in "To change your selection, click **Back**. To start the action, click **Finish**."

- **Run your interface text and messages through a spell-checker.** Spelling mistakes are easy to make, yet embarrassing when not fixed.

Page count

Follow these general page count guidelines:

- **Ensure that your wizard covers only one task**. For example, setting up a printer is one task. Wizards that span more than one task can become overly complicated and lengthy. The individual pages of your wizard should represent subtasks, or steps, that make up the larger task.

- **Keep the page count to 10 or less**. The ideal size of a wizard is 5 pages. Seven or 8 pages are probably okay. If the wizard has more than 10 pages, you need to rethink your design. You might want to re-evaluate the task the wizard is performing to see if it can be broken up into two wizards, or perhaps place optional information in dialogs that can be launched from the wizard.
  For complex wizards, such as a tax preparation wizard, we recommend 10 pages or less for the default path. Ideally, do not create a wizard with a default path of more than 10 pages. For simple wizards, such as a setup printer wizard, which cover simpler tasks, we recommend 3 pages or less.

- **Try to maintain a balance between the number of pages and the complexity (number of controls) of the page.** It is better to have more simple pages with fewer controls and text than a smaller number of complex pages.

Page-specific wizard design guidelines

Wizard pages contain a number of different areas:

- Wizard title area

- Step identification area

- Step description area

- Working area

- Optional graphic area

- Button area

- Navigation (table of contents) area

Figures 5–1 and 5–2 show these areas arranged on a wizard page. The layouts shown in these two figures are samples only; your wizard layout might be different.

Figure 5–2 shows how a wizard page would look if arranged according to the layout shown in Figure 5–1.

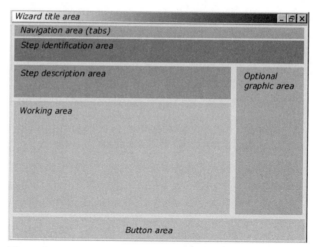

Figure 5–1   *Sample layout showing areas of a wizard page.*

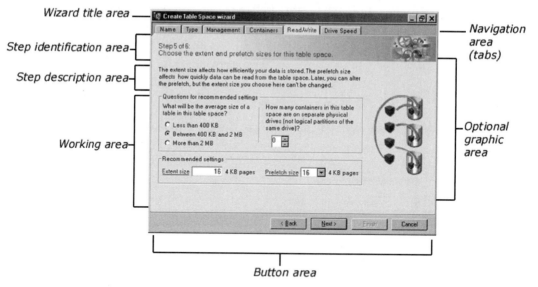

Figure 5–2   *Sample wizard page using layout in Figure 5–1.*

This section provides guidelines for page layout. This section also explains each of the page areas and provides guidelines for each. The navigation area is discussed in Chapter 6, "Navigation." Finally, this section provides guidelines for the first and last pages of a wizard.

Page layout

Using a consistent page layout communicates a sense of order and cohesiveness to users. Consistent page layout provides the following advantages:

- It sets up user expectation of placement of controls, graphics, and buttons on each page. This eliminates the need for users to hunt for the text areas, working area, and buttons.
- It eliminates the perception of flickering when users navigate from page to page because the wizard areas are in a consistent position.

Follow these guidelines when choosing a layout:

- Make the basic page layout consistent in every page of every wizard of the application and associated applications.
- Break the material on the page into bite-size chunks, which can be quickly noticed and processed.
- Do not fill the screen with text and images. Leave white space.
- Distribute the page elements to "force" the eye of the user to go from the more important information to the less important information in the following ways:
  - Place more important information before less important information on a page.
  - Make the order and layout of your wizard page match the sequence in which users perform tasks.
  - Place higher priority items in the upper-left corner of the screen.

    Note: This guideline applies to only those languages that read left to right, top to bottom.
  - Group similar information together.
  - Enclose information that will be used together in lines or boxes. Information used together should also move, change, or look alike with respect to color, shape, size, and topography (Nielsen, 1993).
- Include an initial focus or cursor position on each wizard page. The initial focus position is generally in the upper-left corner control for languages that read left to right, top to bottom.
- Use a consistent grid, consistent typography, and consistent visual emphasis to produce a relationship between words and look and feel.

For more information on layout and grids, see Chapter 7, "Visual design."

Wizard title area

Located in the title bar at the top of the wizard, the wizard title area provides the name of your wizard.

Follow these guidelines for the title area:

- Be specific about what the wizard will do. Make sure that you include a noun and a verb in your title, for example, "Book an Airline Flight Wizard" or "Set Up a Printer Wizard."

- Use headline-style capitalization in the title area, for example, "Create Table Wizard."

- When referring to your wizard in the wizard itself, or in other documentation, avoid capitalizing the word "wizard," except where noted, to avoid possible intellectual property law infringements. The term "Wizard" is another company's trademark and is part of several other companies' trademarks. For example, when referring to your wizard, use "...the Create Database wizard." Capitalize the word "wizard" only when headline-style capitalization is used (such as in the title bar or in a menu choice).

- If your wizard is launched from an application via a menu selection, make the wizard title match the name of the menu selection if possible.

Step identification area

The step identification area provides the user with a quick description of the page (or step) of the wizard.

Follow these guidelines for the step identification area:

- Make the font and color in this area different than the font and color in the rest of the text on the page. This will help the step identification area to stand out.

- Use two lines for the step identification area to allow space for translation into other languages.

- Left-justify the text on both lines with the text in the step description area.

- If you choose to display the total number of steps, use "Step X of N:" on the first line of this area, for example, "Step 2 of 6:". For translation, you can start the second line after the colon on the first line if you need the extra space for the phrase on the second line.

- If the number of pages is dynamic, that is, changes as a function of what the user selects, adjust the total number of steps (N) to the number of pages dynamically.

- Provide a phrase in the form of a question to describe the step for this page on the second line. For example, for a Create Database wizard use:

  > Step 1 of 5:
  > What is the name of database?

  instead of:

  > Step 1 of 5:
  > Name of database.

- Use sentence-style capitalization, for example:

  > Step 1 of 5:
  > What date would you like to travel?

- Display an optional graphic identifier at the right of the step identification area.

Step description area

Use the step description area to provide instructions to the user about how to interact with and complete the current wizard page. If there is no graphic in the optional graphic area, expand the width of the step description area *only* if the text takes up more than four lines.

Follow these guidelines for the step description area:

- Provide guidance to explain how to complete the page, for example, "Select the database to connect to. Provide the user ID and password of a database administrator (optional if the database administrator is the current user)."

  The goal of the step description area is to provide enough instructions to the user so that the user doesn't need on-line help in most cases.

- Provide conceptual help for terms as needed. Underline the terms for which you provide this type of help. See Chapter 11, "On-line help," for more details.

Working area

The working area of a wizard page is where the user interacts with the wizard. It is generally in the center of the wizard page. Even if you have a consistent layout, some pages may not include an optional graphic area. In these cases, you can expand the width of your working area. If you do not include a step description area in your wizard layout, you can expand the height of the working area.

Follow these guidelines for the working area of any page of a wizard:

- Use concrete and meaningful text for field and control labels.

- If possible, provide pop-up help for all controls.

- If needed, provide page-specific buttons in this area, for example, **Clear** or **Undo**.

- When a selection or field is valid only when a certain choice is made on a prior field, disable (gray out) that dependent control until the necessary choice is made. For example, on a tax wizard, there may be a field for marital status. If the user selects **Married**, then the **Name of spouse** field is enabled; otherwise, it remains disabled and is grayed out in appearance.

Follow these guidelines for entry fields:

- Support editing and correcting of values in entry fields. Allow users to correct individual characters within a field without having to retype a field. Support insertion or deletion of characters.

- Provide an audible beep when the user exceeds the length of an entry field.

- If possible, provide validation of user input in entry fields. For example, if a user tries to enter a TCP/IP address in a field, provide feedback if the input is incorrect. This feedback can be in the form of an error beep or a pop-up message, called a smartfield.

- If a field is mandatory, do not enable the **Next** button until any error in the field is corrected.

- Adjust the length of the field to indicate the maximum length allowed for input. However, if the field allows many characters, you will have to scroll the text in the field.

- Provide an example of the intended input or display the format in the field. For example, when requesting the user to enter a monetary value, do not require the user to enter a decimal point, comma, or dollar sign. You can provide these for the user and provide the capability for the cursor to skip from one part of the field, across the decimal or comma, to the next part of the field.

Follow these guidelines for radio buttons and check boxes:

- Use radio buttons when only one selection is allowed and check boxes when more than one selection is allowed.

- Group radio buttons together or check boxes together if they relate to the same information.

- Indicate which radio button is selected or which check box state is the default.

- Ensure that the tab order between the controls on your wizard page is correct. That is, if the user presses the Tab key to move from control to control, ensure that the tab movement is from top to bottom, left to right, or whatever order makes sense for completing the wizard page. See Chapter 13, "Accessibility," for more details.

Optional graphic area

The graphic area is an optional area of a wizard page that contains graphics to help the user understand the content and questions of the wizard page. The graphic area should not be required on every wizard page; there may be some pages that contain graphics and some that do not in the same wizard. If you do not include an optional graphic area on your wizard page, you can increase the width of your working area.

Follow these guidelines for the optional graphic area:

- Always place the graphic area in a consistent location on the wizard page. Because reading takes place from left to right in the majority of countries, placing the graphics on the left would cause the pages to appear to "jump" and disrupt the flow of reading. Placing the graphics on the right has much less of an impact on the flow of the wizard pages in cases where graphics are not used on every page.

- Try to keep the dimensions (width and height) and properties (palette and image clarity) consistent from page to page.

- Make graphics meaningful, attractive, and helpful (for example, to explain a concept). Do not use graphics simply as a decoration. Graphics should reduce the amount of text or description needed in the wizard page and add value to the task.

- Ensure that the graphics are consistent with the metaphors and graphics used in the complete product or application.

- Make your graphics establish a theme for the overall wizard. For example, for a wizard that will create a spreadsheet, you might want to show a spreadsheet as a component in the graphic on each page.

- Make the graphics subtle. They should not be the primary focus of attention, but a visual aid to the user.

- Make the graphics dynamic where appropriate and useful. In some cases, changing graphics (and explanatory text) based on user selections in a page might reduce the user's need for assistance.

  For example, a wizard page might allow the user to select a type of chart—line, pie, or bar chart. If the user selects a pie chart, the graphic shows a pie chart, and the associated explanatory text describes a pie chart and why it can be used instead of some other type of chart. If the user selects a bar chart, the graphic changes to show a bar chart, and the associated descriptive text changes. Figure 5–3 shows an example of dynamic graphics.

- Animate graphics where appropriate. An animated graphic can explain a concept that a static graphic might not be able to explain.

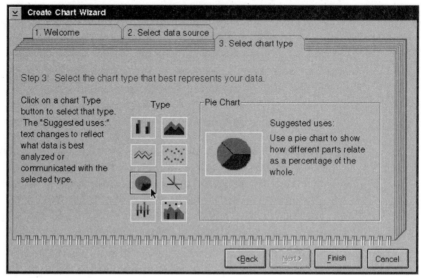

Figure 5–3   *Example of dynamic graphics.*

Button area

The button area contains the push buttons that apply to the entire wizard, not just one individual page. The buttons included in this area generally pertain to navigation, that is, moving back and forth in the wizard, canceling out of the wizard, and completing or finishing the wizard.

The button area usually contains the **Back**, **Next, Finish**, and **Cancel** buttons in a consistent order and right-justified. Table 5–1 describes each of these buttons and their associated accelerator key.

Table 5–1   Definition of buttons in the button area of a wizard

Button name	Access key	Description
Back	The access key for **Back** is usually the B key.	Takes the user back to the previous page. All user input is saved so that users do not need to re-enter all the page information when they return to this page.

Table 5–1   Definition of buttons in the button area of a wizard (continued)

Button name	Access key	Description
Next	The access key for **Next** is usually the N key.	Takes the user to the next page. All wizard processing is tied to this key. This is usually the default action when the user presses the Enter key. Clicking **Next** maintains settings the user provides.
Cancel	Use the ESC key rather than providing an access key for **Cancel**.	Closes the wizard without performing any actions. Generally, clicking **Cancel** should discard user-selected settings. However, if users enter a large amount of data, prompt them via a message box to save the input for later use.
Finish	The access key for **Finish** is usually the F key.	Processes user input only when all required steps of a wizard are completed.

Follow these guidelines for the button area:

- Try to minimize the necessity of including a **Help** button for your wizard. The goal of the wizard is to provide a user interface that is so easy to use that help is not necessary. If help is needed, try to provide assistance in a form that is integrated into the wizard page itself in the form of pop-up help on terms or controls. See Chapter 11, "On-line help," for more information.

- If you must provide a **Help** button, use F1 instead of an accelerator key.

- Do not use **Undo**, **Default**, and **Clear** in the button area because it may not be clear whether these actions apply to a particular page or the entire wizard. However, you can use these buttons (and any others) in the working area of a wizard as needed.

- Place page-specific buttons in the working area of your wizard, not in the bottom area.

Additional guidelines for buttons are described in Chapter 6, "Navigation."

First page

The first page of your wizard should provide an introduction and overview of your wizard. It should explain what the wizard will do and what objects the wizard will create. This orients the users and helps them decide if the wizard is appropriate for them. Follow these guidelines for the first page of your wizard:

- Label the first page with the name of the step, like all the other pages.
- If the wizard performs a number of subtasks, present them in a bulleted form so that each subtask stands out.
- Provide a list of what information, if any, the user will need to complete the wizard.
- Provide any prerequisite steps that must be done before completing the wizard.
- List key limitations of the wizard. For example, in an airline reservation wizard, tell the users that the wizard will not help them reserve a hotel or book a rental car.
- If possible, indicate how much time it will take to complete the wizard.
- Include simple controls in the working area, but only if there is room. This may help reduce the number of wizard pages. Figure 5–4 shows an example of the first page of a wizard containing text and controls.
- Provide a **Do not show this page again** check box if there are no controls on the first page.
- Do not display a **Back** button because this is the first page of your wizard.

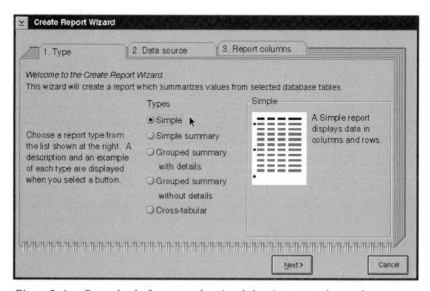

Figure 5–4 *Example of a first page of a wizard showing text and controls.*

Last page

The last page of your wizard should provide a summary of the user's selections, what the wizard will do or create when the user clicks **Finish**, and how to proceed after the wizard finishes processing. The last page of the wizard is the last page for users to catch any errors they may have made. Follow these guidelines for the last page of your wizard:

- Label the last page with the name of the step, like all the other pages.

- Include a **Back** button and a **Finish** button.

  Note: You should include a **Finish** button on any page where the wizard has enough information to complete the task. For example, if you provide enough defaults in your wizard, a **Finish** button could be displayed on the first page.

- If your wizard is complex or contains many pages, provide a summary of the user's choices and what will be created or done when the user clicks **Finish**. The summary could be in the form of a bulleted list, or if there are many options, the summary could be in the form of a scrollable list box. Figure 5–5 shows an example of a wizard summary page.

- If there is room, include controls on this page to help reduce the overall number of pages.

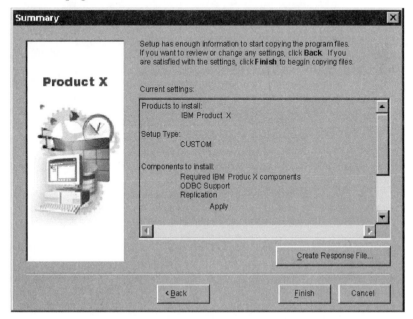

Figure 5–5   *Example of a summary page of an installation wizard.*

- If optional actions can be performed after the wizard finishes processing, include those as check boxes. For example, in an installation wizard, prompt the user to launch a tutorial following installation.

- Optional: Provide a **Show Commands** button to display the commands the wizard will issue before the user clicks **Finish**. See Chapter 12, "Experts and novices," for more details.

- For long-running actions after the user clicks **Finish**, display progress indicators or message dialog boxes. See Chapter 9, "Interactive feedback," for more details.

Guidelines for launching dialogs from wizards

Occasionally, you might find that you need to launch a separate dialog from a button on a wizard page. For example, you might launch a dialog from a wizard page when the user needs to perform some subtask that is not central to the main wizard task and you don't want the user to leave the wizard. Also, you might find launching dialogs useful for providing advanced functions (such as changing defaults) for expert users.

Figure 5–6 shows an example of a separate dialog being launched from an **Options** button on a wizard page.

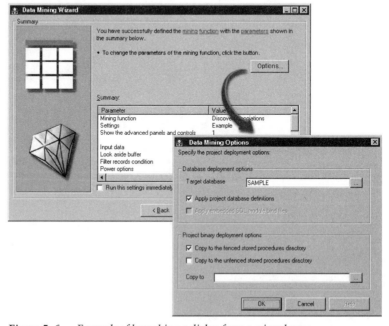

Figure 5–6   *Example of launching a dialog from a wizard page.*

Follow these guidelines for launching dialogs from wizards:

- Launch dialogs sparingly because this might add complexity and may confuse a novice user.

- Try to launch dialogs for optional tasks only. Handle required tasks inside the wizard.

- Avoid cyclic interactions, where the wizard needs the dialog and the dialog needs the wizard.

- Avoid cascading dialogs from a wizard, that is, where one dialog can launch another dialog and so forth.

- Make the dialog modal, that is, do not allow users to interact with the wizard while the dialog is displayed. You do not want the users to advance wizard pages when a dialog from a previous page remains open. Users could misunderstand what the dialog relates to.

Guidelines for wizards on the Web

The guidelines provided for wizard design in this chapter also apply to wizards designed for the Web. However, additional guidelines apply to wizards in this environment. This section lists a few of the most important guidelines for wizards developed for the Web. For a comprehensive look at designing usable interfaces for the Web, see *Designing Web Usability* by Jakob Nielsen.

Follow these guidelines for wizards designed for the Web:

- Allow enough room to accommodate the menu bar, navigation bar, and any other parts of the browser. See Chapter 7, "Visual design," for more details.

- Keep your text shorter than you would in non-Web wizards so that all information can fit on one page. Users do not like to scroll. Nielsen (2000) states that you should allow for 50% less text on Web applications than on non-Web applications.

- Because Web users tend to scan rather than read, use bulleted lists to break up uniform text blocks (Nielsen, 2000).

- Use descriptive links to provide quick understanding.

- Avoid using "click here" for links. Provide more descriptive links, for example, "Would you like to access seat assignments?" Descriptive links are more usable for non-mouse users because they save users from having to click to find out what is on the page. Loading additional pages takes time.

- Avoid the need for links from one area on a page to another area on the same page (anchors) by keeping the page simple.

- Keep feedback times consistent (Nielsen, 2000) to avoid having users think the wizard has stopped responding to their input or has stopped working.

- Cut down on complexity of tables; use ALT attributes so users know what a control is about before it is rendered.

- Use highlighting and emphasis for important words to catch the users' eyes. Users scan information on the Web.

- Provide a different title on each page because the same title in the history list is of little value.

- Use clear page titles because these are used as the main reference to your page in search engines.

Follow these guidelines for reducing the time to load your wizard pages:

- Keep the wizard pages simple.

- Reduce the number of graphics in your wizard pages.

- Keep graphics simple.

- Keep multimedia to a minimum.

- To reduce perceived time to load a wizard page, paint the top of the page first (use width and height attributes on all tables to do this).

Summary of guidelines discussed in this chapter

❏ Follow the general guidelines provided for ease of use, writing style, and page count. Some of the more important guidelines include:

❏ Include as many defaults as possible.

❏ Provide a clear indication of mandatory fields.

❏ Keep the number of wizard pages to 10 or less.

❏ Keep your writing style simple, clear, and concise.

❏ Run your interface text and messages through a spell-checker.

❏ Choose a page layout and use it for all of your wizards.

❏ Follow the detailed guidelines provided for the various areas of each wizard page: wizard title area, step identification area, step description area, working area, optional graphic area, and button area. Some of the more important guidelines include:

- Make the wizard title explain what the wizard will do.

- Make the font and color of your step identification area different from the rest of your wizard to make it stand out.

- Provide enough information in the step description area so that the user does not need on-line help.

- Use concrete and meaningful text for field and control labels in the working area.

- Always place the optional graphic area in a consistent location.

- Place **Back**, **Next**, **Finish**, and **Cancel** buttons in a consistent order and in a consistent location in the button area.

❏ Make sure that the first page of your wizard explains and introduces the wizard.

❏ Make sure that the last page of your wizard summarizes the users' selections and explains what will happen when the users press **Finish.**

❏ Launch dialogs from wizard pages sparingly.

❏ Follow the same guidelines for wizards that will be on the Web, but allow for extra white space and leave room for menu bars and other browser features.

Chapter 6

Navigation

▲ Why optimize your wizard's navigation?

▲ Questions to ask before beginning

▲ Navigation methods

▲ Methods to help users estimate their progress through the wizard

▲ Summary of guidelines discussed in this chapter

U sers *navigate* through a wizard by traveling from page to page to complete their task. To find their way through the wizard successfully, users need to be able to answer several navigational questions, including:

- Where am I now and where can I go?

- How do I get to where I want to be?

- Where have I been?

- What do I have left to do?

To support user progress through the wizard, you must provide controls, such as buttons, tabs, or links, to allow the user to get from page to page. However, you must also provide a roadmap to help users understand their progress through the wizard task.

This chapter will help you to choose a navigation approach for your wizard and to learn how to use cues to meaningfully support navigation. One section discusses choices of controls to allow users to get from page to page. Another section of the chapter provides information on how to create a roadmap to help users understand their position and progress throughout the wizard.

Why optimize your wizard's navigation?

Because a wizard consists of multiple pages, you must allow the user to get from page to page. Dealing with navigational issues early in your design has several benefits:

- **Your wizard will be easier to use.** The proper navigational method will help users to easily understand where they are and what they have left to do.

- **The navigation method impacts your wizard code.** Different navigational methods require very different types of underlying code. **Back** and **Next** buttons do not show an overview of the steps that the user must complete, but tabs do. This difference might result in different rules for redrawing the screen when the number of steps changes.

- **Deciding on a navigational method gives you time to plan your screen layout.** You need to know which method works best, so that you can develop a grid and high-level design that support it. Controls such as tabs and tables of contents will take up real estate and might require you to divide one page into several pages. You want to catch these types of structural impacts as early in the design process as possible.

Questions to ask before beginning

Understanding the structure of the task and the predicted use of the wizard will help you choose appropriate navigational controls and supporting cues. The task and product analyses described in Chapter 1, "Kicking off the project," and Chapter 2, "Gathering requirements," should provide answers to the following questions:

- **How many steps are required to complete the wizard?** The number of steps influences the types of controls you can choose to support navigation. For example, do not use tabs if all tabs cannot be visible on-screen at once.

- **Is the number of steps constant, or can additional steps be added based on user entries?** The constancy of steps influences the navigation method you choose. If the steps are always the same, it is easy to show the user what steps he or she must complete. If the steps change, you will need to redraw and renumber the steps, which will require more programming.

- **Is the order of the steps static, or does it depend on user entries?** If the order of steps changes based on user entries and you show the user the overall task flow in your wizard, you will need to redraw and renumber the steps based on user entries.

- **Must the user perform several steps in a sequential order? Can steps be repeated before proceeding to the next step?** The answers to these questions impact the error checking and coding that you must add to support navigation. For example, if any wizard steps need to be completed in a sequential order, your wizard must prevent users from completing steps out of order.

- **How frequently do users complete the task? Do the users complete the task only a single time, daily, weekly, or other?** If users will reuse your wizard, you might add controls such as tabs to allow users to access each step directly.

- **Can you predict default entries or values for wizard steps or will user entries be needed to complete the steps?** Navigational cues such as enabling the **Finish** button and the addition of checkmarks on completed steps are impacted by the existence of defaults. Default entries make it easier for the user to complete the wizard, but make it harder for wizard code to interpret user actions.

- **Will the wizard integrate with other products or wizards?** If other wizards already exist, be sure that your new wizard's navigation is consistent with previous wizards.

Navigation methods

Several methods can be used to help users navigate through a wizard:

- **Back** and **Next** buttons only
- Tabs
- Table of contents
- Pull-down menu

The method that you provide depends on the underlying task characteristics and user requirements. The most important constraint in this choice is consistency. Wizards in the same product should have consistent navigational approaches and controls *unless* there is a clear reason for the differences.

This section explains the various methods and the advantages and disadvantages of each. This section also discusses other navigational options, such as providing a read-only roadmap.

Back and Next buttons only

The standard navigation method for wizards provides the user with a set of buttons (**Back** and **Next**) to support navigation from one page to the next. These buttons should be present in all wizard designs regardless of any other navigation controls that are provided. Figure 6–1 shows a standard navigation method.

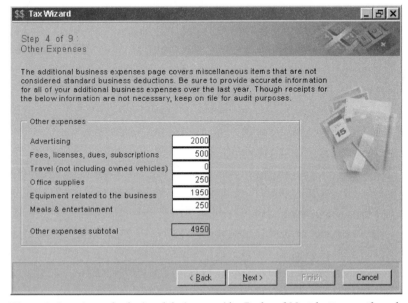

Figure 6–1   *A standard wizard design provides Back and Next buttons as the only means to navigate from page to page.*

Advantages of the standard navigation method are:

- The **Back** and **Next** buttons do not take up much room, leaving a lot of real estate for the working area of the wizard.

- The complexity of the underlying path is hidden. The **Back** and **Next** buttons can make the wizard appear to be very easy to use, even if the path is quite dynamic.

- The user interface tightly controls user navigation through the wizard. It is difficult for the user to jump ahead or skip pages.

Disadvantages of the standard navigation method are:

- User flexibility is limited. Users cannot directly access a specific wizard page.

- Re-entry is awkward for users.

Spool (1999) states that easy-to-use wizards allow re-entry. Re-entry refers to allowing users to save wizard settings and reuse them in the future, either in their entirety (for example, if the user is installing the same software on multiple machines) or in part (for example, if the user is creating multiple similar objects that differ only in one aspect).

The standard navigation method can support re-entry, but re-entry can be quite awkward. For example, to change the setting on the fifth page, the user must click the **Next** button several times to get to the page (and perhaps again to get to the last page of the wizard). Requiring a large number of mouse clicks to make a single change results in poor ease of use. If re-entry or flexibility is an important goal, add other standard user interface controls to allow the user to move about more easily. Three such methods include: tabs, a table of contents, and a pull-down menu.

Tabs

You can add a series of buttons or tabs to the top of the wizard to allow the user to directly access each page. Each tab corresponds to a specific page. If the name of specific pages or the number of pages can change based on user entries, the initial row of tabs should show the path that most users are expected to take. Figure 6–2 shows a wizard with tabs.

Each possible user path should be limited to a single row of tabs, and all tabs for the current user path should be visible. User studies have shown that users have trouble predicting how mechanisms such as scrolling tabs and multiple-rowed tab controls work.

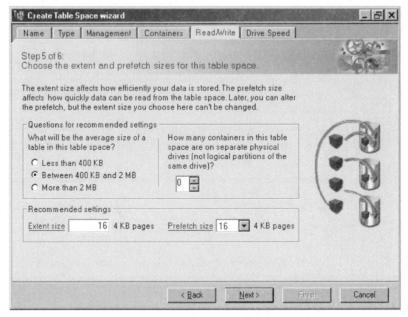

Figure 6–2   *A wizard that uses a tabbed approach for navigation.*

Advantages of the tabbed approach are:

- The tabbed approach uses a common metaphor for navigation. Most users have seen tabbed dialogs before; tabs are used for most Properties dialogs on the Windows platforms.
- Although they take up some room, the tab controls leave a lot of the screen real estate available for the main working area of the wizard.
- The tabbed approach provides more flexibility in navigation than the standard wizard approach. The user can go directly to the step of interest.
- Users can more easily look ahead to view required information on future pages.
- The listing of steps can help the user gain a clearer model of the task approach.
- Users can visually determine their progress through the wizard by viewing where they are in the row of tabs.

Disadvantages of the tabbed approach are:

- Tabs should be used only for wizards with a minimal number of pages.
- Tabs might make a wizard appear harder to use if the underlying path is complex.

- Tabs require additional programming to redraw the tabs as the path changes. The flexibility required to allow the user to jump ahead and skip pages may also make programming more difficult.

- Software performance and response may decrease (become slower), especially if the number of tabs changes based on user selections. The screen and tabs must be redrawn as tabs are added and removed.

Table of contents

The table of contents control consists of a column of buttons or links. You can add a table of contents control to the left side of the wizard to allow the user to directly access pages. This design can be considered a tabbed control in which the tabs are "stacked" rather than horizontally adjacent to each other. Usability test results at IBM indicated that this design was favored above the tabbed, pull-down menu, and standard navigation methods. Two-thirds of the participants ranked the table of contents first for overall preference and first along each of four dimensions for ease of use (ease of understanding how to use the control, ease of using the control, amount of time required to complete the tasks, and number of steps required to complete the tasks). Participants completed tasks using the table of contents wizard significantly faster than with tabs and pull-down menu designs.

Figure 6–3 illustrates a wizard design with table of contents navigational controls.

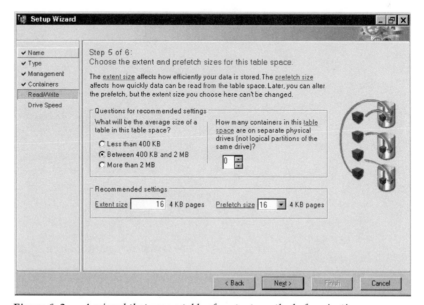

Figure 6–3   *A wizard that uses a table of contents method of navigation.*

As in the tabbed design, each button (or link) corresponds to a specific page. If the names of specific pages or the number of pages can change based on user entries, the initial table of contents should be set to the path that most users are expected to take. Each possible user path should be limited to a single row of buttons, and all buttons for the current user path should be visible on-screen at once.

The advantages of the table of contents method are similar to those of the tabbed method. A key advantage of the table of contents method is that it can support a greater number of wizard steps than the tabbed method. Figure 6–4 shows that more steps can be supported when a table of contents method is used. However, the width of the wizard may also increase to provide real estate for the table of contents control.

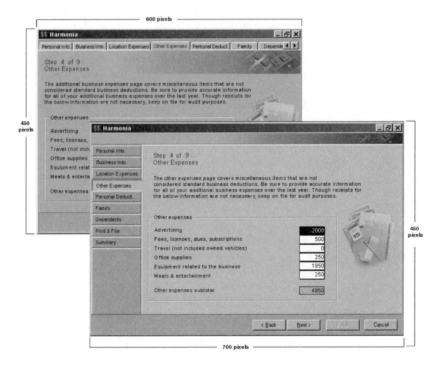

Figure 6–4   *Number of steps visible with a tabbed method versus a table of contents method of navigation.*

Additional advantages of the table of contents method are:

- The table of contents method uses a common metaphor for navigation. This approach is visually similar to frames used on a wide range of Web pages.

- The table of contents method supports a greater number of steps than the tabbed approach.

The disadvantages of the table of contents method are similar to those of the tabbed method. The key disadvantage over the tabbed method is that it requires significantly more real estate for navigation support than the tabbed method.

Pull-down menu

You can add a pull-down menu to the wizard to allow the user to directly access each page. This design reveals a series of steps when the user opens the menu. Figure 6–5 illustrates this method.

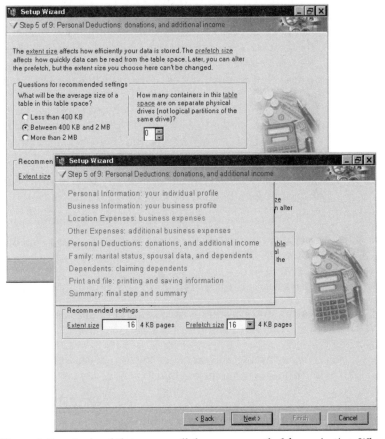

Figure 6–5 *A wizard that uses a pull-down menu method for navigation. When users click on the triangle, a pull-down menu that lists the wizard pages opens.*

The advantages of the pull-down menu method are similar to those of the tabbed method. The key advantage is that it requires significantly less real estate than either the tabbed method or the table of contents method. Additional advantages of the pull-down menu method are:

- The pull-down menu method requires a small amount of real estate. Only a single step (or row of the menu control) is represented on the screen at any time.

- The pull-down menu method supports a greater number of steps than the tabbed approach.

- The pull-down menu method may result in faster performance than the tabbed or table of contents methods because the menu choices need to be updated only when the menu is activated. The screen does not need to be redrawn as the paths change.

Many of the disadvantages of the pull-down menu method are similar to those of the tabbed method. Its key disadvantage over the tabbed method is that it is less visible than either the tabbed or table of contents method. Additional disadvantages of the pull-down menu method are:

- The pull-down menu requires more effort to use than either the tabs or table of contents buttons. The user must click the control, move the mouse to the specific step, and then click again to select that step.

- The pull-down menu is less conspicuous than either the tabs or table of contents buttons. Internal usability tests at IBM showed that most participants didn't notice the pull-down menu control.

- Users must activate the control to view their progress through the wizard.

- During selection, the menu covers the work area of the wizard.

Additional navigational options

You might find that a combination of approaches works best for your wizard. Navigation options include:

- Combining the standard wizard with the tabbed, table of contents, or pull-down menu method

- Allowing the user to define the default path of a wizard

- Providing a read-only roadmap

This section explains each of these options.

Combining the standard wizard with the tabbed, table of contents, or pull-down menu method

One design option is to show only the **Back** and **Next** buttons the first time through a wizard and then show other navigational controls, such as tabs, any future times that the user enters the wizard. This option initially hides the complexity of the path while still affording the users the flexibility to directly access pages of interest upon re-entry to the wizard.

Allowing the user to define the default path of a wizard

You can include several features within the wizard to allow the user to either define all or part of the default path displayed in the wizard. The most basic of these features allows the user to skip the introductory page the next time the wizard is entered. Figure 6–6 shows such an example. Notice that the introductory page includes a check box that allows the user to skip the first page the next time the wizard is launched. If you provide navigational controls such as tabs, the introductory page should still be represented in the navigational control.

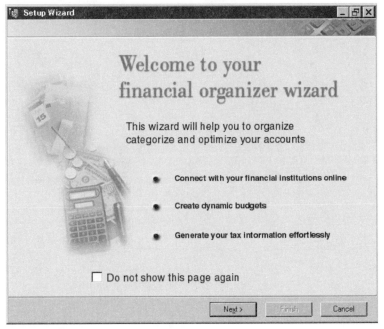

Figure 6–6 * *A wizard with a check box that allows users to skip the introductory page the next time the wizard is launched.*

Users can have a more significant impact on a wizard's default path if they are allowed to choose between basic and advanced functions. For example, on the first page of the wizard, you can allow the user to choose whether to display the pages belonging to the advanced features of the product. Figure 6–7 illustrates one such design.

This option may be useful if your target audience contains both expert and novice users. See Chapter 12, "Experts and novices," for more details on how to support both experts and novices.

You can provide a more intelligent and personal level of customization if you allow the users to specify the default path that they require. Default paths are useful for software applications, such as tax advisors, in which there are many choices to be made and in which there is a high likelihood that user entries will be similar the next time the wizard is used. You can save user answers and use them to generate both the default path and the defaults for individual pages. If it is unclear whether the users will want to

Figure 6–7   *A wizard that allows the user to choose the wizard's default path by specifying whether or not to show advanced features.*

use their current entries as the basis for a default path, you can explicitly ask the users if they want to change the original wizard defaults to more closely match their current path.

For any of the customization options, be sure to allow easy access to the pages that the user did not choose. For example, the tax wizard might have a page that asks the user if any situations, such as a change in marital status, have occurred that would change the default path provided.

Providing a read-only roadmap

Another design option is to provide **Back** and **Next** buttons as navigational controls and to also provide a diagram that helps the users understand their progress through the wizard and their current location in the wizard. For example, Figure 6–8 shows a wizard with a roadmap. The list on the left side of the Sample wizard provides read-only cues to the user's progress though the wizard.

This approach gives the designer more control of the users' motion through the wizard, while providing users with a richer set of cues to understand their progress. The next section discusses how to provide more cues to help the user navigate.

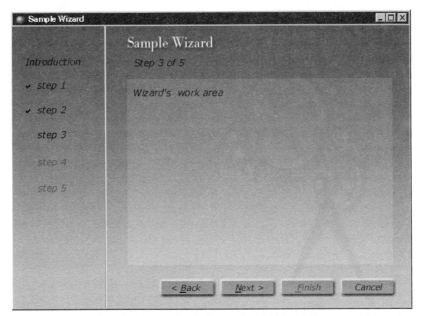

Figure 6–8   *A wizard with a read-only list on the left side to help users understand their progress through the wizard.*

Methods to help users estimate their progress through the wizard

Regardless of the type of navigation control used, the wizard should support the user in understanding:

- Where am I now and where can I go?
- How do I get to the next page?
- Where have I been?
- How much do I have left to do?

This section explains how to design your wizard to help users answer these questions.

Where am I now and where can I go?

Both text cues and control cues can help the user to understand which steps he or she can access and which have been accessed previously. Be sure to use clear visual cues to distinguish active from disabled steps.

Textual cues

Have your design team develop a coding scheme for the textual labels in the actual navigational control to indicate the different states of the wizard pages. One such scheme is shown here:

- Normal text. A page that the user can jump to. This textual cue usually refers to pages that have already been viewed or future pages that are filled with defaults and do not require further user input.
- **Bold text**. The current page.
- Ghost text. An upcoming but unavailable page. This cue is needed for a sequential task in which the user cannot go to the next page or step until the preceding pages are completed.

The scheme used should be consistent with other dialogs in the product.

Control-state cues

You can hide and show controls to support navigation. Hiding and showing the **Back**, **Next,** and **Finish** buttons can minimize confusion about where a user is in the wizard. Follow these guidelines for hiding buttons:

- Hide the **Back** button on the first page. An exception to this condition is if the wizard design allows the users to skip the introductory page the next time they go into the wizard as described in "Allowing the user to define the default path of a wizard" on page 117.

- Hide the **Next** button on the last page.
- Hide the **Finish** button on any pages that the user cannot finish from.

Simply disabling a button does not provide an appropriate cue because the users might think that they can enable the button by changing settings on the current wizard page.

If you use a navigation control such as tabs, a table of contents, or a pull-down menu, be sure that the currently selected choice has visual cues that distinguish it from the other options. For example, you can change its border (use a bevel) or change its color. Figure 6–9 shows examples of a table of contents control with various visual styles. In each example, the selected button looks different than those of the other options. For example, the font in *type b* is different for the selected step than the font of the other steps. Other examples, such as *type a* and *type c* use a different background color for the selected step. In *types a*, *d*, and *e*, one edge of the button is left open so that the color can "bleed" into the working area of the wizard page to provide a further cue about which step is selected.

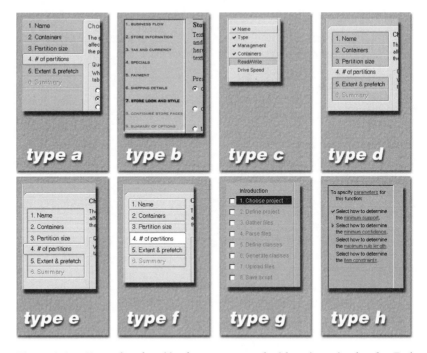

Figure 6–9   *Examples of a table of contents control with various visual styles. Each example shows a method of representing the selected step differently from the other steps.*

How do I get to the next page?

Users may need cues about what they need to do to complete an individual page. Specific mechanisms for providing these cues such as mandatory fields and disabling controls are addressed in Chapter 10, "Error prevention and recovery," and are not discussed here. However, the navigation buttons should change state to provide cues as to their use. Follow these guidelines for button states:

- Hide the **Finish** button whenever the user cannot finish from that page.
- For sequential wizards, disable the **Next** button if there are required fields, and make it selectable when these fields are filled in.

Always allow the user to control navigation. The wizard should *never* advance pages automatically. Also, be sure to allow users to move among or between pages by using keyboard equivalents for mouse actions. Always provide these navigational functions:

- Allow users to navigate to the next page by using the right arrow key.
- Allow users to navigate to the previous page by using the left arrow key.
- Provide mnemonics for all tabs, table of contents buttons, or pull-down menu choices.
- Use N as the mnemonic for the **Next** button.
- Use B as the mnemonic for the **Back** button.

Where have I been?

Icons and text cues can help users understand where they have been. You can place icons such as checkmarks on the table of contents, tab, or menu item when a page has been visited or completed. Figure 6–10 shows a wizard that uses a checkmark as well as text cues to show which steps have been visited.

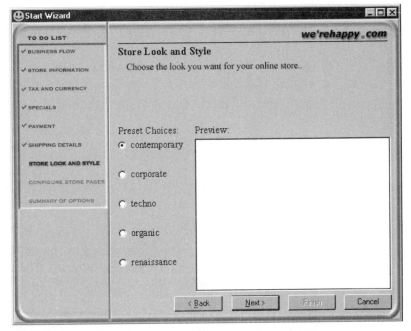

Figure 6–10   *A wizard that uses checkmarks to indicate visited pages.*

You can also change the text color to indicate visited pages. In a Web-based wizard, wizard text should follow the conventions of other links on the Web site. One standard scheme for the Web is shown in Table 6–1.

Table 6–1   *Standard color scheme for Web sites*

Color	Meaning
Purple	A visited link
Blue	An unvisited link

How much do I have left to do?

Users may want to know how far along they are in completing the task. Tabs and tables of contents allow the users to view how far along they are in the wizard just by looking at the navigation control. However, providing redundant cues in the form of page numbering or progress bars can further support navigation. The standard navigation method especially benefits from the progress cues because it does not inherently provide any.

Page numbering

One way to provide cues to progress throughout the wizard is by numbering the pages. You can provide page numbers in two ways:

- Add the text "Step *X* of *N*" to the wizard page.
- Add the number to the title of the page (on the tab, table of contents button, or menu choice), such as "1. Introduction."

Progress bars

Progress indicators are especially useful if the path may change a lot. Numbering pages can cause a problem when dynamic updates to the number of steps are possible. Each tab or table of contents step may need to have its number recalculated and redrawn based on user input, which can dramatically slow performance.

You can avoid this negative performance impact by providing progress bars, which show users a coarser measure of progress. The progress bar can be supplemented with a label that gives a percentage measure of completeness.

Button cues

Show the **Finish** button on the page if the user doesn't need to go to other pages to complete the task. Disable the **Finish** button if the user must first complete something on the page.

Icons to represent completed steps

Using icons such as checkmarks to indicate completed steps is often not possible in non-sequential tasks. Because most wizards contain defaults for control choices, it can become difficult to differentiate between pages completed by the user and pages completed by the computer (defaults). For example, the user action of visiting and reading a wizard page is difficult to distinguish from the user action of visiting a wizard page and agreeing with its original defaults. In the first case, users would not think of the step as completed, but in the second case, they would.

Summary of guidelines discussed in this chapter

- ❏ Ensure that wizards in the same product have consistent navigation approaches, unless there is a clear reason for differences.

- ❏ Always provide **Back** and **Next** buttons.

- ❏ If the user will be allowed to re-enter the wizard, provide navigation controls, such as a table of contents, in addition to the **Back** and **Next** buttons.

- ❏ If at all possible, show all steps (tabs, table of contents buttons, menu choices) on-screen at the same time.

- ❏ Use clear visual cues to distinguish active from disabled controls.

- ❏ Hide the **Back** button on the first page of a wizard.

- ❏ Keep the user in control of navigation. Never automatically advance wizard pages.

- ❏ Provide mnemonics and keyboard equivalents to allow the user to navigate among pages without using the mouse.

- ❏ Provide cues to give users a sense of progress throughout the wizard.

- ❏ If users are allowed to navigate through the wizard in non-sequential order, provide cues to let them know that they have completed a page (if possible) or that they have visited a page.

Chapter 7

Visual design

- ▲ Why does your wizard need a good visual design?
- ▲ Questions to ask before beginning
- ▲ Physical issues
- ▲ Layout design—Defining your grids
- ▲ Typography
- ▲ Color
- ▲ Images
- ▲ Summary of guidelines discussed in this chapter

Visual design is the art of using visual strategies to organize typography and images that communicate information and influence emotion. Design is a cultural practice and highly mutable; it is both the product of society's ideas and an influence on those ideas.

Visual design of software interfaces encompasses engineering, function, and craft, with underlying elements of art. A product's visual design should be subtle and should integrate seamlessly with the behavioral and functional aspects of the product's interface.

In visual design practice, there are three basic aspects to consider—the physical issues, the physical structure, and the semantics:

- **Physical issues.** The physical limitations of your target audience's hardware will influence how you present your design. The section called "Physical issues" on page 129 describes this aspect in more detail.

- **Physical structure.** The physical structure dictates the layout of the components, their shapes, sizes, and common relationships to one another. The physical structure is the beginning of user interface design. Proper knowledge and application of the different elements will ensure that the design serves the functional goals of the interface. This aspect is explained in "Layout design—Defining your grids" on page 131.

- **Semantics.** Semantics evoke emotion, mood, or impression of the essence and purpose of the wizard or application. Through careful selection of the basic elements of the physical structure, the designer creates the wizard's semantics. With consistent patterns of these elements, the viewer learns and differentiates, and ultimately chooses one interface over another, even when the functions of the different interfaces are the same. Throughout this chapter and the CD-ROM interactions, you'll find references to how different visual elements convey specific moods.

This chapter explains the critical aspects of visual design and describes how to use the elements of layout design to construct a visually effective wizard.

Why does your wizard need a good visual design?

A good visual design is always welcome by users. When wizards are well-designed, they invite users to interact with them. On the other hand, a bad visual design discourages users from using the wizards.

Benefits of creating a consistent visual design include:

- **Information is displayed clearly.** A good layout ensures that the information is presented with proper spacing and hierarchy. The user will easily identify the important steps in the task.

- **Distraction is minimized.** Good design takes distractions away, leaving only the relevant information visually available. Bad design has unnecessary elements that can confuse users.

- **Users recognize the different elements easily.** Because the layout is thought out in advance, good design displays each element with its own characteristics. This practice ensures that the user will identify each element consistently in each wizard's page.

- **Users get a consistent sense of organization.** Consistent organization of the visual elements promotes predictability. Users learn to anticipate where information is located.

Questions to ask before beginning

Before you start your wizard's design, make sure you've answered the following questions from Chapter 2, "Gathering requirements:"

- **Is the wizard a new product or is it a new version of an existing wizard or product?** If the wizard is part of an existing product, you need to match your wizard's visual characteristics and metaphors to those of the product. For example, what fonts and color palette does the product use, and how large can the file sizes be? Additionally, you will want to use the same visual references used in icons, launchpads, and manual illustrations.

- **What will the user need to know to use the wizard? What prerequisite knowledge does the target audience need in terms of computers, the task domain, and your software product?** You need to have an understanding of the concepts that the wizards are trying to convey before you begin your visual design.

- **What is the tone that you want your wizard to demonstrate or communicate?** Are your users part of a group that likes classic designs, or are they young people with a need for enticing designs? This information will help you to choose your colors and typography.

- **What equipment do your users have?** Will they use laptops or workstations? You need to design for the majority. Equipment affects color depth and the kinds of images (compression and format) you can use. The screen resolution affects your wizard's page size.

Physical issues

You need to make decisions about your screen resolution, color depth requirements, and other physical limitations based on the kind of equipment your users have.

Table 7–1 lists the different elements you need to consider.

Table 7–1   Physical issues to consider before designing

Element	Issues
Size of the window	According to the display resolution on your target audience's computers, how big will the wizard be?
Fonts	What fonts does the operating system have?
	What fonts is the main product using?
Images	Vector images with minimal color are smaller than 3D (bitmap) images with millions of colors.
Display resolution	Select the display resolution that will work for the majority of your target audience. Choices include:
	• 640x480 dpi
	• 800x600 dpi
	• 1024x768 dpi
	• 1280x1024 dpi
	• 1600x1200 dpi
Color depth	Select the color depth that will work for your target audience. Choices include:
	• 8-bit 256 colors
	• 16-bit 332768 colors
	• 24-bit 16777216 colors
	• 32-bit true color
Browser usage	If your wizard will be displayed on the Web, you need to know how your design displays in different Web browsers. The most popular browsers are: Netscape Navigator and Microsoft Internet Explorer
Connection speed	If your wizard will be displayed on the Web, you need to know at what speed your target audience is connecting to the Web. The connection speed determines how fast can they download the information. The file sizes of your images depend on this information. Big files and slow connection speeds create a real usability problem. Choices include:
	• 14.4K bps
	• 28K bps
	• 33.6K bps
	• 56K bps
	• 56K-1M bps
	• Greater than 1M bps

Table 7–1   Physical issues to consider before designing (continued)

Element	Issues
Platform	How your wizard will look on different platforms is critical. You must a have good understanding of the default fonts and color palettes of each target platform. Choices include: • Microsoft Windows (95, 98, NT, and 2000) • Macintosh • UNIX • Linux • OS/2

At IBM, wizards are designed to meet the minimum requirements of 800x600 pixels resolution and 8-bit (256 colors) color depth. We found that the majority of our customers have these parameters to work with. See "Color" on page 153 and "Images" on page 158 for more details.

To help you understand your users better, you can subscribe to some of the Internet services that provide statistics and surveys specifically targeted at a particular audience. Some of these statistics apply primarily to Internet users. There are, however, a few universal demographics that every designer should track and consider in the design process: browser usage, display resolution, and connection speed.

Layout design—Defining your grids

The layout of your wizard is the heart of its design. The layout communicates a sense of order and conciseness.

Although layout is the combination of various visual components, styles, and ways of interacting with the interface, it must appear as a single entity. Gestalt psychology as applied to visual phenomena suggests that humans see and react to the whole picture before they perceive the parts. The base of the layout is the grid.

A grid is a pattern of horizontal and vertical lines forming squares of uniform size on a defined area. These lines create the foundation used to assemble and organize the different visual elements in a template manner for your wizard page. The grid provides a predefined size, shape, and location for each wizard element. Users will be able to predict the location of the elements on your wizard pages when you employ the use of a grid consistently. Figure 7–1 shows a sample of a grid.

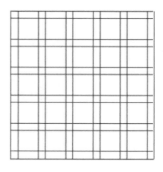

Grid

Figure 7–1   *A grid is group of modular squares formed by horizontal and vertical lines.*

The modular patterns you can create are unlimited. Figure 7–2 shows few of the many combinations of grids in a square.

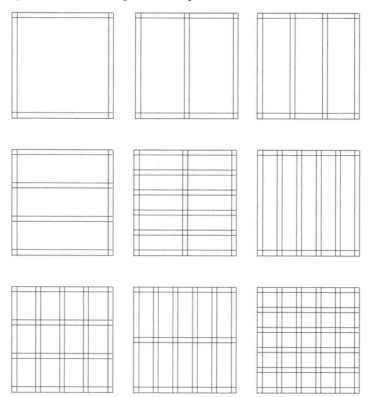

Figure 7–2   *One simple square can have many different ways to divide the space for a grid. Here are nine possibilities.*

Grids allow flexibility for logical alignment, rhythm, and sense of organization. A single grid can provide diverse choices for the placement of elements, as shown in Figure 7–3.

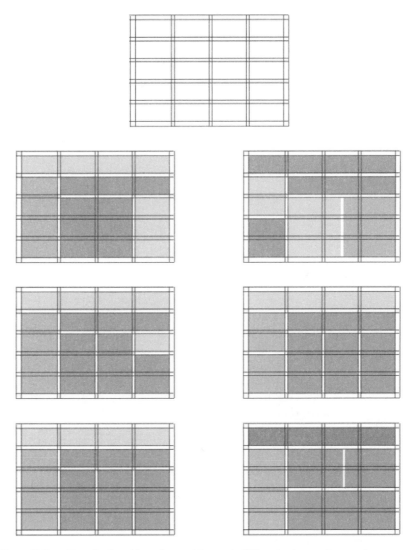

Figure 7–3   *One single grid can be used to create different column placements.*

To create a grid, follow these general steps:

1. Gather all the elements that will be included in the wizard. See Chapter 5, "General wizard design."

2. Choose your navigation method (buttons, tabs, or table of contents). See Chapter 6, "Navigation."

3. Determine the physical size of your window.

4. Choose the orientation of your wizard.

5. Define a general margin. Be sure to analyze the general layout of your product and try to be consistent with the spacing. Explore different divisions of the space.

6. Create the vertical and horizontal lines to define your grid. These lines should maintain regular sizes. Once your grid is ready, you will have the aligned space for your columns for text and images.

7. Allow plenty of white space. See the section called "White space (a divider and a grouping element)" on page 139. Don't cramp your grid.

8. If your wizard will be on the Web, adjust your layout accordingly. See "Web layout" on page 140.

This section explains Steps 3 through 8 in more detail.

Window size of the wizard

One of your first steps is to determine the size of the wizard. The size depends primarily on the resolution for which you are designing. For example, if you are designing for a screen resolution of 640x480 dpi (dots per inch), your wizard is limited to 640X480 pixels to be seen entirely. See Figure 7–4 for size considerations. Currently, the most common setting for screen resolution is 600x800 dpi. If you are designing for a higher resolution, be sure your audience has the right equipment to view what you want them to see.

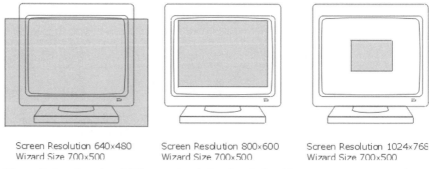

Screen Resolution 640x480
Wizard Size 700x500

Screen Resolution 800x600
Wizard Size 700x500

Screen Resolution 1024x768
Wizard Size 700x500

Figure 7–4   *Samples of different wizard sizes in relationship to common screen resolutions.*

You also need to determine how much real estate you want to occupy on the monitor. For example, you might decide to keep the product visible in the background if you want the user to have access to the application at any time.

In cases where more space is needed for the wizard, you may decide to design the wizard so that it uses all the available space. Figure 7–5 shows different alternatives of wizard real estate.

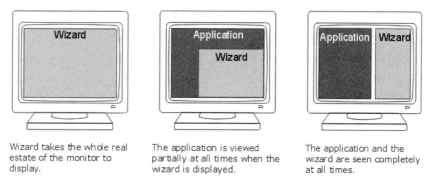

Wizard takes the whole real estate of the monitor to display.

The application is viewed partially at all times when the wizard is displayed.

The application and the wizard are seen completely at all times.

Figure 7–5   *Wizard size is dependent on how you want it to appear in relationship to the application.*

Be sure to choose the size of your wizard wisely because you will probably not provide the ability for the user to resize the wizard. Resizing wizards can disrupt the layout design. The grid no longer exists when the wizard is resized.

Orientation

Orientation is the way your wizard window is presented on the screen. To accommodate the information you want to present, you can choose a vertical or horizontal window. When your wizard's pages have more than 10 lines of text, use a vertical window. Good examples of these formats are wizards for tax information or Web wizards. See Figure 7–6.

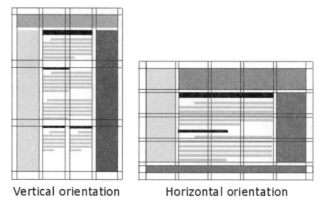

Vertical orientation　　　Horizontal orientation

Figure 7–6 *Vertical orientation is a more common format for the Web. Horizontal orientation is a better choice for applications.*

Once you define the orientation of the window, identify the various elements mentioned in Chapter 5, "General wizard design." Organize the elements in an order that corresponds to the order that the users should read or use them. See Figure 7–7 for an example of a priority list and implementation of the eye scan.

1. Name of the step
2. What is this step about? (Looking at the graphic)
3. How do I navigate?
4. What do I need to do?
5. How do I get out of this window?

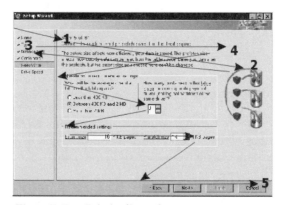

Figure 7–7 *Priority list and eye scan.*

When you define the orientation of your elements, be aware of the following facts:

* A good hierarchy of elements facilitates better understanding and quick comprehension of those elements.

- The mind seeks order and patterns in a display and follows them if they are apparent.

- Most Western languages are read from left to right. Therefore, most people who read in this manner scan the screen from left to right, top to bottom.

- Studies suggest that viewers' eyes move clockwise, influenced by the display's symmetry and other visual cues such as the balance of titles, graphics, and use of space.

- The logical place for a user to start reading a display is in the upper left corner relative to other parts of the display body.

- The eye scans the most dominant sign element, and then proceeds to read the smaller units of information.

For more information about screen design, see *The essential guide to user interface design: An introduction to GUI design principles and techniques* by Wilbert O. Galitz.

Margins

Every wizard page in the product should have consistent margins. Determine the number of pixels to devote to the margins in your wizard page. If the product interface already exists, for consistency, use the same size margins for the wizard's grid as the product uses. For example, ten pixels around the window for margins is a comfortable amount of space when designing for 800x600 dpi. See Figure 7–8.

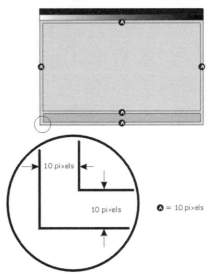

Figure 7–8   *When designing for 800x600 dpi, a 10-pixel margin is a comfortable space to work with.*

Figure 7–9 shows three samples of margins. Choosing a balanced margin ensures that the eye can focus on the content easily.

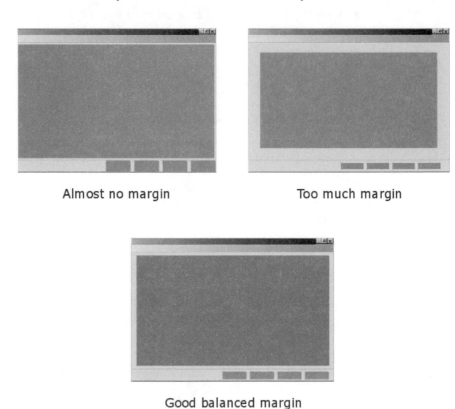

Almost no margin   Too much margin

Good balanced margin

Figure 7–9   *Three samples of margins.*

Columns

Columns are the spaces reserved for your text and images, and they should fit within your grid. Columns spaced within their surrounding margins become the foundation of a distinctive rhythm that distinguishes the wizard from other interface elements and from other products. Because your grids allow flexibility, your wizard can show a combination of columns. Make use of your grid when placing your columns. Figure 7–10 shows two sets of column arrangements.

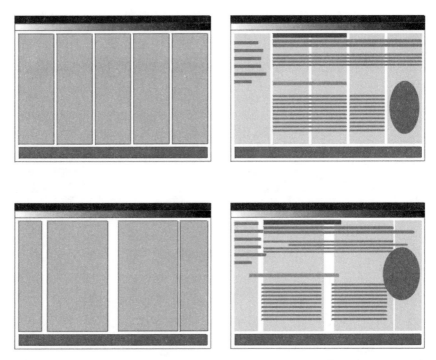

Figure 7–10 *In the first set, the columns have been placed on top of a grid. The text and image are placed within the column alignment. The second set of columns has no grid and the alignment of text and images is not respected.*

Be sure to test your text within columns early in the design phase.

White space (a divider and a grouping element)

White space defines and separates groups of information into a logical and hierarchal form. If this space is interrupted in any way, it no longer acts as a frame or as a divider of the different categories; its character is interrupted, and its effect defeated.

Proper use of white space is critical. The proximity of items on the screen implies associations and leads the eye to consider items as part of a whole. As white space appears between paragraphs and as it fills margins and separates columns on the wizard window, it should promote a balance of occupied and empty space, giving the viewer's eyes a chance to rest as they absorb content.

One more important use of white space is the indentation of the visual elements. Indentation promotes a sense of grouping or belonging.

This space is as important as the text and images. Figure 7–11 shows four uses of white space. Type a doesn't use white space to separate the information. There is no hierarchy. Type b introduces a separation between the two first lines. It shows that the rest of the information belongs to those two lines. Type c shows separation among three groups and indentation in the last group. The indentation suggests a subcategory. Type d uses two columns in the third group to emphasize the concept of belonging.

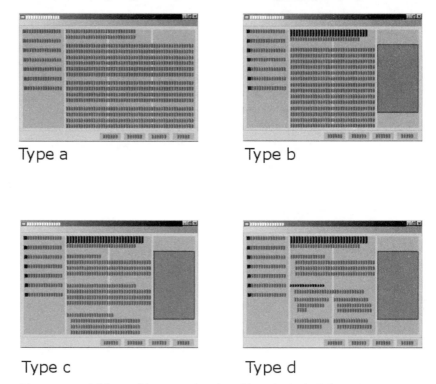

Type a

Type b

Type c

Type d

Figure 7–11   *Without white space, there is no hierarchy in the information.*

Web layout

The Web follows the general principles of layout explained in the previous sections with several exceptions, which are characteristic of the media:

- Wizards created exclusively for the Web are coded in HTML.
- HTML has its own specifications regarding paragraph separation and margins.

- HTML has its own specifications to build tables and frames. These elements will define your columns and spaces.

- Be sure to include space for product banners.

- Be sure to include space for advertising banners. This space is usually located in the top part of the page, before the product banner, but can be situated anywhere on the page.

Figure 7–12 shows a wizard page from grid to layout.

For more information about how to create layouts for the Web, see *Web style guide: Basic design principles for creating web sites* by Patrick J. Lynch and Sarah Horton.

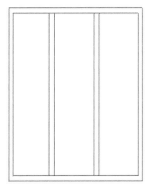

Creation of the grid.

Placement of columns in the grid.

Layout. Placement of text and images using the columns.

Layout with space for advertising banner at the top.

Figure 7–12 *Web layout.*

Typography

Typography is the arrangement and appearance of the textual elements that appear on a page. It is an intensely visual form of communication, which is highly subject to fashion. This visible language communicates subtle information about both the design aesthetic and the reliability of information. Fonts say more than most people realize about content; they communicate formality, casualness, stylishness, sophistication, and emotion.

The different typeface families reflect the history, culture, and fashion of the time. For example, modern sans serif fonts reflect the simple, uncluttered, and technically sophisticated taste of the late twentieth century. In contrast, when we see a poster from the 1840s, it looks dated to us, mostly because of the type of font used. A simple example of how typography plays an important role in communicating the modern level of sophistication is the evolution of the default system font on the Windows interface as shown in Table 7–2.

Table 7–2   Evolution of font sophistication in the Windows interface

Operating system	Typeface	Sample text	Subjective reaction
Windows 2.0	Non-Proportional typeface	This is a Monospaced font used in the Windows 2.0 user interface.	Monospace fonts look chunky and typewriter-like, much less sophisticated than printed characters have looked since the 1500s.
Windows 3.0 and 3.1	Proportional bold typeface	This is a proportional bold typeface used in Windows 3.0 and Windows 3.1.	Proportional fonts are attractive and user-friendly. However, the entire typeface is bold text with an emphasized look, which is heavy. Although it is proportional, it is still a distant from the quality of printed material.
Windows 95	Proportional different weight typeface	This is a proportional typeface with regular and **bold attributes** used in Windows 95.	This typeface is one step closer to the typographic sophistication readers are accustomed to from printed material. It also makes use of highlighting and graying of text to indicate focus or state.

Table 7–2   Evolution of font sophistication in the Windows interface (continued)

Operating system	Typeface	Sample text	Subjective reaction
Windows 2000	Proportional different weight typeface with color attributes to show links	MS Sans Serif typeface is a proportional <u>font</u> used in Windows 2000.	Windows 2000 uses hypertext and rollover effects, moving the characteristics of the font far beyond printed material. These effects are uniquely defined as digital media.

The graphic qualities of type are used to arouse emotions and to communicate integrity or reliability, energy, childishness, brashness, and many other qualitative concepts. Line weight and openness define variations within a font family, while the subtleties of shape and curve communicate powerful associations, which are represented in the following major categories: Old Style, Transitional, Modern, Slab Serif, and Sans Serif (see Figure 7–13).

Figure 7–13   Differences among the typeface categories.

This section explains serif and legibility, attributes and legibility, and how to choose multiple typefaces.

Serif and legibility

The most legible typefaces are those that combine contrast, simplicity, and proportion. Achieving legibility on-screen is more difficult than in print because of jagged edges and low screen resolutions.

In print, serif fonts are always more readable because the strokes at the ends of the characters accentuate the details of the shapes of each letter, making them more easily recognized. However, in general, sans serif fonts are more readable on an interface because the small details of serif are too hard to see when smaller font sizes are used, and thus make for slower reading. This is especially true at low resolutions, when sans serif fonts are clearly easier to see. Figure 7–14 shows the formation, pixel by pixel, of two types.

Serif typeface

Standard deduction

Standard deduction

Sans Serif typeface

Standard deduction

Standard deduction

Figure 7–14 Serif and sans serif typefaces enlarged to show the formation of the font in pixels. Sans serif typeface has fewer changes in the pixels.

A typeface that combines the simplicity of the sans serif and the accents of the serif fonts is the slab serif. Slab serif fonts, such as Egyptian or Lucida, as well as the sans serif Arial, are routinely used on the Web because of their readability on-line.

The most important step in choosing typography, or any other visual element, is to test your choices. To do so:

1. See "Multiple typefaces" on page 151 for better choices of on-screen fonts.

2. Choose your favorite three groups of typefaces in different sizes.

3. For each of your favorite fonts, create fragments of text with the text color and background color you are going to be using in your wizard.

4. Present all three choices on-screen to your test subjects and ask them to read the text. This test should never be conducted on printed text.

5. Choose the fonts whose text is easiest to read.

Figure 7–15 shows a sample of three text groups ready to be tested.

Arial regular 12 pt

> The purpose of typography is to communicate information effectively. The purpose of typography is to communicate information effectively.

Egyptian regular 12 pts

> The purpose of typography is to communicate information effectively. The purpose of typography is to communicate information effectively.

Baskerville regular 12 pts

> The purpose of typography is to communicate information effectively. The purpose of typography is to communicate information effectively.

Figure 7–15   *Different types of text to test legibility. All samples are 12 pts, 300 x 200 pixel space, 72 dpi.*

Attributes and legibility

Typefaces have different attributes, such as boldface or reverse video, that you can use to draw attention. Use these attributes with caution because they can affect the legibility of your wizard. This section discusses the various attributes.

Uppercase/Lowercase

Users read text by scanning the shape of words, using the top halves of letters as the primary cue. Dominant letters within the alphabet that aid in word recognition are those that have either ascenders or descenders (see Figure 7–16). Do not overuse all-uppercase types. Uppercase uses 35% more space. When the characters are all uppercase, there are no ascenders or descenders; the tops and bottoms of letters align, and viewers can't use the shapes of the words to recognize them.

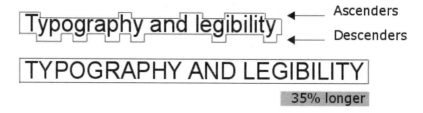

TEXT AND LEGIBILITY

All uppercase. No ascenders and descenders make recognition difficult.

Text and legibility

Mixed case. Ascenders and descenders aid in recognition.

Figure 7–16 *The use of ascenders and descenders is critical in legibility.*

Bold/Light

Most typefaces have three levels of thickness: light, medium, and bold. Use medium typefaces for most text.

Heavier typefaces, or bold, are commonly used in titles, captions, or other instances to draw attention or indicate separation. Bold typefaces are most readable when used to stand out from medium type. Avoid using bold type for all your text because you won't be able to use contrast to emphasize importance.

Light typefaces are rarely used on-screen because they are less legible than medium and bold typefaces. Figure 7–17 shows a typeface family with different weights.

Regular typeface with only few italics for emphasis.

The purpose of typography is to *communicate* information effectively. The purpose of typography is to communicate information effectively.

The purpose of typography is to *communicate* information effectively. The purpose of typography is to communicate information effectively.

All italics diminish legibility, especially when using serif typefaces.

The purpose of typography is to communicate information effectively. The purpose of typography is to communicate information effectively.

The purpose of typography is to communicate information effectively. The purpose of typography is to communicate information effectively.

Figure 7–17   Sample of bold, medium, and light fonts. All samples are Helvetica 12 pts, 300 x 200 pixel space, 72 dpi.

Italic

Limit the use of italic typefaces to specific purposes. They are used primarily for emphasis and differentiation. Try not to use more than two lines of italic text, because italic text diminishes legibility considerably (see Figure 7–18).

Regular typeface with only few italics for emphasis.

The purpose of typography is to *communicate* information effectively. The purpose of typography is to communicate information effectively.

The purpose of typography is to *communicate* information effectively. The purpose of typography is to communicate information effectively.

All italics diminish legibility, especially when using serif typefaces.

The purpose of typography is to communicate information effectively. The purpose of typography is to communicate information effectively.

The purpose of typography is to communicate information effectively. The purpose of typography is to communicate information effectively.

Figure 7–18   *The first sample shows a good use of the italic attribute. The second sample slows down the reading due to the overuse of italic type, especially when using a serif typeface.*

Reverse video

Reverse video is a relative attribute. If most of your text is dark and presented on a light background, reverse video text is light on a dark background; and if your text is light on a dark background, reverse video text is dark on a light background. Figure 7–19 shows two samples of the reverse video attribute.

This is the text to show the reverse video attribute when text is black and the background is white.

This is the text to show the reverse video attribute when text is white and the background is black.

Figure 7–19   *Samples of reverse video.*

Most fonts read very well on light backgrounds, except those with very thin strokes or a combination of strong and light strokes. Only a few are legible with a dark background.

Use reverse video with caution. It adds emphasis and draws attention, but if used excessively throughout the text, it becomes tiring for the eyes.

Underlining

Underlined words may reduce legibility, but when used discretely, they can be a very effective visual tool to draw attention. Users with any Web experience will interpret underlined words as links, especially when they display in a blue color.

Size

Size is a relative attribute. Not only is it relative to the resolution and the user's font size choice in the operating system, but it is also relative to the proximity of other typeface sizes. Most fonts are fairly legible at 10 points in the Windows operating system because there are enough pixels to render the shapes of the characters clearly. Figure 7–20 shows different font sizes in a wizard page.

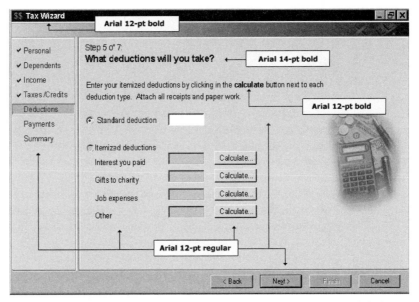

Figure 7–20 *The contrast in typeface attributes in this wizard page is subtle, but very effective.*

Figure 7–21 shows the font sizes used in Figure 7–20.

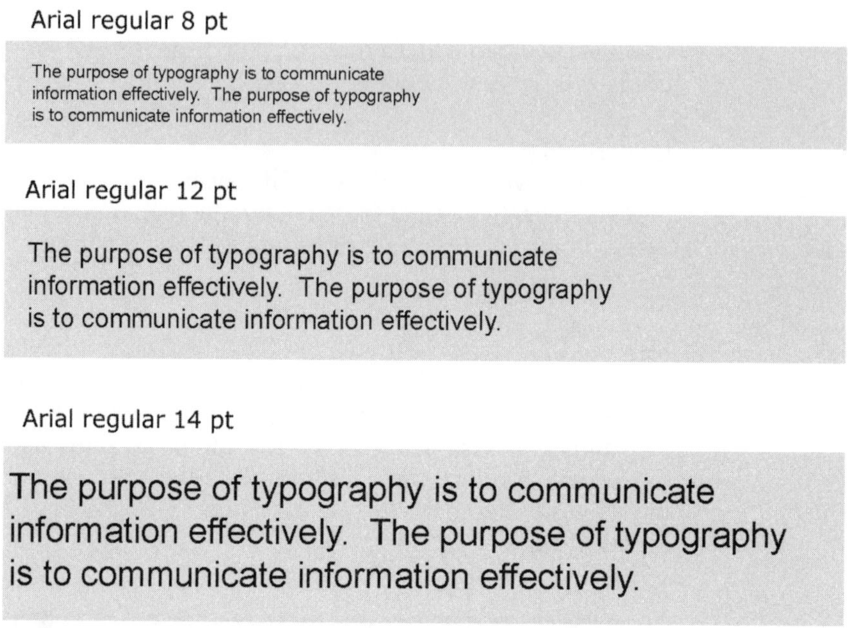

Arial regular 8 pt

> The purpose of typography is to communicate
> information effectively. The purpose of typography
> is to communicate information effectively.

Arial regular 12 pt

> The purpose of typography is to communicate
> information effectively. The purpose of typography
> is to communicate information effectively.

Arial regular 14 pt

> The purpose of typography is to communicate
> information effectively. The purpose of typography
> is to communicate information effectively.

Figure 7–21 *Difference of type size. All samples are Arial regular, 300 x 200 pixel space, 72 dpi.*

Smaller than 10 points and too few pixels per character cause many fonts to become distorted. However, if you are designing for multiple platforms or for the Web, be aware of how size differs on each platform. Figure 7–22 shows the size differences between Windows and Macintosh operating systems.

In general, typeface sizes in Windows appear about two sizes larger than the equivalent sizes on Macintosh. Thus, a line of 12-pt Times type on a Macintosh looks more like 14-pt Times on a Windows screen.

Windows	Macintosh
Arial	Arial
Arial Black	**Arial Black**
Arial Narrow	Arial Narrow
Helvetica	Helvetica
Helvetica Black	**Helvetica Black**
Verdana	Verdana
Times New Roman	Times New Roman
Baskerville	Baskerville
Book Antigua	Book Antigua
Garamond	Garamond
Egyptian	Egyptian
Courier	Courier

Figure 7–22   A sample of 12-pt typefaces on two different platforms.

For Web applications, you can use the FACE attribute to specify type. If you don't have ready access to a machine with another operating system, use the "FONT SIZE" HTML tag at the top of your HTML code to globally change the type size for a quick preview: Macintosh users should try <FONT SIZE="+2">. Windows users should try <FONT SIZE="-2">.

Multiple typefaces

Using more than one typeface is another way to draw attention. A wide variety of typefaces are currently available. Digital typography has introduced a new variety of typefaces for you to use. Using two typefaces, well combined, is a common practice; for example, you could use Garamond bold 16-pt for a title and Verdana bold and regular 12-pt for content text. Using more than two typefaces can create problems, however. You need to have experience working with typography to successfully blend more than two families. The use of many or poorly chosen typefaces may both fracture the information and communicate it weakly. This can make the interface less usable or visually uninviting. For more information about typography, see *Typography design: form and communication* by Rob Carter, Ben Day, and Philip Meggs. Figure 7–23 shows a few different typefaces.

Old Style	Garamond	Times New Roman
	The purpose of typography is to communicate effectively the information. **Typeface bold.** *Typeface italic.*	The purpose of typography is to communicate effectively the information. **Typeface bold.** *Typeface italic.*

Transitional	Baskerville	Century School Book
	The purpose of typography is to communicate effectively the information.	The purpose of typography is to communicate effectively the information. Typeface bold. *Typeface*

Modern	Bodoni	Korina
	The purpose of typography is to communicate effectively the information. *Typeface italic.*	The purpose of typography is to communicate effectively the information. *Typeface italic.*

Slab Serif	Serifa	Egyptian
	The purpose of typography is to communicate effectively the information. **Typeface bold.** *Typeface italic.*	The purpose of typography is to communicate effectively the information. Typeface bold.

Sans Serif	Switzerland	Arial
	The purpose of typography is to communicate effectively the information. **Typeface bold.** *Typeface italic.*	The purpose of typography is to communicate effectively the information. **Typeface bold.** *Typeface italic.*

Figure 7–23   *All these typefaces are displayed at 12 points. The legibility of the sans serif typefaces is higher than the rest of the group.*

Choosing a typeface

One pragmatic consideration when choosing a typeface is using the fonts that are available on the user's computer. In Windows, there are three common font families in TrueType format: Arial, Courier New, and Times New Roman. The system also includes several other specialty fonts: MS Sans Serif and MS Serif (bitmap fonts for the screen), Wingdings, and Small Fonts (for small screen text). If you want to use another font, such as Lucida Sans or Bookman Old Style, you'll need to ship the font and install it on the user's computer as part of your application setup. For most applications, it's better to use the system defaults, remaining consistent with the operating system and the user's choices.

Follow these guidelines when choosing typefaces:

- Choose one typeface family and make use of the bold and medium weight, size, italics, underline, and color attributes to show differentiation.
- For content-based applications and games, where fonts have greater aesthetic impact, consider using more attractive fonts than the default operating system fonts. Don't forget to ship the fonts with your application in this case.
- Don't use fonts smaller than 10 points.
- Consider using slab serif typefaces for screen fonts. Your second choice should be the sans serif family.
- Use serif typefaces only when they are bigger than 16 points. They look great in titles.
- If you need a traditional look, use a serif typeface in titles.
- If you need a modern look, use sans serif.
- Always test your choices.

Follow these guidelines for typography on the Web:

- Avoid creating text as a graphical file.
- Consider the issue of the font size on the Web for different operating systems.
- Use standard link colors—blue for links not visited and purple for links visited. Users are familiar with these colors and can quickly see where they have been.

Color

Color is the most controversial of all the visual elements of screen design. People assign a name to a color according to previous experiences and associations with specific visual sensations and color names. Therefore, a color can only be described in terms of a person's report of his or her perceptions. The color "green," for example, can be one of a thousand "greens." Exact measurements for color are rarely reported in literature. We are attracted to colors instinctively, and we all have opinions about colors.

A pleasant and effective use of color can be more powerful than animation, interactivity, or on-line graphics. Proper use of color has these benefits:

- Color adds a new dimension to screen usability.
- Color draws the eye to specific areas.

- Color emphasizes the logical organization of information.
- Color facilitates the discrimination of screen components.
- Color accentuates differences among elements.
- Color makes displays interesting.
- Color can diminish fatigue when used properly.

This section explains some facts about color, how the screen displays color, and color disabilities. This section also provides tips for using color in wizards and on the Web.

A glossary of color terminology is located in the color section for your reference. The CD-ROM contains an interactive color wheel and color palettes to better illustrate color attributes.

Color facts

Several color systems have been developed to categorize and explain how colors affect our perception and interaction. These systems are used in science, technology, art, and business. In addition to experiments on the anatomy of the eye and the physics of light, scientists have also conducted studies of the psychological effects of color. Color information is received in the eye and transferred to the brain, where the individual responses vary a great deal.

The diverse classifications and categorizations of color are sometimes conflicting. This section explains the following aspects of using color:

- Color is emotional.
- Color draws attention.
- Colors relate or group elements.
- Colors influence other colors.

People in different cultures may interpret colors differently. For more information on this aspect of color, see Chapter 14, "Worldwide audiences."

Color is emotional
Color has emotional properties; some reds excite the eye, and some blues calm it. It's easy to associate feelings with colors. People instinctively evaluate the state of the world around them based on color cues.

The level of emotional response to color, and the fact that it varies considerably from person to person, has important implications for the design of visual interfaces. If the wizard has primary colors (red, blue, and yellow),

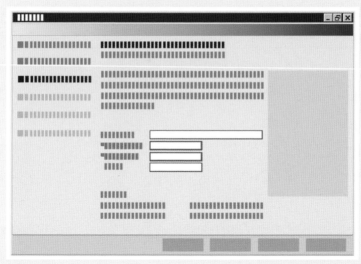

Color Figure–1   *Red color is used to highlight mandatory fields.*

Color Table–1   *Color Glossary*

Term	Description	Visual sample
Spectrum	All possible colors in a color space such as RGB or CMYK.	
Hue	Simply pure color or any color but white or black.	
Tint	White added to a hue. For example, pink is a tint of red.	
Shade	Black added to a hue. For example, maroon is a shade of red.	
Value	A number that describes the lightness and brightness of a color.	
Saturation	A number that indicates the intensity of a color in a percentage. For example, muted colors are hues with very little intensity of color. These are some of the best colors to display on-line.	100% 50% 20%

Color Table–2 *Color palettes and color schemes (see the CD-ROM for implementations of these color palettes).*

Palette	Description	Visual samples
Achromatic	This scheme consists of black, white, and the vast range of grays in between.	
Primary	The most basic color palette: the pure hues of red, yellow, and blue are combined. The elementary nature of this color scheme makes it a favorite for children's themes.	
Secondary	This palette combines the orange, green, and violet hues, providing an uplifting, refreshing quality.	
Complementary	Uses direct opposites in the color wheel (green-red, blue-orange, yellow-purple, and so on). These colors produce almost a vibratory visual sensation when seen side by side. Be careful using this palette; it may be annoying and stressful to the eye.	
Split complementary	Often more pleasing than true complementary colors. Choose a hue; the hues on either side of its complement create a split complementary scheme (orange with blue-green and blue-violet, for example). Use this palette to show strong contrast, accents, and strong statements. If you add a big percentage of tint (add white), this palette becomes a romantic palette.	
Tertiary triad	The two tertiary triad palettes are: red-violet, yellow-orange, and blue-green and red-orange, yellow-green, and blue-violet. These palettes are almost as difficult to use as the complementary palette due to the vibration quality.	
Monochromatic	This restrained, peaceful color palette consists of a single hue combined with any of its tints or shades. This palette is very safe to use.	
Analogous	Use any three adjacent hues in the color wheel. These hues have a harmonious, pleasing effect on the eye. You can't go wrong with this palette in your design.	
Clash	This palette has a surprising effect. The clash palette is formed by combining a hue with the color found on either side of its complement: for example, blue with red-orange or orange-yellow. This palette is difficult to control easily. If you feel uncertain about your choices among this palette, you can mute them (decrease the amount of color in percentage).	

users might feel as if they are being treated like children. If you use the gray color of the operating system, users might feel that the wizard is not any different or special. The wizard will look like just another dialog window.

Color draws attention
In a black-and-white field, we will instantly see a colored object. In a field of colors, we'll see the brightest (most saturated) color first. Color attracts the eye, and once the eye is engaged, attention quickly focuses on the object.

In your wizard, you can define one color to convey status, or to highlight the mandatory fields as a guide for the user. In both cases, color must be relevant and known to be effective. If the users do not understand the meaning of the color, or if it is not known, the purpose is defeated and the users must rely on their memory or a manual.

Figure Color–1 in the color section of the book shows an example of how color draws attention.

Colors relate or group elements
Researchers have found that we often use color for grouping or relating things to each other. In a field of abstract shapes, many people will assume that all red objects are related in some way, all blue objects in another, and so on. Conversely, color can also be used to separate different groups of information. You can use a specific visual code to define different wizard components.

One of the most common uses of the color grouping relationship is color-coding. Color-coding works when we mentally group objects by color. Color codes are most effective when there aren't too many of them, when they are used repetitively, and when they are associated with a common cultural use of color.

Colors influence other colors
The brain combines all color cues when seeing a group of different colors as a whole. When we see each color in detail, our perception of each color is different. If pixels of different colors are placed next to each other, a third color is generated. This effect is referred to as dithering. You can use this optical illusion when you are limited to a certain amount of color.

Colors next to each other may lead to color misinterpretation; a green can look more brown, or a yellow more orange depending on what color is next to it.

Colors placed next to each other in certain configurations can't be focused on at the same time; they create vibrating or irritating effects (this happens with complementary colors like green-red and orange-blue). Colors that are very similar in both hue and value will also cause visual discomfort when seen next to each other because the eye has to strain to distinguish the slight difference.

Colors also can lead to misinterpretation of an object's size in relationship with the other colors around it. Dark colors tend to give the illusion of smaller size than light colors. If your image size area is small, use light colors to create the illusion of a larger image. On the other hand, if your image appears too big, use dark colors to make it look smaller.

Color on-screen

Color monitor displays are based on the RGB color modes. RGB combines red, green, and blue pure colors in various combinations to create the many colors we see on-screen. Users can adjust the amounts of red, green, and blue light presented in a pixel and millions of colors can be generated. This color mode is different than CMYK, which is used to design for print work. There are other modes to work with color, but RGB is the most commonly used. For more information about color spaces and calibration, see *Designing web graphics.3: How to prepare images and media for the web* by Lynda Weinman.

To control the color of each pixel on the screen, the operating system must dedicate a small amount of memory to each pixel. This kind of memory is known as video RAM, or VRAM, and is also commonly referred as the color depth of the monitor. When 8 bits of memory are dedicated to each pixel, each pixel could be one of 256 colors (2 to the eighth power = 256). These 256 colors are not fixed, but there are only 256 colors that can be seen at once in a monitor with 8 bits of VRAM. These colors include background, fonts, and all the colors that are in the images used. Due to hardware limitations, the easiest solution is to design for 256 colors. Indexing your colors to a 256-color palette will ensure good display of your wizards on-screen and on the Web.

Newer computers can display color depths greater than 8 bits (16 bits and 24 bits); however, many users own computers that are limited to 8 bits. True-color images (24-bit) are typically much larger than 8-bit images in their compressed state, because 24 bits of memory are dedicated to each pixel.

For more information about color palettes and compression techniques see "Images" on page 158.

Using color in wizards

When choosing your colors, especially when the color is emphasizing important information for the user, be sure to use color with different values between light and dark. This way, even if the users are color-blind, they can see the difference among grays. For more information on color blindness, see Chapter 13, "Accessibility."

Blue is difficult to read in text because the human eye is not designed to see blue well. This means that blue is a great background color, but it does not work well in small areas, thin fonts, or narrow lines. Use blue for text only if it is linked to other information. In this case, the text must be underlined.

Watch out for color customizing. Users can often change their color preferences. Do not refer to parts of the screen by specific color, for instance, do not include an instruction such as "Enter data into the green box." You cannot be sure that the box will always be green.

Use colors consistently. Decide on the specific meanings of colors within an application and use colors and their coding techniques consistently.

Don't use too many colors in the screen design. Color is still a novel capability for many designers. There is a tendency to use it just because it is available, to overuse it when it adds no particular value to a display, and to use it as a substitute for other design techniques that might actually be more effective in certain circumstances. Use a distinctive color only to attract attention, to communicate organization, to indicate status, or to establish a relationship.

Some books advise not to use colors when designing your interface. When you design in a monochrome environment (white-grays-black), you ensure readability. After you choose your values in the gray scale, then substitute with colors. You can also use the reverse technique to test your color choices; once the design is done, save your image in the gray scale and evaluate the contrast.

Choose background colors carefully. Follow these guidelines:

- In general, display typefaces in dark color on an achromatic background (gray, white, or any other color with little pigmentation).

- Avoid using a black background because it requires large fonts to have proper readability.

- Use light backgrounds. Color discrimination is easier on a light background than on a dark background. On a light background, colors are perceived as more saturated and thus more dissimilar to one another.

- Avoid color images as a background unless they have almost no saturation (watermark style). Backgrounds with images compete and interfere with the main purpose of the other visual elements (like text, for example).

Color on the Web

When you work with color in the Web, you have two choices: create colored artwork or use an HTML tag to specify a hexadecimal color. When you create artwork, you have control over what the user will see at all times; however, artwork takes longer to download than text. If you use HTML to choose your colors, remember that users can always change their preferences and alter the original design.

The color management scheme used by Web browser software is based on an 8-bit, 216-color (not 256) palette. The browser software makes a decision about which colors to display not by pooling colors from the Web image, but by choosing colors from its own fixed palette.

For more information about how to use the browser-safe palette, see *Web style guide: Basic design principles for creating web sites* by Patrick J. Lynch and Sarah Horton.

Images

Images can enhance your wizard pages not only by stylizing them, but by increasing the user's understanding of the task. Handled badly, images can make a page busy, distracting, or confusing. The images in a wizard are especially helpful if they convey and clarify meaning, and orient the users to the task they are about to perform.

This section explains how to create images for your wizards. Topics include types of images, resolution and color depth, compression techniques, image size, and semantics.

Types of images

The images used in your wizard page can vary in style, format, look, and size. Regardless of what your choices are, avoid unnecessary graphic embellishments. Besides the optional graphic, you could add other graphic elements such as divider lines, graphic bullets, and other visual markers to your wizard page. Our recommendation is to stay away from these extra graphics to avoid a patchy and confusing window. However, we do recommend the use of a graphic identifier. This image is constant through each of your wizard pages and acts as a subtle but constant reinforcement of the product brand. You can also use this graphic as a hot link to the Web site of the product.

Attributes to choose from when designing images include:

- Generic versus specific
- Illustrative versus abstract
- Decorative versus functional
- Photographic versus linear

Generic versus specific
Do not use generic images that remain the same through the different wizard pages. Use images that add information and change based on the content of the wizard pages. The user "reads" these images as part of the information presented in the wizard. In many cases, the image becomes as important as the text.

Illustrative versus abstract
It's difficult to determine the level of abstraction an image should have in a wizard. When an image is too abstract, users have difficulty recognizing the information you are trying to convey. Abstract graphic representations can provoke misinterpretations or force users to try to memorize associations like math symbols. Eventually, users can lose interest in trying to interpret abstract graphics, and they will end up ignoring your graphics altogether.

Illustrative images can also be hard to read if they provide too much information for the user to absorb. Be specific and direct about the message presented by your image, and use only the necessary elements to convey that message.

Decorative versus functional
Decorative images can make your wizards look cheerful and fill the optional graphic area of your layout. However, much of the power of the images is lost if the image is not functional. As tasks become more complex, images

159

must become more functional. Knowledge of your product, knowledge of your target audience, and an understanding of the graphic language used by this audience are needed to create a functional graphic. For example, a cylinder in a graphics program identifies a way to create a 3D shape of a cylinder. In a database product, a cylinder is associated with a database.

A simple functional image that illustrates the task itself can be very useful. It can also orient the user to the most important information by highlighting elements you decide to emphasize.

Photographic versus linear

Highly detailed images, such as photographic images, are large files that take up a lot of memory and disk space. They can add a very important level of sophistication, but they can be slow to load and full of colors that can't be displayed correctly in low-resolution monitors. When displayed on the Web, highly detailed images can frustrate your users because large images take longer to download. If you absolutely must use large images, use image compression that can shorten download time. For basic compression techniques, see "Compression techniques" on page 161.

Linear images (or line images) are graphics that do not use gradations. They are built with defined areas of solid color. Working with line images simplifies the amount of information to display, and helps to keep your wizard efficient. Figure 7–24 presents the difference between a figure with high detail in gradations and an image with three solid colors.

For detailed information about types of images to use in interface design, see *Visual interface design for Windows: Effective user interfaces for Windows 95, Windows NT, and Windows 3.1* by Virginia Howlett.

Photographic image   Line image

Figure 7–24   *A photographic image and a line image of a cube.*

Resolution and color depth

Most visual designers work in 24-bit color, but as mentioned before, unfortunately most users don't. In a less-than-optimal viewing environment—the user's hardware—the image loses its original attributes. Design for the most common resolution used by your target audience.

The same graphic can look different on different platforms or resolutions. When working in an 8-bit (256 colors) environment, you need to take into consideration that any color in the original graphic that is not part of those 256 pixels of color will display dithered (two or more colors of the 256 palette are combined to approximate the real shade). Dithering doesn't create a problem for photographic images, but it does when you want clean, flat colors or a combination of both photographic and linear images. You can avoid or minimize dithering by using Equilibrium Debabelizer, Macromedia Fireworks, or by indexing to a common palette.

The 256-color allowance on 8-bit monitors has to cover all the images that are shown on the screen at one time. Once 256 colors are used, any remaining colors will be mapped to the closest equivalent among the first 256 colors. If you are using several photographic images or complex illustrations with different color palettes in your image-processing program (Adobe Photoshop or other), combine all the images you expect to show on a single pane in one Photoshop document and convert it to an 8-bit indexed color image with an adaptive palette with dithering.

Compression techniques

Working with photographic images or complex colors imposes tight limits on the images. The first limit is the size of the file; the second is the format. Applications are able to handle different bitmap formats; BMP, GIF, and JPEG are among the most commonly used. GIF and JPEG formats have gained in popularity, mostly through their use on the Web.

- **BMP.** BMP, also referred to as "bitmap," is a graphic format that creates an image using an array of pixels of different colors or shades by mapping a series of discrete dots. The compression can be at 8-bit, 16-bit, or 24- bit.

- **GIF.** GIF, also referred to as Graphic Interchange Format, is a common format for on-line 8-bit graphics (256 colors). There are two kinds of GIF files: gif87a and gif89a. The second one is used for gif animations and images with transparent backgrounds. GIF files are appropriate for images with few colors and no gradation.

- **JPEG**. JPEG, a compressed bitmap format, is best for photographs and continuous-tone images. It is easier to create small JPEGs than small GIFs. There are no dithering, indexing, or color depth issues to be concerned with during compression. Adobe Photoshop implements three kinds of JPEGs:

  - **JPEG standard**. You can manipulate this kind of JPEG on a scale of 1 to 10; the higher the number, the higher the file size. Older browsers do not support this format.

  - **JPEG optimized.** This is the most versatile JPEG version. Older browsers support this type of format. The file size is still small compared to the JPEG standard, but less dithered.

  - **Progressive**. This version supports interlacing as well as 24-bit color depth (16.7 million colors). This format is ideal for compressing photographs and complex images with shades and gradients, but it is not good for 8-bit color depth. Due to the color depth, older browsers do not support this format.

For applications that deal with compression issues and more advanced techniques of compression, see *Designing web graphics.3: How to prepare images and media for the web* by Lynda Weinman.

Image size

The real estate of the screen is always at a premium. If the screen is too small, the resolution is too low, and there are too many elements to display in perfect harmony. The solution is to work with different iterations. The image is part of the information and should not take priority over the rest of the layout. It should integrate with the text.

Semantics

Styles such as futuristic, playful, conservative, technical, classic, and so on are aesthetic, often emotionally generated, and go in and out of fashion. It's important to define what kind of style your product requires. In a classical style, for example, keep the design clear, minimalistic, understated, and sophisticated. All the elements must follow a simple alignment, and must be spaced and placed evenly. The images should have few colors, and those colors should usually be neutral with one contrasting color (black, burgundy, or navy blue, for example). There is no space for extraneous elements in the design.

Ensure that the metaphors you use in your images are consistent with those used in the rest of the product, launchpads, and icons, as well as the illustrations in the manuals.

Summary of guidelines discussed in this chapter

❑ Use grids to enforce consistent alignment of the different elements: text, images, and navigation elements. This practice promotes position predictability.

❑ Avoid visual clutter. Use only necessary elements in your wizard. Too many visual elements create chaos.

❑ Eliminate purposeless graphics.

❑ Group related elements in proximity to each other.

❑ Use indentation to reinforce grouping.

❑ Avoid italic and small serif fonts; these are often hard to read, especially at low resolutions.

❑ Design for your target audience. Currently most users have a monitor that can display 256 colors (8-bit) or more. We recommend designing for this audience.

❑ Use colors that have a visual connection with the rest of the application.

❑ When choosing colors, remember not to use too many. Your best choices of color are monochromatic, in the analogous palette, or simply muted colors.

❑ Use color to show relationships or groupings.

❑ Create visuals that have a function in the interface. Generic or ambiguous images might distract the attention of the user.

❑ Make your wizard visual design "feel" like it is part of the whole product. Wizards are only part of a whole application that runs under an operating system.

❑ Follow the visual rules of the operating system and application before integrating new visual strategies.

❑ Choose colors carefully. Interpretation of color meanings varies by culture.

❑ Avoid the use of generic images. Use images that add information and change based on the content of the wizard page.

❑ When designing for the Web, use the optimized JPEG format to compress photographic images and the GIF format for line images.

Chapter 8

Launchpads and linking wizards

- ▲ Why link wizards?
- ▲ Questions to ask before beginning
- ▲ Methods of linking wizards
- ▲ Design issues for launchpads
- ▲ Additional functions that can be supported by a launchpad
- ▲ Summary of guidelines discussed in this chapter

A launchpad is an interface that groups related wizards or dialogs in one central access point. A launchpad can provide additional benefits over individual wizards. For example, if a task is too complex for a single wizard, a launchpad can be used to connect the series of steps necessary to complete the complex task from one central access point. A launchpad can contain elements to help novice users, such as descriptive text to explain how to complete the wizards or tasks. A launchpad can also provide features, such as a graphical overview and interactive preview of the entire process, to help users understand where the wizard fits into a larger task.

Our usability tests show that users respond positively to launchpads. They like having a task-oriented graphical user interface (GUI), and they like having a central access point for multiple tasks.

In fact, one design alternative to creating a series of wizards is to create a launchpad that links together individual dialogs. If dialogs already exist to enable users to complete tasks, then a launchpad can provide a large usability improvement without the development cost of multiple wizards. However, wizards in conjunction with a launchpad offer greater task support than either one alone.

This chapter explains how to choose a navigation approach for linking wizards, design issues for launchpads, and how to add interesting features to your launchpad that help users to learn about your product as a whole.

Why link wizards?

Enhancing usability is the main reason for linking or grouping related wizards together. Benefits of linking or grouping wizards include:

- **You can break a single wizard into multiple smaller wizards.** This situation may occur if your original wizard design has too many steps. The user should *never* have to scroll to reach steps in a wizard. For example, if the number of steps cannot be represented by a single row of tabs that are always visible on-screen, then you should restructure the wizard.

- **You can accommodate tasks that require multiple users.** You may have a situation in which different users often complete subsets of the original wizard steps. For example, at some companies, database administrators separate the responsibilities for creating data objects and monitoring those objects. In other companies, the same person would complete both tasks. A wizard that encompasses the entire task of creating an object and specifying a monitor for that object would not be useful for the database administrators at the first type of company. However, a design that breaks the task into two separate wizards, one for creating the object and one for specifying a monitor, and that clearly links the two wizards, would accommodate target users at both types of companies.

- **You can put tasks in order.** You may begin with several smaller wizards and decide that users would benefit if the wizards were linked together. Sometimes individual wizards are not enough to help the user successfully complete a complicated task. Your user tests may show that users are having trouble grasping the "big picture." If users do not understand the order in which wizards should be completed or are having problems finding individual wizards, then you should consider adding an aide to help users link together the required wizards.

- **You can organize related wizards.** The software application may contain a variety of wizards, which are spread throughout the menu structure and interface, but which users feel are related in some dimension. For example, you might create a launchpad to provide access to wizards that create various graphical objects, such as pictures, graphs, and animations.

Questions to ask before beginning

The structure of the task and the predicted use of the wizards significantly impact the choices that you, as a designer, have in creating individual wizards and linking them. The task and product analyses in Chapter 1, "Kicking off the project," and Chapter 2, "Gathering requirements," should provide the information you need to answer the following questions:

- **How many steps are required to complete the entire task?** If the task consists of more than 10 steps, you might choose to break the task into multiple, related wizards.

- **Do the steps fall into natural groupings (subtasks)?** If the steps fall into natural groupings, you might divide your task into multiple, related wizards.

- **Does the task have multiple commit points?** The best approach is to have each wizard have a single point where code is run or actions are committed. If your task has multiple commit points, then you might want to break it into multiple wizards.

- **Does the product contain other methods or dialogs that allow the user to complete some of the subtasks? How likely is it that the user may have already completed some subtasks before starting the wizard?** If it is likely that the user has completed some subtasks, then your wizard must be flexible enough to recognize the completed subtasks. One approach is to provide a launchpad with multiple wizards that allows users to explicitly skip wizards and steps that they have completed.

- **Does the same target user complete all of the subtasks in your wizard design?** If not, then you should break your subtasks into separate wizards.

- **Must the user perform several subtasks in a sequential order? Can subtasks be repeated before proceeding to the next subtask?** If the user can complete subtasks multiple times before proceeding to the next subtask, then you may want to provide a wizard for each subtask.

- **Does it make sense to link the wizards? Would a tutorial, improved help, redesign of the underlying architecture of the product, or other intervention be more effective at helping users to complete the entire task?** Linked wizards may not be the best approach for helping users complete a complex task. You should examine other options to ensure that it makes sense for you to design and implement linked wizards.

Methods of linking wizards

Once you decide that it makes sense to link wizards together, you must determine which approach to use. There are two main approaches to linking related wizards together. The first approach is to launch one wizard from within another wizard. The second approach is to create a launchpad. From a launchpad, users can launch multiple, related wizards, dialogs, or a combination of the two. You can extend the launchpad concept to allow one launchpad to launch secondary launchpads.

Launching one wizard from within another wizard

One option for linking related wizards is to allow users to launch one wizard from within another wizard. This option is useful if your users do not finish all the prerequisite steps before launching a wizard or if they want to redo a prerequisite step after completing the wizard. If your wizards are sequential, your users may change their minds about settings in earlier wizards when they are working in subsequent wizards. If this situation occurs in your task flow, you might want to allow users to launch a wizard that lets them change earlier settings, from within the context of a later wizard.

Figure 8–1 illustrates a scenario in which one wizard, a Data Mining wizard, launches a second wizard, a Change Parameters wizard. In this scenario, the Data Mining wizard helps users create appropriate statistical functions to analyze their data. The Change Parameters wizard allows users to set or change default parameters such as user IDs, passwords, database names, and execution options for functions that they create. When the users finish

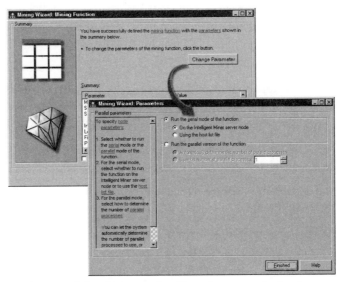

Figure 8–1   *An example in which one wizard launches a second wizard.*

specifying a statistical function in the Data Mining wizard, they may opt to change some of the default parameters that they set earlier. To allow users to easily change these parameters, the last page of the Data Mining wizard contains a button that launches the Change Parameters wizard.

Launching wizards from within wizards works best when:

- **It is the exception, rather than the rule, that users will need to launch the secondary wizard.** One such situation may occur if a wizard used for on-line purchases uses a customer profile to fill in default billing addresses and so forth. While users are completing a purchase, they may discover that their profiles are inaccurate. As a result, the user may launch a profile wizard to update the profile before continuing on with the purchase.

- **The prerequisites are outside of the usual end-to-end task flow.** This situation is also common in wizards used for on-line purchases. For example, the first time users attempt to make a purchase, they may be given the option to store default information within a profile. Then, in subsequent uses of the wizard, the users will not need to concern themselves with the create profile task.

- **Your product is part of an integrated offering and the prerequisite tasks are outside the scope of your product, but are within the scope of the integrated offering.** For example, you may have a database package that allows users to create and administer database objects and also conduct analyses on the data. There may be limited situations in which it would be useful to launch a database wizard from the analysis tool, and vice versa.

Launching wizards from launchpads

A launchpad is a GUI that groups in one central access point the series of wizards or dialogs necessary to complete a single complex task. One common use of a launchpad is to help users through the task of installing software.

Launching wizards from within a launchpad works best when:

- It is the rule, rather than the exception, that users will need to launch multiple wizards.
- The wizards exist as part of the usual end-to-end task flow. The users would benefit from understanding the order and dependencies among various wizards.
- The wizard tasks all lie within the scope of your product.

Design issues for launchpads

Launchpad designs can vary greatly in their look and feel, the type of features they support, and how users interact with them. The most basic launchpad consists of a panel with multiple buttons or labels, each of which launches a different wizard. More sophisticated launchpads support exploratory user behavior and may allow users to interactively preview the contents of a wizard or to learn about the high-level concepts of the task.

Figure 8–2 shows a sample of possible designs for a basic launchpad.

Regardless of the launchpad approach chosen, you must address several issues to create a useful and usable design:

- The appropriate number of steps for your launchpad
- Navigation among wizards, the launchpad, help windows, and other supporting dialogs
- Dependencies between steps
- Progress-related cues
- Task progress and dependency cues
- Consistency between the launchpad and its wizards
- Access to your launchpad

These issues are discussed in this section.

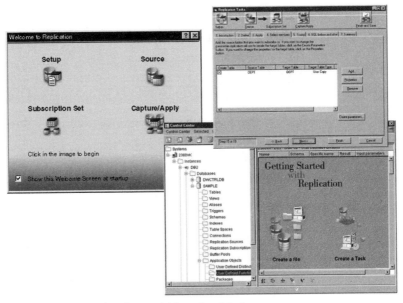

Figure 8–2 *Samples of potential launchpad designs.*

The appropriate number of steps for your launchpad

Participants in our usability studies felt that the launchpad should contain a group of related functions and that it should take them though the *entire* process or task. However, they also felt that the launchpad should have a limited number of tasks to "keep it simple." A large number of tasks on one panel can seem overwhelming to users.

The factors determining the maximum number of wizards to launch from a launchpad are similar to those that determine how many steps to include in a single wizard:

- **All steps (tasks) should be visible on-screen at all times.** If the task contains too many steps or wizards to fit on a launchpad, consider showing only the necessary or most common default steps. Two ways of doing this are to:

  - Leave expert functions or optional functions off the launchpad.

  - Re-think the task definition and provide multiple launchpads, each of which supports a more limited set of tasks. For example, instead of providing a single launchpad that allows users to complete state and federal tax returns, provide two launchpads. One launchpad could assist with federal tax returns, and the other could assist with state tax returns. Upon completion of the federal return launchpad, the software could ask users if they would like to continue with the state launchpad.

- **The launchpad should support a coherent and useful set of tasks.** The following tips may help you select an appropriate set of tasks:

  - Don't provide shortcuts to all tasks in the product. Unless the product is very limited in scope, showing the user shortcuts to all wizards or functions will be overwhelming.

  - Perform a task analysis to identify a useful subset of product functions.

  - Ensure that the user can complete an entire task without leaving the launchpad.

  - Ensure that wizards or dialogs accessed from the launchpad are functionally related and that this relationship is communicated to the user. For example, a good rule for including wizards on a launchpad is: "all wizards that allow users to create a report." If your software allows users to create five types of reports, the launchpad can provide a shortcut to these options. A better rule for including wizards is: "all wizards that are needed for software installation." This type of launchpad helps users to learn task dependencies. A poor rule for wizard inclusion on a launchpad is: "all wizards that are more than seven pages long." This type of rule should never be used.

Navigation among wizards, the launchpad, and other supporting dialogs

As discussed in Chapter 6, "Navigation," successful navigation requires the users to understand: Where am I now?, Where can I go?, Where have I been?, What do I have left to do?, and How do I get to where I want to be? Users must also answer these questions as they attempt to navigate through a launchpad. See Chapter 6, "Navigation," to learn how to apply cues such as text states and control changes to support navigation.

Launchpads have an additional layer of navigation that does not exist in single wizards. This layer refers to how a user navigates among the launchpad, wizards, and other supporting dialogs. There are two possible overall structures for a launchpad: a container style and a multiple window style. When a user launches a wizard from a container-style launchpad, the wizard appears within the launchpad window. Figure 8–3 shows a container-style launchpad. A single window exists at all times; subsequent wizards replace

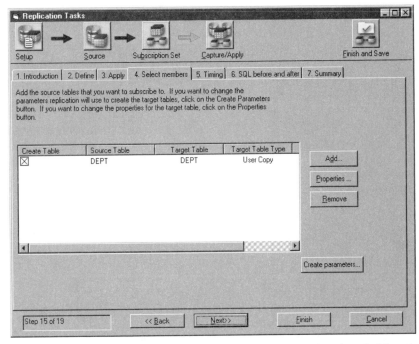

Figure 8–3   *A container-style launchpad and a wizard that has been launched from it.*

the previous content of the launchpad. The container-style launchpad can provide a mechanism for the user to easily move from one wizard to the next by clicking the **Next** or **Back** button.

When a user launches a wizard from a multiple window-style launchpad, each wizard appears in its own dedicated window. Multiple windows are open at once; one for the launchpad and one or more for the wizards. Figure 8–4 illustrates the multiple window-style launchpad.

During a series of usability tests, we found that participants slightly preferred having the wizards launched as separate windows. They felt that the launching of separate windows helped to enforce a clearer division of where one wizard ended and the next began. Participants stated that understanding where each wizard ends is very important, because earlier tasks must be completed before later steps are attempted. Participants also felt that the separate windows would help to provide clear cues that **Finish**, **Save,** and **Show SQL** (code to be run) buttons applied only to a single wizard (task).

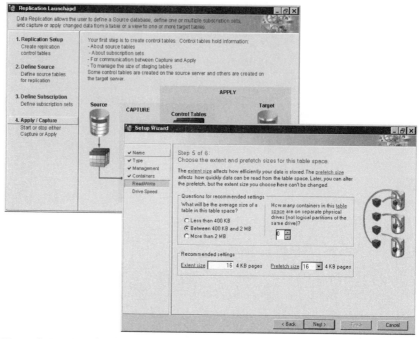

Figure 8–4 *A multiple window-style launchpad and a wizard that has been launched from it.*

Participants stated that it was acceptable to launch secondary dialogs such as dialogs that showed SQL commands or help dialogs from the wizards. When the secondary dialog is dismissed, focus should return to the wizard. Similarly, focus should return to the launchpad after a wizard that it launched is completed.

Some participants felt that that the multiple window-style launchpad may be better for novices, but that the container approach was more efficient. If a central goal of your launchpad implementation is to teach the conceptual structure of the task, use the multiple window-style.

Dependencies between steps

A vertical arrangement implicitly denotes a linear sequence of the tasks from top to bottom, whereas a horizontal arrangement suggests non-linearity in the tasks. You can use these launchpad arrangements to reflect the underlying task characteristics.

You can disable links to steps whose predecessor tasks are not yet completed to provide further information about dependencies. You can also use numbers, indentations, or arrows to visually denote task dependence. Figure 8–5 illustrates a launchpad design that uses numbering and indentation as cues to task dependencies. In this design, task 2 consists of three subtasks, a, b, and c. These subtasks can be completed in any order. Task 3 cannot be started until all of the subtasks in task 2 are completed.

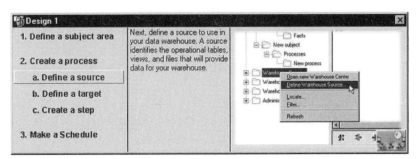

Figure 8–5   *A launchpad that uses numbering and indentation to demonstrate task sequence and dependence. Task 3 cannot be started until tasks 2a, 2b, and 2c are completed.*

Progress-related cues

You can design a launchpad to provide progress cues for various levels of granularity. However, some levels of feedback are too dynamic and low-level for launchpads. Participants in our user studies wanted a general sense of progress; they did not care about the exact number of steps. You can provide general progress information through a completion bar or progress indicator.

Participants in our usability studies tended to favor having clear cues indicating when one wizard ended and another began. As mentioned previously, participants preferred the multiple window-style approach for this reason. The launchpad itself should also provide a clear visual indication of which wizard is currently being used. For example, graphics can be filled in as tasks are completed. Participants also indicated a slight preference for restarting the step numbers when a new wizard is entered.

Task progress and dependency cues

Providing information about task dependencies and progress can become quite complicated. These complications are due to the issues of persistence, context or scope of the launchpad, and recognition of objects. For example, suppose that you were designing a launchpad to take users through a series of database tasks. You would like to place a checkmark next to each completed step. This simple design requirement turns out to be quite complicated because the interpretation of "completed" depends on issues such as:

- Will the checkmark state persist after the computer is turned off?

- Will each launchpad "belong" to a specific database? For example, the launchpad for database1 may show four completed steps, while the launchpad for database2 may show only two completed steps.

- If a user completed a task without using the launchpad, would the launchpad recognize that the necessary prerequisites for a step were completed?

- If the user went through the launchpad wizards, but saved the scripts to run later, would the checkmarks appear? What would checkmarks mean in this context?

The answers to the questions above rely heavily on the underlying task characteristics. If the tasks to be supported by the launchpad will be completed only once per software installation, in a sequential order, and only through the launchpad, then the launchpad should show information such as task dependencies and progress. However, if the task dependencies are not as stringent, then it may be more usable not to show task dependency and progress information. For example, a travel agent launchpad may allow the user to make hotel reservations and buy airline tickets. A launchpad that forces the user to make airline reservations first would be too stringent. Users may want to make hotel reservations before airline reservations if they are afraid that the hotel may fill up, if they are expecting someone else to make their airline reservations, or if they are trying to coordinate flights with other travelers. For this type of launchpad, you may decide to allow the user to access any task at any time. In this case, your launchpad design can assume that the user will know (or will be able to determine) if previous tasks were completed and if they need to be completed.

Consistency between the launchpad and its wizards

The launchpad should be consistent in both look and behavior with the wizards it launches. You can achieve consistency in look by using similar color palettes, fonts, and styles. Icons should also be consistent. However, to prevent confusion between the launchpad and the wizards, you may choose to use different layouts for each. For example, your launchpad might have a table of contents layout, and individual wizards might have a horizontal, tabbed layout.

The launchpad and wizards must be consistent in behavior. User actions in each should have the same results. For example, if positioning the mouse over a word in the wizard displays a definition of the term, the same action should do so in the launchpad.

Access to your launchpad

You need to provide easy access to your launchpad. Methods to launch your launchpad include:

- **Automatically launching the launchpad upon starting the product.** Because the launchpad provides a broad overview of the product and helps the user understand dependencies among tasks, you might consider automatically launching the launchpad upon starting the product. If you take this approach, give your users the option to *not* have the launchpad displayed automatically in the future. A check box with a label such as "Don't show this window next time the product is started" can fulfill this design requirement.

- **Allowing the user to launch the launchpad through shortcut menus.** If your software is structured with a tree view on the left and a details view on the right, the launchpad should be accessible from shortcut menus on the relevant objects. Figure 8–6 shows such an approach to accessing a launchpad. In this scenario, the pop-up menu is on the topmost object in a tree hierarchy to allow users to quickly access it without needing to expand the lower objects.

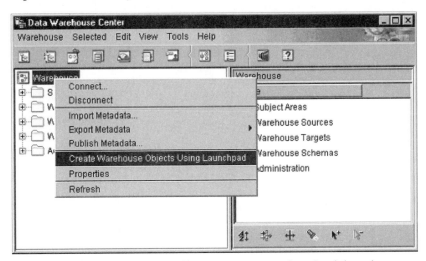

Figure 8–6   *An application that allows users to access a launchpad through pop-up menus on objects in its tree view*

- **Allowing the user to launch the launchpad through a list of wizards or list of launchpads.** Some products include a list of wizards in their menu bar or **Help** menu. You can add your launchpad to this list or create a similar list of the launchpads found in your product.

Additional functions that can be supported by a launchpad

The features and issues described so far apply to a "bare bones" launchpad design, which simply links various wizards into a central access point. However, launchpads also afford an opportunity for teaching concepts, providing practical information about using the product, and supporting user exploration. You can use launchpads to:

- Teach the user the conceptual model of how the product works.
- Support user exploration.
- Show the user how to do the task without the launchpad.
- Allow users to personalize or build their own launchpads.

Ideas for taking advantage of these opportunities and giving the user a richer experience are described in this section.

Teaching the user the conceptual model of how the product works

Launchpads can provide information that may help the user learn the underlying conceptual model of a product. This information can be presented by textual descriptions or graphical features.

Conceptual graphics

At IBM, the launchpads in our database and data warehousing products contain an interactive, conceptual graphic of the end-to-end task. This graphic changes as the user moves the mouse pointer over the buttons corresponding to each task. These changes illustrate which objects are impacted by or involved in each step. Graphical changes must be salient to ensure that users notice the differences in the graphic and understand what is being affected by each wizard as they proceed through the launchpad. Figures 8–7 and 8–8 show how a conceptual graphic changes as the user moves the mouse pointer over different steps. Figure 8–7 illustrates the objects that will be impacted by the second task on the launchpad. These objects—Source, Log, and Change Data Table—are brightly colored, while other objects in the conceptual diagram are faded. The textual description at the top of the graphic explains what will happen in this task.

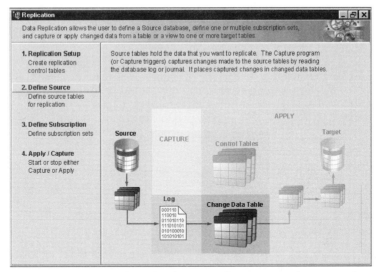

Figure 8–7 *The conceptual graphic changes as the user moves the mouse pointer over different tasks. The Source, Log, and Change Data Table are impacted during task 2.*

Figure 8–8 illustrates the objects that will be impacted by the third task on the launchpad. When the user moves the mouse pointer over task 3, Define Subscription, the Change Data Table and Target objects become brightly colored, while the Source and Log objects become faded. The textual description at the top of the graphic also changes to explain what will happen in task 3.

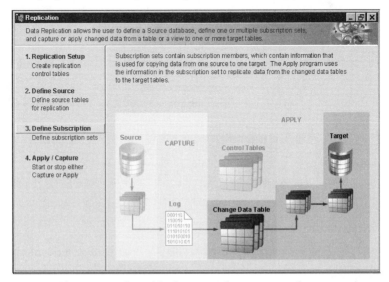

Figure 8–8 *The conceptual graphic changes as the user moves the mouse pointer over different tasks. The Change Data Table and Target are impacted during task 3.*

You can view an interactive sample of the launchpad shown in these figures on the CD-ROM.

Our usability tests have provided consistent, positive feedback on this feature. Participants in the tests found the conceptual graphic useful and visually attractive. Several participants were able to describe the complete process for setting up a complex database task after using that launchpad a single time. Some even claimed that they would use it as a teaching resource for new database administrators!

You can personalize the conceptual graphic to reflect user entries. For example, the graphic might begin with generic labels, such as "database" or "table." As the user completes steps using the launchpad, these labels can be replaced with the actual object names, such as "payroll database" and "employee table." This automatic personalization can further help the user understand and relate to the conceptual graphic.

Development of a useful conceptual graphic requires many iterations and usability tests to ensure that the correct concepts are being communicated. Guidelines to help begin the process include:

- If there are a large number of tasks, say 10 tasks, do not include a visual symbol or representation for each task. Providing a symbol for each task would decrease the overall impact of the conceptual graphic, making it appear too cluttered and complicated.

- Make the visual approach of the conceptual graphic simple and easily identifiable. Users want to be able to relate it to other visual elements in the overall user interface. The images or symbols in the graphic should be used as anchors, familiar landmarks, or metaphors.

- Rather than providing a flowchart of steps, use the conceptual design to display the relationships among objects impacted by the wizards and launchpad.

- Make sure that the dominance of visual elements in the conceptual graphic is directly related to their level of functional importance.

- Consider using color to highlight the active aspects on the conceptual graphic.

- Avoid using gray graphics if you want the user to click the graphics. As with other objects, gray graphics do not appear selectable. Participants were not tempted to click on grayed objects in the conceptual graphic. Some participants did click on the colored objects in the graphic.

Textual descriptions of each step

A launchpad can teach users the conceptual model of the product by providing textual descriptions as the user moves the mouse pointer over specific tasks or icons. For example, in Figures 8–7 and 8–8, the textual description at the top of the conceptual graphic describes what objects will be impacted by the task. This text changes as the user moves the mouse pointer over each step.

Graphics that are versions of the icons used in the product

Even if a conceptual graphic is not provided, the launchpad can introduce the user to the key icons or images used in the product. The launchpad shown in Figure 8–9 illustrates how a launchpad can be used to familiarize a user with the toolbar icons. The graphics used for the launchpad steps are simply larger versions of the toolbar icons. The first launchpad image and the third icon in the toolbar both launch the same wizard—the Set Up Member Only Analysis wizard.

One advantage of this approach is that the launchpad itself contains enough real estate to allow descriptions of the icons to co-exist with the graphics.

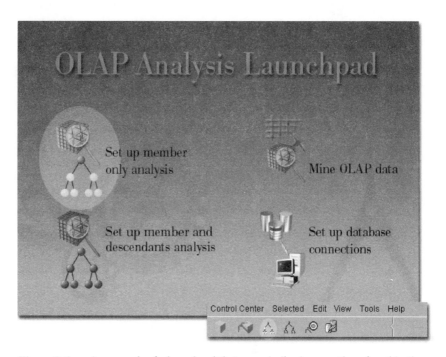

Figure 8–9   *An example of a launchpad that uses similar icons as those found in the toolbar for the product. The third icon in the toolbar launches a wizard to set up member only analysis.*

Supporting user exploration

Anecdotal evidence collected during usability tests at IBM suggests that the Web has significantly impacted users' expectations of what software can and should do. Participants express expectations that are consistent with Web applications, such as the use of mouse rollovers to provide additional information and the use of color to denote previously visited links. Participants also rated "Web style" designs more positively than traditional software designs. For example, participants stated that launchpad designs that used beveled buttons to launch wizards were "too 80s." The Web also seems to be impacting user's interaction with computers in a more general fashion. Participants expect the computer to provide an interactive environment for them. They do not want the computer to simply provide a passive display of information.

The conceptual diagram and textual descriptions described in the previous section are two examples of how launchpads can encourage and support user exploration. Another method is to provide pop-up help, or special text boxes that appear when the user pauses the mouse over an important term or phrase. Figure 8–10 shows an example of how a pop-up help window would look on a launchpad. For more information on this type of help, see Chapter 11, "On-line help."

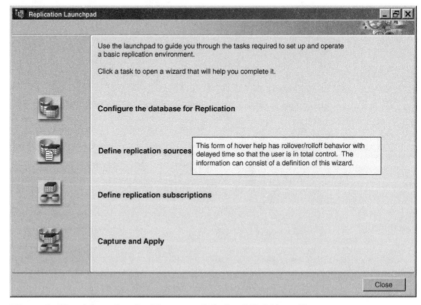

Figure 8–10   *A launchpad with pop-up help for definitions of key terms.*

Launchpad designs can also help users understand which wizard or dialog will be launched by each button or label. The launchpad should contain brief textual descriptions of what each wizard will do. This information can help users understand the scope of each option and determine which is the correct one without having to launch the actual wizard.

Participants in usability tests at IBM often want to know what information is required before they start. They also want to understand the approach that a user interface takes to dividing up a task, even if they are not going to complete the task immediately. Launchpads can provide a framework for presenting this information. You might allow users to view the contents of a wizard even if it cannot be completed at the current time. To prevent confusion, use visual cues to inform the user that the wizard cannot be completed. For example, you can disable the controls and text on each wizard page. This approach allows the user to explore without the risk of making mistakes or of having to create "dummy" objects just to see how things work. A similar approach is to provide a textual description of what information or user action is needed to enable a particular wizard page. Figure 8–11 demonstrates this second approach.

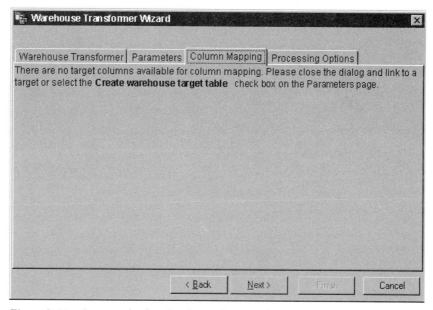

Figure 8–11   *An example of a wizard page that describes what needs to be done to enable the page.*

Showing users how to do the task without the launchpad

One of the criticisms of wizards is that they do not help users learn how to do tasks without the wizards. This is not surprising because learning how to do a task requires two levels of knowledge: understanding the underlying conceptual model of the product and having the practical knowledge of where functions exist in the interface. Launchpads can be designed to provide both of these types of information. Features that help the users gain a conceptual understanding of the product are described in "Teaching the user the conceptual model of how the product works" on page 178.

You can also add practical information to the launchpad to help the user understand how to complete the task without the launchpad. The alternate method for completing the task might involve launching wizards, using dialogs, or entering commands. This information may be quite useful if users are likely to want to access the individual steps from the product interface. For example, if users do not need to complete all launchpad steps each time, users might prefer to launch one or two dialogs or wizards from the software product rather than to launch the launchpad first and then launch these dialogs for the steps.

This section describes three approaches to showing users how to do the tasks without the launchpad: textual descriptions, graphics of the interface, and help mechanisms:

- **Textual descriptions.** You can add a textual description to the main panel of the launchpad. Figure 8–12 shows such an approach.

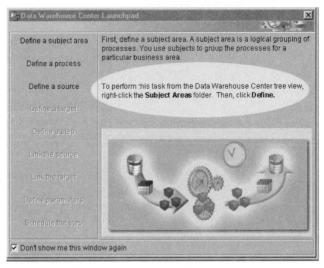

Figure 8–12 *A launchpad that provides a textual description of how to complete the task without using the launchpad.*

Textual descriptions have the advantage of being relatively inexpensive to implement and maintain. Additionally, the text is easily accessible to the user. The user does not need to leave the launchpad or enter a special mode to obtain the information. However, it may be difficult to concisely describe how to access a wizard or dialog.

- **Graphics of the interface.** You can provide a series of graphics that show the user how to complete the tasks without the launchpad. Figure 8–13 illustrates a graphical approach.

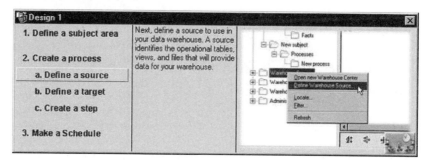

Figure 8–13 *A launchpad design that incorporates screen captures to demonstrate how to complete the task without the launchpad.*

This graphical approach is much more time-consuming and expensive to implement. Additionally, the number of graphics required to show the user what to do may slow down performance. If the product is translated into multiple languages, the graphical approach may also cause additional problems. And finally, this graphical approach occupies more screen real estate than the textual description, and therefore does not allow enough room for you to also show the practical information with a diagram. You might consider providing two launchpad modes: one for the conceptual diagram and one for the "how to" information. However, this option runs the risk that the users might never notice that a second mode exists.

- **Help mechanisms.** You can use a help mechanism, such as a tutorial, coaching feature, or on-line help, which is directly accessed from the launchpad. Design guidance for some help mechanisms is addressed in Chapter 11, "On-line help."

Allowing users to personalize or build their own launchpads

As with wizards, you can include several features within a launchpad that allow the user to define all or part of the path displayed. For example, your launchpad might include a check box that allows the user to choose whether to display the steps belonging to the advanced features of the product. Similarly, you can allow the user to choose whether the launchpad launches dialogs or wizards. You might even allow users to build a personal launchpad by selecting wizards or other functions that they would like to have ready access to. This extended function could be difficult to code, especially if the launchpad maintained information about task dependencies. However, it would be useful in work scenarios where the end-users have varying levels of expertise. For example, for educational software, the instructor might want to remove certain functions that would not be used in the classroom. Building launchpads would also be useful when a product is being installed across an entire company. The software administrator might want to remove advanced functions due to licensing considerations or to prevent users from installing pieces of a product that are not used at the site.

Summary of guidelines discussed in this chapter

❑ Allow users to launch secondary wizards from within wizards in rare cases only.

❑ Use a launchpad to organize wizards that must be completed in a specific order.

❑ Limit the number of steps on a launchpad to ensure that all are visible on-screen.

❑ Support a coherent and useful subset of tasks.

❑ In most cases, launch wizards as separate windows and return focus to the launchpad after the wizard is completed.

❑ Use visual cues to denote dependencies between launchpad steps.

❑ Always provide cues to give users a sense of progress throughout the tasks supported by the launchpad.

❑ Ensure that the launchpad and wizards behave consistently.

❑ Allow users to easily access the launchpad.

❑ Optional: Help the user to form a conceptual model of how the product works.

❑ Optional: Include graphics that are versions of the icons used in the product.

❑ Optional: Support user exploration by providing additional useful information when the user positions the mouse pointer over the steps and by allowing users to view the contents of the wizard even if it cannot be completed at the current time.

❑ Optional: Inform users of how to do the task without the launchpad.

❑ Optional: In situations where one user may manage software usage by others, allow users to personalize or build their own launchpads.

Chapter 9

Interactive feedback

▲ Why provide feedback?

▲ Questions to ask before beginning

▲ General feedback guidelines

▲ Auditory feedback

▲ Feedback while interacting with the wizard

▲ Feedback at the completion of the wizard

▲ Summary of guidelines discussed in this chapter

One factor that is often overlooked during the design phase is feedback. Feedback provides acknowledgement to the users that the wizard has accepted their input.

Feedback should be provided at the following times:

- **As the user is interacting with each wizard page**. For example, when a user clicks a radio button, that button should receive focus; that is, it should be highlighted.

- **While the wizard is processing user input after the user clicks the Finish button**. For example, a pop-up message can be displayed telling the user how much processing time is left until the task is complete.

- **At the completion of wizard processing**. For example, if the wizard processing is successful, you can display a pop-up message letting the user know that the wizard processing is complete.

This chapter presents general guidelines for providing feedback in wizards and for providing auditory feedback. This chapter also describes detailed methods of providing feedback for processing wizard information. These detailed methods are divided into two sections: feedback while the user is interacting with the wizard and feedback methods when the wizard is complete.

Why provide feedback?

Feedback in any form is necessary so that users feel that your wizard is interacting with them and recognizing their input.

Benefits of feedback include:

- **Feedback lets users know that the wizard is functioning**. Feedback is an acknowledgement that the wizard has received or accepted input as the user progresses through each page of the wizard.

- **Feedback lets users know they have completed the wizard successfully.** This allows them to move on to the next task or wizard.

- **Feedback informs users of errors.** Feedback can also explain what caused the errors and how to resolve them, and it can provide links to additional information if necessary.

Questions to ask before beginning

Gather the answers to the following questions from Chapter 2, "Gathering requirements," before you begin:

- **Does the target audience include users with visual or auditory disabilities?** The answer to this question will help you determine which form of feedback to use. For auditory disabilities, avoid sound as a method of feedback. For visual disabilities, you might want to consider sound or speech synthesis as a form of feedback.

- **Is noise a concern in the target audience's work environment?** If so, then you will want to avoid the use of sound as a method of feedback.

- **Does the task have multiple commit points?** Provide feedback at every commit point in your wizard to let the users know whether their input is successful or unsuccessful.

- **What errors might the users make?** You will want to optimize your wizard design to prevent errors or help users recover from them. However, errors may still be possible and you will want to identify those situations and design feedback to inform the users of those errors.

General feedback guidelines

Feedback is a key aspect of wizard design because it informs the user that the wizard recognizes his or her input, what the wizard is doing with the input, and whether the input is correct. Follow these general guidelines for providing feedback:

- Provide users with positive feedback in addition to informing them of error situations.

- Provide feedback immediately to let users know if actions are successful or unsuccessful. Miller (1968) provides these guidelines for response times and the necessity for feedback:

  - 0.1 seconds is the limit in which users feel any processing is immediate and no feedback is necessary.

  - 1.0 second is the limit where users start to notice that there are delays in processing. Processing times between .1 and 1 second do not require feedback; processing or response times greater than 1 second do require feedback.

- For long processing times, provide a progress indicator that tells the user how much longer the processing will take, what actions are being processed, or what percent is complete. Ten seconds is the limit for keeping the user's attention on your wizard.

Auditory feedback

Auditory feedback is an audible sound that can be used as feedback to let your users know the wizard is processing and that a wizard task is complete. There are a number of guidelines to take into consideration when using sound as a method of feedback:

- Do not use sound as the only cue to wizard processing because users can turn the sound on their computers off, and sound does not provide specific information about wizard processing.

- Do not use sound as a feedback cue when you know your wizard will be used in noisy environments.

- Use sound if you know your users will not be dedicated to watching their computer screens. Sounds can alert them that wizard processing is complete or that processing is still continuing.

- Consider having different auditory cues for successful and unsuccessful wizard processing.

- Depending on the task that your wizard is performing, consider making the sound fun. For example, for a create postcard wizard in a children's drawing program, you could use the *1812 Overture* (with cannon) when a process is complete. However, if your wizard is performing a critical task, then you probably do not want to implement sounds that are not serious.

- Use auditory cues for users who might be visually impaired.

Feedback while interacting with the wizard

There are many points within the wizard pages where you should provide feedback. This section describes the various methods for providing feedback for controls on a wizard page and feedback for subtasks related to the wizard.

Feedback for controls

Follow these guidelines for providing feedback when users interact with controls on a wizard page:

- **Provide focus on a control when the user selects the control with the mouse or keyboard.** Focus is indicated by highlighting the control by providing a darker, thicker outline around the control, or by providing a dotted outline around the control.

If the control is actually a group of radio buttons or check boxes, highlight the default value. If the control is an entry field and the entry field is blank, change the cursor to a blinking cursor as feedback. If the entry field contains text, use reverse video to show focus (that is, changing dark text on a light background to light text on a dark background, and vice versa). Figure 9–1 shows an example of focus on a blank entry field, focus on an entry field with text, and focus on a group of radio buttons, respectively.

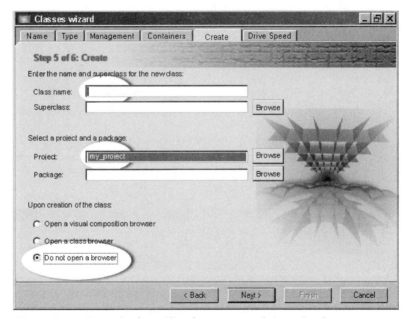

Figure 9–1   *Example of providing focus on controls in a wizard page.*

- **Provide focus on the first control of a wizard page when the page is first displayed.** This lets the user know where to begin and that the page has focus.

- **Highlight items that the user selects from a list.** Highlighting list items provides feedback that the item is selected. Figure 9–2 shows an example of highlighting a list item.

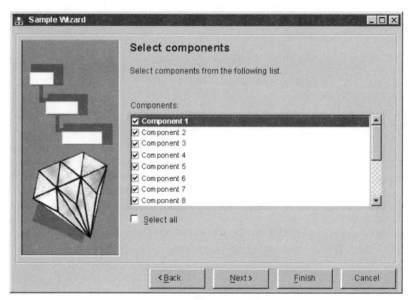

Figure 9–2   *Example of highlighting a list item that is selected.*

- **Change the cursor style as users tab or move the mouse over links.**
  Changing the cursor style provides feedback that the underlined text is a
  link. Figure 9–3 shows an example of changing the cursor icon as the user
  navigates to a link.

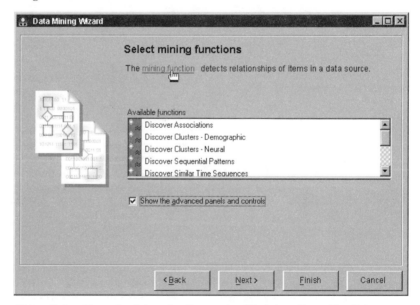

Figure 9–3   *Example of changing the cursor while interacting with a link.*

- **Enable or disable controls based on related selections the user makes.** For example, in a tax wizard, there are two radio buttons: one indicating the user will take the standard deduction and the other indicating the user wants to itemize deductions. If the user chooses to take the standard deduction, all fields and controls related to itemizing are disabled. Figure 9–4 shows an example of interactions between controls.

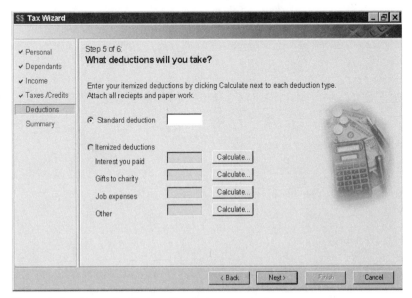

Figure 9–4   Example of interactions between controls.

- **Enable or disable the Next button as feedback that all mandatory fields are or are not completed on a wizard page.** See Chapter 6, "Navigation," for more details. Follow these guidelines for enabling and disabling the **Next** button:

  - Disable the **Next** button if all mandatory fields are not completed.

  - Enable the **Next** button when all mandatory fields are completed.

  - Enable the **Next** button when enough defaults are provided on a wizard page to allow the user to simply take the defaults. This guideline applies to the **Finish** button as well.

  - Tie any necessary page-level processing to the **Next** button. For example, if page 1 of your wizard asks users to select the type of chart they want to create, the contents of page 2 can vary depending on the type they select on page 1.

    Figure 9–5 shows two pages of a wizard. The selection made on the first page affects what appears on the next page. The processing is done when the user clicks **Next** on the first page.

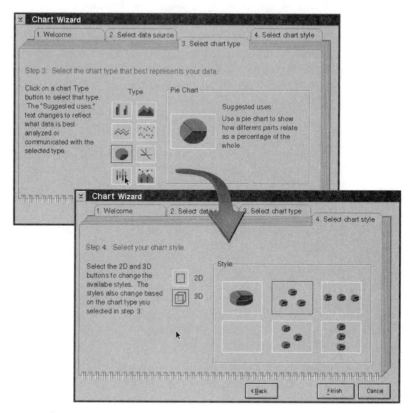

Figure 9–5 *Processing information on one page of a wizard affects subsequent pages.*

Feedback for subtasks related to the wizard

As described in Chapter 5, "General wizard design," you sometimes need to launch a dialog from the main wizard to allow users to perform a subtask related to the wizard. If your wizard contains such a subtask, you might find it necessary to process that subtask's information and provide feedback prior to returning to the main wizard.

For example, a tax wizard might have one page that contains a field to enter the interest the user paid. You can provide a **Calculate** button, which launches a dialog that allows your users to calculate the interest. When the user completes the information in this dialog and clicks **OK**, the information in the dialog is processed and fills in the field in the main wizard. Figure 9–6 shows an example of processing for related subtasks.

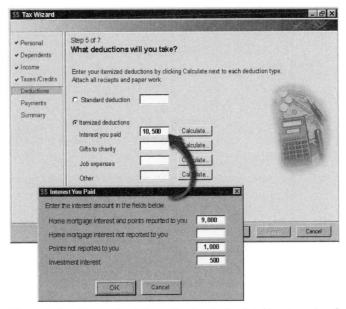

Figure 9–6 *Processing information in a task related to a tax wizard.*

Follow these guidelines for providing feedback for subtasks related to your wizard:

- **Make the subtask dialog modal.** Do not allow users to interact with the wizard while the dialog is displayed. This provides feedback that your users must complete this dialog or click **Cancel** before returning to the wizard.

- **Update the wizard entry fields when the user closes the subtask dialog.** This provides feedback that the subtask completed successfully.

Feedback at the completion of the wizard

After the user enters information on each wizard page, the information is stored as the user progresses, and it is finally submitted when the user completes the wizard by clicking the **Finish** button.

Display the wizard while it is creating an object, launching a long-running process, or issuing a command. Close the wizard only when the object is created or the task completes successfully. Keeping your wizard open during processing provides strong visual feedback that the wizard is still processing information. Also, if errors occur during the processing of information, keeping the wizard open allows the user to modify responses and resubmit the wizard again.

You can use these methods of providing feedback both while the wizard is processing information and after it completes its task:

- Progress indicators
- Billboards
- Status line
- Confirmation dialogs
- Displaying the object that your wizard created

Progress indicators

Progress indicators inform users that wizard processing is taking place. These indicators draw the user's visual attention and should be used in cases where the completion of the wizard launches a long-running process. We have found that progress indicators work best when used to display the following types of information:

- **How much time remains until the process is complete**. This information can be difficult to provide because it might be difficult to predict system processor speed or the effects of other applications running on the user's machine.

- **Specific details on what the wizard is doing during processing**. For example, the progress indicator for a create database wizard could provide the following details: "Creating database," "Creating tables," and "Inserting data." Figure 9–7 shows an example of a progress indicator.

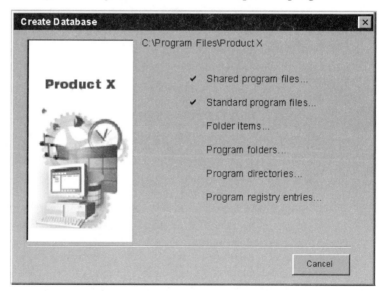

Figure 9–7   *Example of a progress indicator for the Create Database wizard.*

- **The percentage of processing complete**. This information can also be difficult to provide due to non-wizard influences. This type of progress indicator "fills up" when processing is 100% complete. Figure 9–8 shows an example of a progress indicator showing percentage complete.

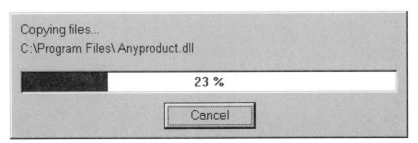

Copying files...
C:\Program Files\ Anyproduct.dll

23 %

Cancel

Figure 9–8   Example of a progress indicator showing percentage complete.

Billboards

For long-running processes such as those encountered in an installation wizard, you can provide "billboards," which are separate windows containing information about your product, marketing messages, or any kind of information to hold the user's attention while the wizard is processing. Users will understand that the process is still running and that the product is still working as long as the "billboard" is changing. Figure 9–9 shows an example of a billboard message.

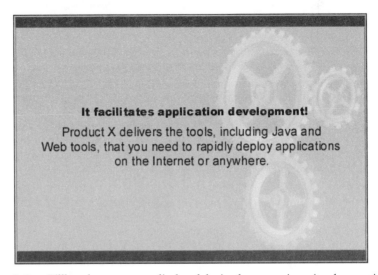

It facilitates application development!

Product X delivers the tools, including Java and
Web tools, that you need to rapidly deploy applications
on the Internet or anywhere.

Figure 9–9   Billboard messages are displayed during long-running wizard processing.

Status line

The status line is a text area that is used to present feedback to users. It is usually located at the bottom of a window or wizard page. It can be used for displaying feedback while the wizard is processing and after the wizard is complete.

The status line is usually a single-line, ready-only text area. Status lines are commonly used in non-wizard applications; their use in wizards is less common. Figure 9–10 provides an example of a status line. Status lines can display:

- **Field-level help**. The status line can display field-level help as the user moves the mouse or cursor over the various entry fields and controls, and can provide information as to what type of data to enter or a description of the field.

- **Progress.** The status line can display the status of processes launched from the dialog or page. For example, in a wizard to set up a new printer, the status line might display such information as "Setting up printer."

- **Information about process completion**. Status lines can display process completion information and whether the process was successful or unsuccessful. For example, in the Printer Set Up wizard, the status line could display information such as "Printer setup successful."

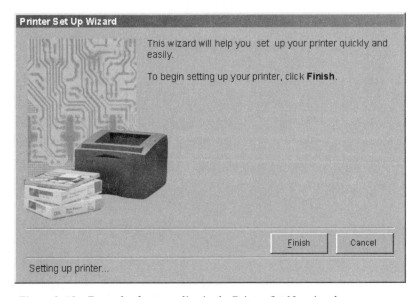

Figure 9–10   *Example of a status line in the Printer Set Up wizard.*

Although the status line is a very useful and versatile method of displaying feedback information, there are some disadvantages to consider:

- Because the status line can be used for so many purposes, it can be awkward to determine where and how to display these different types of information. For example, suppose the wizard for creating a new printer is processing the user information and is creating the new printer. The status line is displaying "Creating printer..." The user then moves the mouse over an entry field with field-specific help enabled. Does the help information override the progress indicator or is the information displayed in a separate area of the status line? When there are several types of information being displayed in the status line, the general practice is to break the status line into sections to display the various types of information.

- Because the status line is a small area at the bottom of the screen or wizard page, the user's visual attention is not usually drawn there. The user might overlook some messages.

- If wizard processing is successful and the wizard closes, you still need to provide an additional confirmation message.

Confirmation dialogs

Confirmation dialogs are separate message boxes or dialogs that are used to provide feedback that the wizard has completed processing. Follow these guidelines for confirmation dialogs:

- **Be specific**. Provide information about exactly which objects were created or which processes were completed. For example, if you design a wizard to create a new printer, the message could say, "MyPrinter set up was successful." Figure 9–11 shows an example of a specific confirmation dialog.

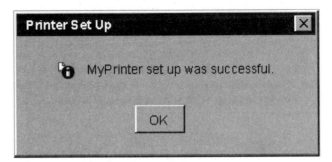

Figure 9–11   *Confirmation dialog indicating successful printer set up.*

- **Tell the user if the process or object creation was successful or unsuccessful**. If unsuccessful, you should:
  - **Provide information about why the object creation or process failed and how to recover from the error situation**. For example, in the Create Table wizard, the failure information could say, "Create table 'Personnel' failed. Database connection not established. Connect to database 'MyDatabase' and resubmit information."
  - **Provide links to additional information or help to assist the user**. Figure 9–12 shows an example of a message dialog that provides a **Help** button to provide additional information in an error situation. See Chapter 10, "Error prevention and recovery," for more details on this topic.

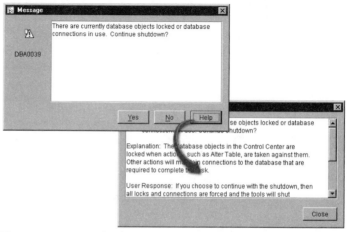

Figure 9–12   Example of confirmation dialog in an error situation with links to additional information.

Displaying the object that your wizard created

If the purpose of your wizard is to create an object, for example, a database, you can display the object your wizard created in the work environment or on the computer desktop. This type of feedback informs the user that the wizard is complete and that the task was successful.

Generally, it is not a good idea to use the display of the newly created object as the *only* feedback cue because:

- The user may not be looking at the desktop or larger work environment.
- There might be many existing objects and the user might not notice one more object being displayed.
- There might be cases where the user must manually refresh the application to view changes or additions.
- The application might not be open.

Summary of guidelines discussed in this chapter

❑ Ensure that feedback is immediate.

❑ Provide feedback for successful and unsuccessful processing.

❑ Use sound as a method of feedback if you know your users will not be dedicated to watching their computer screens.

  • Do not use sound as feedback when you know your wizard will be used in noisy environments.

  • Do not use sound as the only cue to wizard processing because users can turn the sound on their computers off. Sound does not provide all the feedback information your wizard needs.

❑ Provide focus on a control when the user selects the control with the mouse or keyboard.

❑ Provide focus on the first control of a wizard page when the page is first displayed.

❑ Enable or disable the **Next** button as feedback that all mandatory fields have or have not been completed on a wizard page.

❑ If users need to perform a subtask related to the wizard, process information after the subtask is complete, before the user returns to the wizard.

❑ Use progress indicators to provide information about how much processing time is left, the percentage of processing completed, and what steps the wizard is taking while it is processing.

❑ Provide special progress indicators, such as billboards, for long-running processes.

❑ Use status lines to provide feedback to users that the wizard is processing and when it is complete.

❑ Use confirmation dialogs to:

  • Provide specific information about what objects were created or what processes were completed.

  • Tell the user if the process or object creation was successful or unsuccessful. If unsuccessful, provide additional information to assist the user in error recovery.

❑ Display the object or objects that your wizard created as feedback of successful and completed wizard processing. Provide another method of feedback, however, in case users do not have the application open.

Chapter 10

Error prevention and recovery

▲ Why predict, prevent, and recover from errors?
▲ Questions to ask before beginning
▲ Predicting errors
▲ Preventing and reducing errors
▲ Recovering from errors
▲ Summary of guidelines discussed in this chapter

The goal of most wizards is to simplify a task. As a result, an easy-to-use wizard is one in which the user is not likely to make any errors. If your users do not understand how to input data or do not understand which choices to make, they will find your wizard difficult to use and will make lots of errors.

The best method of dealing with errors is to take an iterative approach of predicting and handing errors:

1. Use categories or lists of possible errors to help predict errors.
2. Rate your errors in terms of likelihood and severity.
3. Design your wizard to eliminate the most severe and most likely errors.
4. Design your wizard to make it easy to recover from errors that cannot be prevented.
5. Repeat this process for your new design.

This chapter will help you predict, prevent, and recover from errors that users are likely to make. It discusses guidelines for decreasing the likelihood that users will make errors. It also includes guidelines for handing errors that users do make and for ensuring that it is easy for them to understand how to correct problems.

Why predict, prevent, and recover from errors?

Each time you change your wizard design, you should predict errors again and follow the iterative process. This cycle of error prediction, error prevention, and error recovery has several benefits:

- **Your wizard will be easier to use.** The goal of a wizard is to make things easier. If you do not predict and prevent errors, your wizard will be difficult for the user to use.

- **The quality of your wizard will improve.** The exercise of predicting errors helps you to identify potential coding errors early in the design cycle. You will be able to structure your code to be more efficient and bug-free if you take a systematic approach to identifying errors.

- **Your usability testing will be more cost-effective.** By examining your design and brainstorming about where the user may make mistakes, you can identify design flaws without needing to pay for users. You should never eliminate user feedback, but you should be intelligent in your testing approach, especially when users are expensive to recruit. Error prediction helps you ensure that your design is ready to be tested and that you will gain insights from participants that you would not have been able to predict. The process of predicting errors will also help you identify tradeoffs in your design. These tradeoffs are often exactly what you'll want to test.

- **Errors can be a good measure of your wizard's success.** Because one goal of your wizard is to make a task easier, one measure of its success is whether it can prevent users from making common and severe errors. If representative users do not make errors during usability testing, you can be reasonably sure your design is good.

Questions to ask before beginning

Before you can begin to predict errors, you must understand your target audience's experience and knowledge. Additionally, because errors are closely related to tasks performed, you must also understand the user's tasks. Before beginning to predict errors, you should complete a user definition and task analysis. Both of these types of analyses are described in Chapter 2, "Gathering requirements." These analyses answer questions such as:

- **Who will be using your wizard and what are their characteristics?** Previous experience shapes our expectations and how we think about things. If you can determine what your audience expects, you can identify mismatches between your wizard and audience expectations. These mismatches are likely to cause errors.

- **What is the user's task?** To answer this question, you need to ask questions such as: What tasks will the wizard support?, What tasks are supported by the application?, What tasks do the users complete as part of their job?, and What is the underlying structure of the task? The answers to these questions will help you understand the differences between how users think about the task and how the software represents the task. Errors are likely to occur when there are mismatches between how the wizard presents the task and how the user thinks about the task.

- **Are there aspects of the tasks that can be simplified?** The answer to this question will let you know what features and functions may be added to your wizard to make the task easier for users. Users are less likely to make errors when the task is easy.

- **Can you predict default entries or values for wizard steps or will user entries be needed to complete the steps?** Default entries can reduce certain types of errors such as typos and accidentally leaving out needed information. However, defaults make certain types of errors more likely, such as forgetting to enter a non-default entry.

- **Can aspects of the task be automated?** If you can eliminate an aspect of the task, then you can eliminate the chance for a user error to occur during the completion of that aspect.

- **What errors might the users make?** You may not know this information before design begins.

Predicting errors

The first step in preventing errors is to predict errors using categories or lists of possible errors. Ideally, you should predict errors before you design your wizard. However, if you already have a rough design, you can still benefit from predicting errors.

You can begin by creating a list of types of errors that you can use to evaluate your wizard design for possible errors. The goal of this list is to help you think more broadly when you are going through your wizard design. If you want to, you can use a formal model of human error as the basis for your list. For example, Norman (1988) and Reason (1990) developed models for the types of errors that people make. However, you can also design your own categories of possible errors.

Figure 10–1 provides a set of categories that you can use as a starting point for your list of errors. To use this table for your list of errors, first add rows for error categories that are possible in your wizard's task or domain area. Then, add a column so you can list specific errors that might occur.

Error type	Definition
User errors	
User knows the correct answer or action	
Data entry	User makes a data entry error.
Missing data	User "forgets" to enter needed data.
User does not know the correct answer or action	
Misinterpretation of wizard choices	User misinterprets wizard choices.
User is stuck	User does not know correct answer and realizes it.
User is mistaken	User thinks he or she knows the correct answer, but is wrong.
System errors	
Incorrect wizard assumptions	Wizard makes the incorrect assumptions.
Other	Network error, system crash and error in code (bug).

Figure 10–1   *A categorization scheme that you might use to predict errors.*

Preventing and reducing errors

After you predict the possible errors, you should design your wizard to prevent or reduce the likelihood of the most common and most severe errors. Many of the design guidelines in other chapters help to reduce user errors and are not repeated here. For example, clear labeling, consistent behavior, and proper help design will reduce the probability that the user will make an error.

This section describes guidelines for preventing these types of errors:

- All categories of user error
- Data entry errors
- Missing data errors
- Misinterpretations of wizard choices
- User-is-stuck errors
- User-is-mistaken errors
- Incorrect wizard assumptions
- Other system errors

Because you will not be able to prevent all errors, prioritize and prevent the most dangerous or most common errors. If you cannot prevent an error, you should help the user recover from it easily. Guidelines for error recovery are discussed later in the chapter.

All categories of user error

Your wizard structure determines what control combinations users can choose as well as how they think about the task. Structure your wizard to prevent invalid or error-prone combinations of control options. Additionally, the consistency between your wizard structure and how the user naturally "thinks" about the task can impact the number of errors. Do not directly map your wizard structure to the way the system "thinks" about the process (or the way the code is structured to complete the process). Instead, map your steps to how users naturally think about the task. Guidelines for reducing user errors via the wizard structure include:

- Reduce the number of steps and actions required.
- Prevent users from submitting input on one page that would invalidate input on an earlier page.
- Order controls so that early controls help to limit future inputs.

Reduce the number of steps and actions required

One of the most effective ways of preventing an error is to eliminate the need for the step that might cause the error. This is especially true for wizards because the primary motivation for creating a wizard is to automate parts of a task. Three methods to reduce the number of actions are:

- **Organize the wizard such that any repetitive processes are removed.** For example, do not require users to type both a mailing address and a billing address each time they use your wizard. Instead, provide an option to specify that the mailing address and billing address are the same.

- **Check for prerequisites or other settings, rather than have the user input them.** For example, rather than having your users verify that they have a certain version of Web browser software installed, have your wizard code check for the existence of the Web browser and its version automatically.

- **Allow users to use the finished wizard as a template for the next task or to create default settings that work for them.** For example, if your wizard helps users create graphs, let users select a previously created graph as a template instead of starting from scratch.

Prevent users from submitting input on one page that would invalidate input on an earlier page

For some tasks, user choices for one option might invalidate certain choices for other options. Make sure that your wizard is designed such that early pages drive the choices that are presented on later pages. User choices on later pages should never invalidate choices that the user made previously.

This rule also applies if your wizard provides tabs that allow the user to skip pages in the wizard. Tabs may become tricky if you have pages that have dependencies on other pages in the wizard. For example, suppose your wizard is structured so that page 3 is dependent on page 2. Three design options for this wizard are:

- Do not allow users to access page 3 until page 2 is completed.

- Allow users to access page 3, but tell them that page 2 needs to be completed before page 3 is enabled. This option allows users to browse the page and see what is expected of them.

- Allow users to fill in page 3, assuming they will take the defaults for page 2. If they later go to page 2 and change the settings to be non-default, warn them that page 3 needs to be completed again before they can click the **Finish** button. This option is the least preferred of the three.

Order controls so that early controls limit future inputs

This guideline is similar to the previous guideline. Structure individual pages so that controls near the top of the page impact controls displayed lower on the page (for cultures that read left to right, top to bottom). Figure 10–2 provides an example of a payment information page where the order of the controls on the page helps limit inputs. In this example, users need to enter credit card information. The design has users choose the type of credit card first. If a user selects Discover/Novus, the number 6011 is displayed (because all Discover cards begin with this number), and the user needs to type only the remainder of the Discover card number.

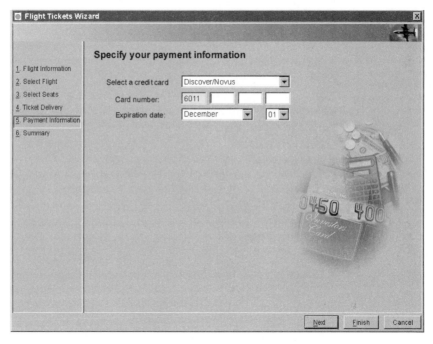

Figure 10–2 *A wizard page where the selection of the type of credit card changes the information presented later on the page.*

Data entry errors

Typing mistakes are one of the most common errors because they can occur for lots of reasons. One reason is that your users may not be good typists. Another reason is that the users may not be familiar with the format of information that needs to be entered, such as a calendar date. Guidelines to help reduce data entry errors when users understand what needs to be entered, but do not understand how to enter it, include:

- Use selectable choices rather than text entry fields where possible.

- For text fields, represent the length and format of the needed data.

- For text fields, use matching routines to complete data entry when possible.

Use selectable choices rather than text entry fields where possible

Rather than requiring users to type information, provide a control that allows users to select the option they want. If the set of choices is finite and predictable, use drop-down lists, selectable lists, radio buttons, or check boxes instead of text fields. This guideline is especially important if the proper input format is unclear and if it requires special characters in the middle, such as "( )" or "/".

Two common situations are when the user needs to select a date or time span within your wizard. If the user needs to enter a specific date, such as the departure date of a flight, a text field does not provide enough cues for the user to easily understand how to input the correct date. The user may have several questions such as: Does the month come before the day, or vice versa?, Should a slash (/) be placed between the month, day, and year?, Should the year be four characters long? Instead of providing a text field, provide a calendar control, which looks like a monthly calendar and allows the user to select a date by clicking on it. This type of control has the advantage of eliminating the uncertainties associated with the text field. Calendar controls also prevent other errors by allowing users to see which dates fall on which days of the week.

Another common error is when users type 12:00 AM (midnight) when they mean 12:00 PM (noon). Figure 10–3 illustrates a control that can be used in place of a text field. This control allows the user to select the start time and end time of an event. Users see the length of the span and can quickly notice if the event is longer than they expected.

A similar control can be used for selecting a time of day. Users who aren't sure if 12 PM is midnight or noon can tell by the surrounding times (11:00 AM and 1:00 PM) that they are selecting noon.

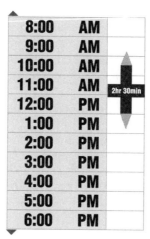

Figure 10–3   *A control that allows users to select specific meeting times rather than having them type 12:00 AM or PM.*

This guideline also applies if the needed input requires long or cryptic text strings. For example, if the user needs to specify a directory in which to store a file, do not require the user to type the entire file path. Instead, provide a **Browse** button that allows him or her to select the file by navigating through the file structure.

For text fields, represent the length and format of the needed data

If your user needs to type data such as a credit card number, check number, or airline ticket number, size your text boxes so that they reflect the length of the input you expect. Additionally, separate text boxes so that their grouping reflects the grouping of numbers that appears in the original item or document.

Figure 10–4 shows a control for inputting a credit card number. The format of the data entry text boxes matches how the numbers appear on the card. This format illustrates that credit card numbers are four groups of four numbers each. Each text field is the same length as the "6011," which gives users a strong cue about how many numbers are required. You can automatically take users to the next text box as they finish each set of four characters.

Figure 10–4   *An example of matching the controls for inputting credit card numbers to how the numbers appear on the actual credit card.*

If your wizard allows users to add code, such as code for their own filters or macros, provide a template that represents the expected format. For example, if the user is writing a procedure, automatically provide the keywords for beginning the procedure, punctuation for input variables, and proper keywords for ending the procedure.

For text fields, use matching routines to complete data entry when possible

Some text fields and combination boxes allow the user to type a few characters and then the program automatically completes the remainder of the entry by matching against valid choices. This can be a useful feature, but it can also be annoying if the matching is done incorrectly or if the matching routine slows down wizard performance.

Missing data errors

Another error category is when users neglect or forget to enter necessary data. Guidelines to help reduce missing data errors include:

- Identify mandatory information.
- Prevent the user from leaving the page.

Identify mandatory information

Ideally, your wizard should contain only mandatory fields. However, in certain cases, optional fields play a valuable role. Two such cases are when the users are able to enter an optional description for an object they are creating and when they can provide a hint to help them remember a password and user ID.

If your wizard has both mandatory and optional information, be sure to provide visual cues that clearly differentiate the two types of information. One common approach is to mark mandatory fields with a bold, colored border. Other visual cues, such as an asterisk placed next to the mandatory field or the use of a bold font for the field's label, could be used instead of or in conjunction with the bold, colored border. Figure 10–5 shows a wizard page that contains two text entry fields. The first field is a mandatory field. Its label is in a bold font and contains an asterisk. The field itself is surrounded with a bold, colored border. The second field is an optional field. Its label is shown in regular font and its text field does not have any additional cues.

If your wizard is part of a larger application that differentiates mandatory from optional information, continue this practice within your wizard, even if your wizard contains only mandatory information. In this situation, all wizard fields will be marked with the same visual cue.

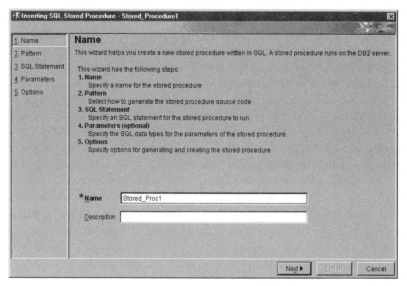

Figure 10–5 *An example of a wizard that uses a bold, colored border, an asterisk, and a bold font to differentiate mandatory from optional information.*

See Figure Color–1 in the color section of this book for an example of a mandatory field.

Prevent the user from leaving the page

Disable the **Next** button until all mandatory fields have been completed. If you are using a drop-down menu style of navigation, you can disable the menu. This guideline becomes more difficult if your wizard has tabs or a table of contents control to support navigation. In these cases, you can disable the other tabs or table of contents choices or you can give the users a warning message when they attempt to leave the page. (For more information on different approaches for supporting navigation, see Chapter 6, "Navigation.")

Misinterpretations of wizard choices

Sometimes the users may know what they want, but they misinterpret the choices in your wizard. Providing clear descriptions and labels on your wizard pages can reduce these types of errors. In some cases, you can also provide graphical examples of what the results of the choice will be. For example, if your wizard requires the user to select a type of chart from a menu of chart styles, include icons of what each chart will look like in the menu. Alternately, after the user selects a chart type, you can display what the chart will look like in the optional graphic area of the wizard page where the selection was made.

User-is-stuck errors

Sometimes users do not know what the correct answer or choice is and realize that they lack this knowledge or understanding. You can reduce these errors by providing appropriate help both on the wizard page itself and also in supporting documentation and on-line help. Chapter 11, "On-line help," describes help design in more detail.

Errors can also be reduced by matching the input control's length and format to the required information, as described earlier. For example, users may not be familiar with the format of information that needs to be entered—such as their airline ticket number or their bank's routing number. A layout that shows users how numbers are grouped in the actual physical object from which they need to get the information can help them determine which numbers are correct through a process of matching the actual object to the layout in the wizard page.

The guidelines in the next section also help to reduce the probability of this error category.

User-is-mistaken errors

Sometimes users do not know what the correct choice is, but do not realize that they lack this knowledge or understanding. Guidelines for reducing these types of errors include:

- Provide appropriate assistance.
- Reduce the amount of information that the user needs to remember.
- Do not require users to write code.
- Offer tools to eliminate complex calculations.

Provide appropriate assistance

Always use clear and intuitive labels. The more clear the labeling, the less possibility of confusion. Test all labels and on-screen text with your intended users to ensure they are clear.

As discussed in the previous section, you can also reduce errors by providing appropriate help both on the wizard page itself and also in supporting documentation and on-line help. Information on tradeoffs or common misconceptions is especially useful to help users avoid common mistakes. Chapter 11, "On-line help," describes help design in more detail.

Reduce memory load

People are bad at remembering information that they rarely use. However, people are good at recognizing the correct choices. This is why fill-in-the-blank questions tend to be harder than multiple-choice questions. To reduce the amount that users need to remember:

- Use selectable controls rather than text entry fields.

- Match the size of the text field to the expected input's length. For example, if your text field requires a four-digit PIN, do not make it the same length as a text field that will contain the user's address.

- Give rules for valid values, such as the lowest and highest numerical values allowed.

- Use visual aids to clarify choices. For example, if your wizard asks users to print, include a visual representation of "landscape" versus "portrait" so that users do not have to remember which setting results in the output they want. Similarly, if your wizard allows users to create charts, use visual representations of what the final product will look like.

Do not require users to write code

Wizards simplify tasks. Therefore, wizards should eliminate the need for users to know the details of the code required to perform the actions that the wizard will perform. For example, if you are creating a database wizard that requires a view of two tables, allow the user to build this view through actions such as dragging and dropping and clicking on columns. Do not require the users to write the SQL statement from scratch. Users are likely to mistype a column name or forget the exact syntax needed for the SQL statement.

Offer tools to eliminate complex calculations

If your wizard requires a mathematical entry, provide a calculator "link" or provide fields that allow users to enter values and then have the wizard do the calculations for them. Don't force users to do mathematical operations. You can avoid errors by having your wizard do computations instead of expecting users to complete the calculations in their heads.

Incorrect wizard assumptions

The previous sections discussed errors that users may make in interpreting your wizard design and the choices it provides. This section discusses a different category of errors—those in which the designer or coder made incorrect assumptions for the users. In these cases, the users must discover that their situation does not match the one for which the wizard was designed. Guidelines to help the user catch these mismatches include:

- Tell the users what your wizard will do and allow them to cancel out of it.

- Allow users to examine and edit the code that your wizard will run.

- Provide defaults, but allow the user to override the defaults.

Tell the users what your wizard will do and allow them to cancel out of it

Before the user clicks the **Finish** button, he or she should understand what your wizard will do. One way to provide this information is to use the last wizard page to summarize his or her choices on the previous pages. If your user clicks the **Finish** button without going to the last page, which is possible if you provide defaults for the controls on the other pages, you might consider showing the summary information on a separate confirmation dialog. With either approach, allow the user to cancel out of the wizard action if he or she does not like what the wizard will do.

Allow users to examine and edit the code that your wizard will run

This guideline assumes your audience has a certain level of expertise. It also assumes that users have certain restrictions or rules in their work environment and they want to be sure that anything that the wizard creates will obey these rules. For example, many companies have specific databases and computers that they use when creating and testing new objects. Database administrators would never create a new object outside of these databases. In this situation, the users would want to check to make sure that the default object location and name matches their company standards. Users also want to make sure that you are not configuring their systems or altering their application data without their knowledge.

Provide defaults, but allow the user to override the defaults

When there is a clear, common choice for most users, provide it as the default choice. This approach helps your users to complete the wizard more quickly and easily. With some sophisticated programming, you can determine more about the user's system and needs, and then use that information to determine what would be an appropriate default for each user. Although defaults are useful, you do not want to force the user to be stuck with the default that you choose because you will not be able to choose correctly all the time.

For example, if you have a wizard that helps users buy goods on-line, assume that each user's mailing address is same as the credit card address. This will prevent your users from needing to input the same address twice and will provide less opportunity for users to make typing errors. However, there will be times when a user wants to send a gift and will need to override this default assumption.

Other system errors

There are other types of errors that might be caused by your wizard design or by other aspects of the computer system that your user is using to access the wizard. These errors include, but are not limited to, network errors, system crashes, and errors in your wizard code (bugs). To reduce the bugs in your wizard code, be sure to test the code under a variety of situations. Although you do not have any control over network errors and system crashes, design your wizard code to help minimize the impact of these situations so that the user can easily recover from a system error. Guidelines for error recovery are discussed in "Recovering from errors."

Recovering from errors

If you cannot "design out" the possibility of making an error, minimize its potential impact and allow the user to fix the problem easily. To help users recover from errors, wizards can:

- Inform the user that an error occurred.

- Help users fix any errors that are made.

- Avoid all destructive actions.

- Allow users to cancel and reverse actions.

This section describes some guidelines for each of these ways of helping users easily recover from errors.

Inform the user that an error occurred

A user must realize that an error was made before he or she can take action to recover from it. Some guidelines for informing a user that an error was made either by the user or by the system include:

- Tell the user that an error was made as close as possible to the point at which the error occurred.

- Help users understand *where* the error was made.

- Avoid nuisance messages.

- Provide error messages in a separate dialog.

Tell the user that an error was made as close as possible to the point at which the error occurred

In most cases, tell the user about the error immediately after the error is made. The closer in time that a user finds out about an error, the less work he or she needs to do to find and fix the problematic data. For example, if a user finds out before leaving a page, the user can limit the search to the current page. If the user finds out at the end of the wizard, he or she will need to navigate to the problematic page and then find the problematic data. However, early and continuous error detection usually requires more processing than later error detection. You must weigh the benefit of informing the user about the error against the cost of slower wizard performance.

You can inform users of errors at several points in the wizard:

- **During field completion.** You can check for errors when the user is entering data into a text field. For example, the user might type a numeric character when only alphabetic characters are allowed. We recommend that you avoid informing users about errors they make while typing information into a text field. Often, users will catch the error before they continue to the next control. They may consider any error beeps or messages to be a nuisance if they are not done typing. Field-level validation is usually sufficient.

- **Upon field completion.** You can check for errors when the user changes focus from a field to another control on the wizard page. Inform the user if an error was made in the field.

- **Upon page completion.** You can check for errors when the user attempts to leave the page, such as when clicking the **Next** button, clicking the **Back** button, or pressing a tab control. Inform the user if an error was made with any controls on the page.

- **Upon wizard completion.** You can check for errors when the user clicks the **Finish** button, but before any scripts or code are actually run. Inform the user if any of the wizard inputs are erroneous.

- **During wizard code processing.** You can check for errors when the code that the wizard generated runs. Inform the user if any of the wizard input is erroneous and temporarily stop processing the wizard code.

Ideally, tell the users before they leave a page or before they click the **Finish** button that an error occurred. If this is not possible, provide information after they click the **Finish** button, but before any code or scripts are run. Finally, if an error is caught while the code is being run, tell the users when the first error is caught and ask if they want to continue. Always allow the users to cancel the wizard actions and to undo any actions that the wizard has already performed.

Help users understand where the error was made

Ensure that the user understands where an error was made. Your error message should include information that helps the user identify which input was incorrect. This information is especially important if your wizard allows users to create or work with multiple objects at once. For example, Figure 10–6 illustrates an error situation where one or more drop actions failed. The **Details** button allows the user to discover which objects could not be dropped and why these objects could not be dropped.

You may supplement your error message with a visual cue on the wizard page. For example, a red border around a problematic text field can help the user to quickly hone in on a control with a problem.

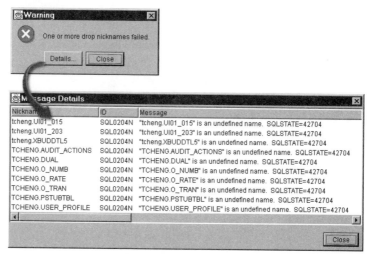

Figure 10–6   *An error message that allows the user to view further details about which objects were problematic and why.*

Avoid nuisance messages

Ensure that your error messages are not a nuisance and do help the user identify an error situation. Nuisance messages occur when users are not done with their action or if they realize that they made an error and are in the process of fixing it. For example, if a user has made a typo and is correcting it, a message about how the input is not valid is a nuisance message.

Provide error messages in separate dialogs

Do not provide error messages at the bottom of the wizard page; users will not notice them. To ensure that users notice an error message, provide it in a separate error dialog and require them to dismiss the dialog by clicking either **Yes** or **No** (or **Cancel** or **OK**). Error dialogs may also contain an icon to indicate the severity of the error and a **Help** button to allow users to access information that they may need to make a decision. Figure 10–7 shows a typical error message dialog.

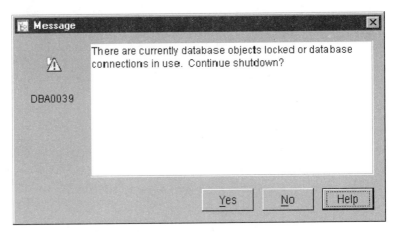

Figure 10–7   A typical error message dialog.

Help the user fix the error

After users understand that an error occurred as well as where the error occurred, they need to fix the error. Guidelines for helping users correct error situations include:

- Tell the user *how* to fix the error.
- Provide a shortcut to fix the error.
- Provide a button to automatically fix the error.
- Allow users to resubmit the information easily.

Tell the user how to fix the error

The first step in fixing an error is understanding how to fix it. You can help the user by providing information about how to correct the error in the error dialog itself or in secondary dialogs that can be launched from the error dialog. Another approach is to provide field-level information on how to fix errors in pop-up help messages that appear as the user moves the mouse over the problematic text entry field. This approach is best if the error is caught during field validation.

If the error occurs after the user clicks the **Finish** button, you may want to provide a sequence of steps that the user should follow to correct the situation. If the explanation requires a lot of detailed information, you may want to include links to on-line manuals or reference specific sections in the hardcopy manuals.

Provide a shortcut to fix the error

If an error occurs after the user clicks the **Finish** button, you may want to provide a shortcut, such as a button, to help the user get to the correct wizard page and correct the error. This way, you do not force the user to navigate in search of the problematic page and control. A shortcut is especially important if your wizard has a lot of pages.

You can also provide this type of shortcut on the last page of your wizard along with the summary information. With this design, if the user discovers an error while verifying the summary information, he or she can go directly to the appropriate page to change it.

Provide a button to automatically fix the error

In some cases, such as problems in the data format, the action to fix the problem will be quite predictable. In these cases, provide a button to automatically fix the error. For example, if the user typed data in capital letters, but your wizard requires the data to be in lowercase letters, provide a button that allows the user to correct the problem with a single click.

Allow users to resubmit the information easily

If an error occurs while the wizard code is being run, give the user an option to fix the error and then have the wizard continue processing. Sometimes this fix can be done within the actual wizard or while the code is being run. At other times, you may not know about the error until after the code runs. For example, suppose that your wizard helps people order airline tickets. One possible error situation is that the credit card is rejected. To help users recover from this error, you might allow them to input another credit card and then rerun the ticket request without forcing them to start over from the beginning with a new flight search.

Avoid all destructive actions

Do not allow your wizard to perform destructive actions such as overwriting existing files or deleting objects, especially without the user's knowledge. One exception to this rule is a wizard that uninstalls a product and needs to delete files. However, no wizard should delete non-empty files that were created by users. Your wizard code should stop if it encounters a situation that may be destructive and cause the user to lose data.

Allow users to cancel and reverse actions

Never allow users to get into a situation where they are stuck. Always allow them to cancel or reverse the actions they have made. Some ways to do this are:

- Allow users to cancel out of the wizard altogether and not create anything.

- Allow users to cancel an action after the wizard begins its back-end processing. For example, if the user tries to create a report with the same name as a previous report, do not automatically overwrite the first one. Ask the user how to proceed.

- Provide an undo function to take the user back to the last set of saved changes. This function aids users who made a lot of changes and don't want them anymore.

- Provide a return-to-defaults function to allow users to start over on any page or to start over for the entire wizard.

Summary of guidelines discussed in this chapter

- ❏ Create a list of potential errors. Use this list to predict errors.
- ❏ Design your wizard to prevent or reduce the likelihood of common or important errors.
- ❏ If you cannot prevent an error, help users recover from it easily.
- ❏ Reduce the number of steps and actions required.
- ❏ Prevent users from submitting input on one page that would invalidate input on an earlier page.
- ❏ Order controls so that early controls limit future inputs.
- ❏ When possible, use selectable choices rather than text entry fields.
- ❏ For text fields, represent the length and format of the needed data.
- ❏ For text fields, use matching routines to complete data entry when possible.
- ❏ Identify mandatory information.
- ❏ Prevent the user from leaving a page without providing needed data.
- ❏ Provide appropriate assistance.
- ❏ Reduce memory load.
- ❏ Avoid the need to write code.
- ❏ Offer tools to eliminate complex calculations.
- ❏ Tell the users what your wizard will do and allow them to cancel out of it.
- ❏ Allow users to examine and edit the code that your wizard will run.
- ❏ Provide defaults, but allow the user to override the defaults.
- ❏ Reduce other system errors, such as programming bugs.
- ❏ Tell the user that an error was made as close as possible to the point at which the error occurred.
- ❏ Help users understand where the error was made.
- ❏ Avoid nuisance messages.
- ❏ Provide error messages in separate dialogs.
- ❏ Tell users how to fix errors.
- ❏ Provide shortcuts to fix errors or provide a **Fix** button to automatically fix an error.
- ❏ Allow users to resubmit information easily. Avoid all destructive actions. Allow users to cancel and reverse actions.

Chapter 11

On-line help

▲ Why provide help?

▲ Questions to ask before beginning

▲ Should you provide help for your wizard?

▲ Types of help

▲ Implementing help

▲ Summary of guidelines discussed in this chapter

B uilding on-line help for wizards of larger products can be as challenging and involved as building the wizards themselves. If your wizard requires a help system, you will want to plan the design of the help system as early in your development cycle as possible—preferably when you first begin planning your wizard.

This chapter explains the different types of help that you can provide and the advantages and disadvantages of each. This chapter also lists different types of help implementations and issues to consider. For a deeper discussion of on-line help implementation and design, see *Designing and Writing Online Documentation: Help Files to Hypertext* by William Horton and *Developing Online Help for Windows 95* by Scott Boggan, David Farkas, and Joe Welinske.

Why provide help?

On-line help in a wizard is a safety net for the minority of users who cannot complete the wizard while the majority can. Ideally, a well-designed wizard should be so easy to use that it doesn't require a help system. Realistically, though, the only wizards that don't require some type of help system are those that are either extremely simple and provide sufficient explanatory text on each page or those that are adjuncts to a help system itself.

The benefits of providing help include:

- **On-line help can explain how to use the interface controls.** Some of your users might be unfamiliar with the interface controls used in your wizard. With on-line help, you can explain every control without cluttering your interface with text.

- **On-line help allows you to provide users with additional information that can guide them through their task.** If your wizard is detailed, complex, or very large, or if it attempts to simplify a long or involved process, the interface alone might not be able to clearly relate all of the concepts the user needs to be aware of. For example, if you design a wizard that allows database administrators to create user profiles for a database tool and some users need explanations of the concepts of database security before using the wizard, on-line help could provide that information. Although that information could help some users avoid errors, those concepts are not critical to the completion of the task itself. The wizard is designed to simplify task completion, and the information that the user needs cannot always be incorporated into the wizard interface.

- **On-line help can aid users who reach an impasse. Users who cannot complete a wizard are at an impasse.** If you identify such impasse points in your wizard during usability testing and you cannot redesign the wizard, you can provide information in the on-line help to aid users who reach these points. For example, if a field in your wizard requires the user to enter values that are dependent on options that the user selected in a previous step, the user might not understand why the values they are trying to enter are unavailable or are causing an error during the current step. By providing on-line help, you can explain each control and how decisions in early steps will affect options in later steps.

Questions to ask before beginning

Before you choose the type of help that you will provide and before you begin writing your help content, you must understand your target audience's experience and knowledge. Additionally, you must understand the user's task and what makes it difficult. Finally, you need to understand the overall product and the role the wizard plays in it. The user definition, product definition, and task analysis discussed in Chapter 2, "Gathering requirements," should provide the information to answer the following questions:

- **What is your audience's education level and what is their experience level with: computers, the Internet, the tasks that your wizard will support, previous releases of your product, other software that supports the task, other software products, and specific operating systems?** The answers to these questions determine what you need to provide in your on-line help. Previous experience shapes our expectations and how we think about things. If you can determine what your audience expects, you can identify mismatches between your wizard and their expectations. Your on-line help should contain information to help users overcome these mismatches.

- **What is the age range of your target audience?** The age range will impact graphic style and vocabulary used in your on-line help.

- **Does your target audience speak English?** What is the primary language? Do your users speak multiple languages? If your users speak a variety of languages, you will need to design your on-line help to support these languages.

- **What role will your wizard play with respect to other products and wizards?** Clarify the role your wizard plays in relation to your help system and your product. Is the wizard an extension of the user interface or an outside tool? Is it tightly or loosely integrated with the product, an extension of or supplement to the help system, or the help system itself? The role your wizard is designed to play will directly affect your available resources and the design limitations of your help

- **What will the user need to know?** The answer to this question determines the content you need to provide in the on-line help.

- **What tools will the user use to access the wizard?** The answer to this question determines the type of content that you can provide. For example, connection speed, monitor size, and display settings will impact the number and type of graphics that you can provide in your on-line help.

- **Will the users receive any training or support on your product, the wizard, or both?** Service or training agreements might alter the level of help that you need to provide with your wizard.

Should you provide help for your wizard?

Four factors impact whether you should provide on-line help for your wizard:

- **Complexity of the wizard.** If your wizard is very complex or is the entire product, then you need on-line help to deliver content that cannot fit on the wizard pages. Additionally, if your wizard is sequentially related to other wizards, you may want to provide on-line help to explain these relationships. However, if your wizard is quite simple and is only two or three pages long, you will probably not need to create separate on-line help for it.

- **Available real estate on the wizard pages.** If your wizard pages have a lot of white space left on them, you may be able to fit all needed information on those individual pages. However, if your pages are quite full, then you will need to provide useful information via an on-line help mechanism.

- **Success during usability testing.** If your wizard fares well during your usability tests and users do not have problems completing it, then it's unlikely that you'll need to provide much additional on-line help. However, if user testing reveals conceptual gaps or problems and you cannot redesign your wizard, then you will need to provide on-line help. Additionally, if your error prediction exercise (see Chapter 10, "Error prevention and recovery") predicts severe or frequent errors, then you will need to design some on-line help to prevent these errors and help users recover from them.

- **Time and resources.** If you do not have time to redesign your wizard, you may need to provide on-line help to compensate for any problems found during usability testing. However, this is *not* the recommended approach. You should not use on-line help as a bandage for a poor design. Additionally, you will need time and resources to write and test your on-line help.

Types of help

One of the first decisions you need to make about your help system is what type of help content you will provide to your users. Not all of these types may be necessary, and you may want to integrate content from each of these types as appropriate.

Types of help information include:

- **Control-level help.** Provides explanations of the page and interface controls on which the user is working.
- **Conceptual help.** Provides explanations of the concepts behind the tasks, controls, and product.
- **Task help.** Provides information that explains the steps for performing a task or recovering from an error.

This section explains the different types of help information and the advantages and disadvantages of each. Your help system can provide any of these types of help or a combination of them to meet the needs and expectations of your target audience.

Control-level help

During usability testing, we found that control-level help is the first type of help users look for. If your wizard is part of a larger product that has its own on-line help system, then you may plan on providing only control-level help for the wizard controls. Control-level help is also important when your target audience contains users with little computer and software experience.

Control-level help is help in the context of where the user is on the wizard page. In other words, control-level help explains how to use the pieces of the interface. It consists of brief explanations of the controls and their function. You can change the content of your control-level help based on the state of the control that it describes. For example, you might present one description if a check box is checked and another description if it is unchecked. Control-level help does not explain how to do a task, just how to use a control or page that might or might not be part of the user's larger task.

If you are building an on-line help system for your wizard, control-level help should be provided for the wizard pages, secondary dialogs, and launchpads.

Writing control-level help

Follow these guidelines for writing control-level help:

- Use a simple and direct writing style.

- Be consistent in both level of detail and format. Once users become accustomed to one format for control-level help, they will expect it to be the same across your wizard and across the entire product.

- For each control, keep your description distinct and specific to a predictable user need.

- If the control is a text entry field, provide details about what data format is valid, such as the number of characters and type of characters that the field accepts. Try to provide examples of typical input.

- Explain why some options may not be advised or available in the wizard's current state based on previous user decisions.

- Keep control-level help accurate as you progress through your development cycle. Every visual change to a dialog or addition of a dialog may require changes and corresponding additions to help content.

Delivering control-level help

You can deliver control-level help in different ways:

- From a **Help** button in your wizard that launches a help dialog

- As a pop-up over the control on your wizard page

Figures 11–1 and 11–2 represent the same control-level help content in two delivery formats—a help window and "pop-up" help, respectively. Figure 11–1 shows a help dialog that contains control-level help for the fields on the Create Alias page of a wizard.

Figure 11–2 shows the same control-level help in the form of a pop-up window that appears when the user positions the mouse over the **Alias name** field.

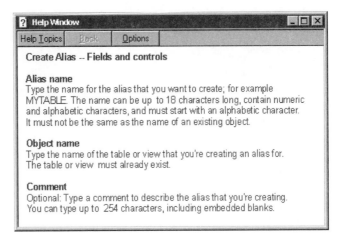

Figure 11–1   *A help dialog.*

Type the name for the alias that you want to create; for example MYTABLE. The name can be up to 18 characters long, contain numeric and alphabetic characters, and must start with an alphabetic character. It must not be the same as the name of an existing object.

Figure 11–2   *The same help in "pop-up" format; appears when the user positions the mouse over the Alias name field.*

Conceptual help

Conceptual help explains how the user can accomplish overall goals with the product or wizard. Conceptual help describes why the user would do a task, the terms used in the wizard, and the relationship between the wizard and other wizards or dialogs in the product. You might include some conceptual help on your wizard pages, especially on your introduction page.

Figure 11–3 shows a wizard with underlined terms—"user tables," "containers," and "Space management." When the user clicks a term, the conceptual help appears in a help dialog.

You can also launch conceptual help from a **Help** button or from links inside other help dialogs.

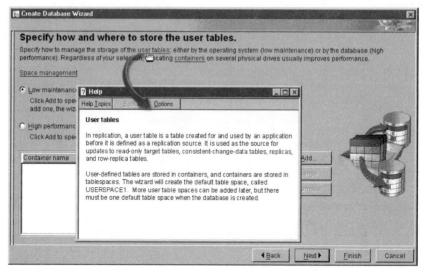

Figure 11–3 *A wizard page that uses underlined terms to link to conceptual help for those terms.*

Writing conceptual help

Follow these guidelines for writing conceptual help:

- Educate your users on how using the wizard can help them reap certain benefits.

- Help your users understand the task.

- Explain how your wizard fits in with the rest of the product or with other methods for completing the same task.

- Help users recognize mismatches between the way they think about the task and the way the wizard presents the task.

- Explain terms used in the wizard.

Delivering conceptual help

Because conceptual help tends to be longer than other types of help, it is usually not provided on the wizard page or in pop-ups. The most common methods for delivering conceptual help are:

- A **Help** button in your wizard that launches a help window

- A launchpad (See Chapter 8, "Launchpads and linking wizards," for more information about designing launchpads.)

- A **Help** menu for the entire product

- Underlined terms on a wizard page

Task help

Your wizard is designed to take a user through a task. Therefore, it is unlikely that you'll need extensive task help for your wizard. However, some users might want an overview page that explains in general terms what the wizard does. Additionally, even with a well-designed wizard, some users may reach an impasse or make an error and need task help to assist them in completing the task. Task help is also used for providing help on error message dialogs.

Task help provides steps to follow to perform a task. Task help is usually provided in a help window and can link to help for other tasks or subtasks. Task help often includes modest amounts of conceptual information about each task or provides links to higher level conceptual help documentation. Task help can also provide some control information or links to control-level help.

Figure 11–4 shows a wizard layout in which some task help is provided on the left side of the wizard page. This help provides links to additional task help or subtasks.

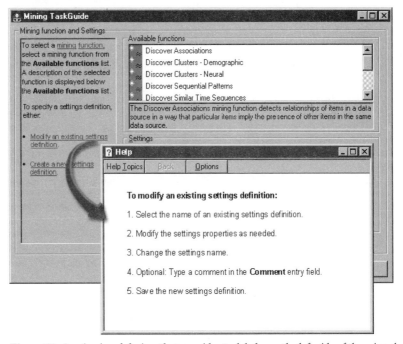

Figure 11–4   *A wizard design that provides task help on the left side of the wizard page with links to more task or subtask help.*

Writing task help

Follow these guidelines for writing task help:

- Explain the goals of the task and the nuances of how to avoid various types of errors.

- Use synonyms. Sometimes users do not understand the text provided on the wizard page. Synonyms can help users think about the task a bit differently, which may be all they need to understand what to do.

- Expand and rephrase the task-level information that you provided on the wizard page. This additional content can help users who did not understand the information provided on the wizard page.

- Fit task help that is specific to one wizard page into a single help file. Use multiple files that link to one another to provide help for users with varying levels of experience without overwhelming users with too little or too much information.

Delivering task help

The most common methods for delivering task help are:

- A dedicated task help area on the wizard page

- A **Help** button in your wizard that launches a help dialog

- A **Help** button on an error dialog that launches a help dialog

Implementing help

Once you determine the type of on-line help you'll provide for your wizard, you'll need to determine how the user will access this content. You can provide on-line help as:

- Pop-up help

- Smartfields

- Help dialogs

- On-line books

- Printed manuals

- Reference cards and brochures

Printed manuals, reference cards, and brochures are outside the scope of this chapter. However, you might want to use them to support your users.

Pop-up help

Pop-up help is the most convenient type of help for the user to invoke. It is generally invoked when the user positions the mouse pointer over a control on the wizard page. Since users do not need to explicitly launch a help page, they are more likely to see this type of help than other types. Figure 11–5 shows how pop-up help would look on a launchpad.

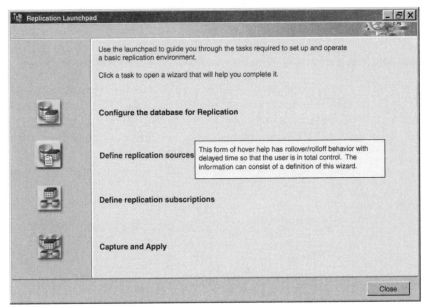

Figure 11–5   A launchpad with pop-up help.

Follow these guidelines when implementing pop-up help:

- Allow time to code and test your pop-up help. Pop-up help may require additional coding or third-party software and tools that must be tested.

- If you must select a default time period before the pop-up window is launched after the user moves the mouse pointer over the control, choose a setting between 750 milliseconds and 2 seconds. Be aware that some help tools and operating systems will not let you set the default time.

- Allow your users to disable pop-up messages if they find them distracting.

- Be sure that your text will fit in the pop-up window for practical viewing. We have found that 560 characters, or 150 words (15 lines with 10 words per line), is an optimal length. If the pop-up window grows with

237

the amount of text, try to keep its size to less than 50% of the underlying window. This size allows the user to see parts of the dialog while reading the pop-up help and to make connections between the pop-up help text and dialog controls.

- Be sure that you leave enough space in your pop-up help to account for word growth. Translation can expand the width of your text between 30% and 80%.

- Refer to or link to other types of help from your pop-up help.

Smartfields

Smartfields are a special type of pop-up help that provide assistance according to the current state of the field due to previous selections. For example, smartfields can provide tips for preventing errors. Smartfields can also help prevent errors by matching the first few characters that a user types to a valid entry and completing the entry automatically. Figure 11–6 illustrates a wizard text field with its smartfield visible. The smartfield explains the rules for creating a valid entry.

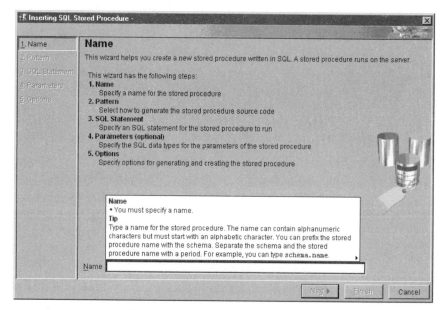

Figure 11–6   *An example of a smartfield.*

Follow these guidelines when implementing smartfields:

- Allow time to code and test the smartfields. Smartfields require more coding than standard pop-up help. They are usually triggered by an error condition, rather than by a default time period.

- Be sure that your smartfields can be interpreted by assistive technologies.

- Allow your users to disable smartfields if they find them distracting.

- Implement smartfields for all text entry fields, or for none at all. Consistency is important. Users may interpret the lack of smartfield guidance as a cue that their input is valid.

- Allow users to choose the level and format of smartfields. For example, you may want to simply provide a beep when the user makes an error and then provide additional information upon user request.

Help dialogs

Help dialogs are easy to write and test. An intentional action from the user in the form of a menu selection or a button click is required to invoke a help dialog. Help dialogs are good places to put task or conceptual help, which tend to be longer than control-level help.

Follow these guidelines when implementing help dialogs:

- Make it easy for the user to launch the help dialog. For example, provide a **Help** button on your wizard or on your error dialog.

- Ensure that your text fits into the help dialog. Try to avoid the need for scrolling.

- Allow different users to access different levels of content in or from your initial help dialog. For example, you may want to allow users to drill down into deeper levels of conceptual help or understanding.

- Take advantage of the expanded real estate of a help dialog to list all controls on the wizard page.

On-line books

On-line books are electronic versions of printed books. In most cases, you would not need to provide an on-line book for a simple wizard. However, if your wizard is an entire product, such as a tax completion wizard, you may want to provide a large amount of supporting information. An on-line book is a good delivery mechanism for a large amount of information.

Users often prefer on-line books to printed books because on-line books support search capabilities and can contain hyperlinks that make it easy to navigate through a book. Also, you may save quite a bit of money by not having to pay the costs associated with printed books.

Follow these guidelines when implementing on-line books:

- Provide your on-line book in formats (such as PDF, Bookmanager, eBook, or HTML) that your target audience can read and print.
- Make it easy for the user to launch the on-line book. For example, provide a **Help** button on your wizard or a shortcut icon for the user's desktop.
- Make it easy for users to get your on-line book. Be sure that your on-line book fits on the same CD as your wizard. If the user will download your wizard, allow him or her to download the on-line book from the same Web page.
- If you want to use a specific viewer or player for your book, provide the player with your wizard and provide easy instructions for installing the player. This approach is *not* recommended for simple wizards.

Summary of guidelines discussed in this chapter

❏ Determine whether you should provide help. Evaluate the four factors (complexity, real estate, ease-of-use, and time and resources) for providing help in your situation.

❏ Identify which types of on-line help (control-level, conceptual, and task) you'll be providing before you determine how to deliver it.

❏ Provide control-level help for wizard pages, dialogs, and launchpads.

❏ Provide a consistent format for your control-level help and be sure to provide it for all controls.

❏ Keep control-level help short and specific. Use a simple and direct writing style.

❏ If the control is a text entry field, provide details about what data format is valid, such as the number of characters and type of characters that the field accepts. Try to provide examples of typical input.

❏ Provide conceptual help to help users understand the wizard task and to explain terms and concepts.

❏ Use synonyms in task help and expand on the text provided on the wizard pages.

❏ Create one task file per wizard page and link to other task or subtask help.

❏ Provide task help for error dialogs.

❏ Use a default time period between 750 milliseconds and 2 seconds for launching pop-up help.

❏ Try to keep pop-up help to under 560 characters and allow for translation.

❏ Allow users to disable pop-up help if they find it distracting.

❏ Be sure that your smartfields can be interpreted by assistive technologies.

❏ Allow your users to disable smartfields if they find them distracting.

❏ Implement smartfields consistently across your wizard.

❏ Ensure that your text fits into help dialogs to avoid the need for scrolling.

❏ If you provide an on-line book in addition to on-line help, make it easy for your users to get, launch, and print.

Chapter 12

Experts and novices

▲ Why design wizards for both experts and novices?

▲ Questions to ask before beginning

▲ Designs that support experts and novices

▲ Guidelines for supporting experts

▲ Summary of guidelines discussed in this chapter

The traditional notion of a wizard is one of a simple interface for simple tasks. In the past, wizards were developed for novice users rather than highly skilled or expert users. There was a mistaken belief that highly skilled users did not need an interface that simplified their tasks. It was thought that expert users would want to be able to specify every setting and parameter, view all options, and use a more complex user interface, which would exclude a wizard.

Because of this belief, many products provided two ways of performing tasks: a non-wizard GUI that allowed experts to see and set all options and parameters, and a simple wizard method of performing the same task for the novice users. The thought behind these products was that the novice users would prefer the simpler, wizard method of task completion until they mastered the subject matter and then they would move to the non-wizard method of performing tasks.

The reality, however, is that most users do not acquire expertise in all areas of a task or system, and therefore, even an expert user may, at times, need novice-type assistance. This is especially true for complex wizards with many subtasks and controls.

Of course, some wizards are designed only for novices because they are only used a few times. These wizards, for example, installation programs or programs that help you prepare your taxes, assume that there are no expert users for these tasks. However, most interfaces are designed for both expert and novice users, and wizards should accommodate both user types.

Expert users that we surveyed felt that providing both wizard and non-wizard methods of performing tasks was of value. They liked using wizards and also saw value in an alternative wizard interface for reducing the amount of time and training they must provide their novice users.

For each wizard that you design, you must decide whether to support both expert and novice users or to support novice users only. If the goal is to keep the novice away from expert functionality, support only novice users with your wizard and provide a separate approach for expert users. If only novice users will perform the task, aim the wizard at novice users only. However, if you can extend the wizard to accommodate both novice and expert users, consider doing so.

This chapter provides alternative methods for designing wizards that support both expert and novice users and additional guidelines for supporting expert users.

Why design wizards for both experts and novices?

Given that the goal of a wizard is to provide a simple interface that performs complex actions "behind the scenes," wizards can indeed be readily extended to expert users.

Benefits of supporting both types of users include:

- **You can help users learn all aspects of the task.** Providing an interface that supports both experts and novices allows users to first interact with wizards as novices. Users can then use the same interface to perform expert tasks as they become more experienced.

- **You can extend the marketability of your product.** Wizards are a key selling point for any product. Extending your wizard to expert users will increase the number of potential users for your wizard.

- **You can simplify the experts' complex tasks.** Our usability evaluations of database products showed that expert users typically rated the usability and usefulness of wizards very highly for performing tasks.

Questions to ask before beginning

Gather the answers to the following questions from Chapter 2, "Gathering requirements," before you begin:

- **How much experience does your audience have with computers**? This information will help you determine what types of controls to use or paths for novices and experts. For example, although novices can make use of mnemonics and accelerator keys, these methods of interacting with your wizard tend to be geared more toward expert users.

- **How much experience does your audience have with the Internet**? If your wizard resides on the Web, remember that Web sites behave in certain ways. If your users are not familiar with mechanisms such as underlined phrases being links and the use of the **Back** and **Next** buttons, you will have to provide user assistance such as explanatory text or hints and tips.

- **How much experience does your audience have with the tasks that your wizard will support?** This information will help you determine which of the design alternatives your wizard will support.

Designs that support experts and novices

There are a number of design alternatives you can follow to help you design a usable wizard interface for both expert and novice users. These design alternatives fall into two major categories, each with its own advantages and disadvantages. The first design category, explained in "Integrating expert and novice functions in wizards" integrates expert functions in the wizard pages themselves. The second design category, explained in "Separating expert and novice functions in wizards" on page 249 separates expert functions either in additional wizard pages that are optional or in dialogs that are launched from the wizard pages.

No matter which of the designs you choose, always provide user assistance (control-level help, explanatory text on the wizard pages, or hints and tips). Although user assistance helps the novice user, expert users can benefit from help too because no one user is an expert in all aspects of a task. See Chapter 11, "On-line help," for more details.

Integrating expert and novice functions in wizards

This section discusses design alternatives that provide expert functions on the wizard pages themselves.

The advantages of integrating expert and novice functions in wizard pages are:

- There is no need to design, develop, and test additional windows or pages because both expert and novice functions are integrated into the wizard pages.
- The overall size of your product is reduced because of fewer wizard pages or dialogs.

The disadvantages of integrating expert and novice functions in wizard pages are:

- Providing many options for users to select from (trying to satisfy everyone) may slow novice users down, require more time for them to learn, and therefore increase the probability for errors. As Nielsen (1993) states, "less is more."
- Expert users may need a different vocabulary and different level of help than novice users.
- Extra controls might cause problems with translation due to "busy" pages. See Chapter 14, "Worldwide audiences," for more details.

This section explains three separate design alternatives for wizards that integrate expert and novice functions in the wizard pages:

- Design alternative 1: Provide default values that can be modified.

- Design alternative 2: Provide expert functions in optional controls or groups of controls.

- Design alternative 3: Do not separate expert functions.

Design alternative 1: Provide default values that can be modified

Display defaults whenever possible, but allow expert users to modify the defaults if they have the knowledge.

This design method has advantages for both novice and expert users. Defaults decrease the number of fields that the novice users must complete. However, this design alternative allows them to see what the default values are, thus helping them to learn and understand the task. The experts can view the defaults and do not need to change them unless necessary. Figure 12–1 illustrates this design point.

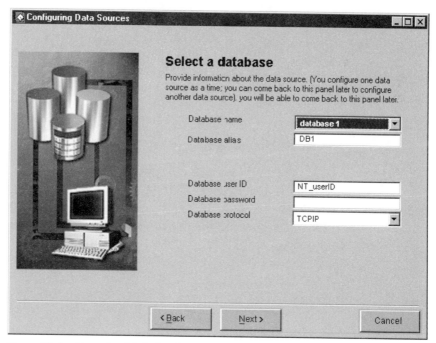

Figure 12–1   *Example of default values on a wizard page.*

Design alternative 2: Provide expert functions in optional controls or groups of controls.

Provide expert functions in the wizard pages, but separate them from novice functions via physical grouping or the use of group boxes. Figure 12–2 shows an example of grouping expert functions.

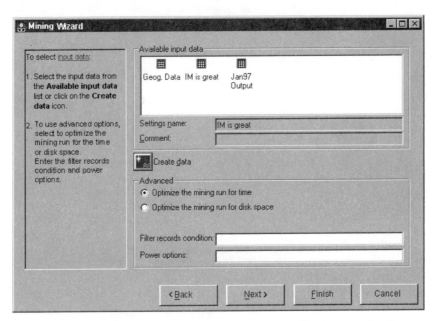

Figure 12–2   *Figure showing grouping of expert controls within the same wizard page.*

Design alternative 3: Do not separate expert function

Integrate expert functions into the wizard pages themselves and do not attempt to separate them in any way. For example, in a Create Database wizard, expert controls consist of settings for performance, which novice users would not be expected to modify. We do not recommend this design alternative because it clutters the page and makes the novice task more difficult.

Separating expert and novice functions in wizards

This section discusses design alternatives that provide expert functions, but place them on separate wizard pages or in optional dialogs and windows launched from the wizard.

The advantages of separating expert and novice functions are:

- Separate dialogs or pages keep each wizard page simpler and less cluttered, which improves usability and reduces errors.

- Expert users can be given different on-line help and different vocabulary than novice users.

- If you plan to translate your wizard, the usability of your translated user interface will be improved because the expert functions are not crowded onto the main wizard pages.

Disadvantages of separating expert and novice functions are:

- Additional windows, dialogs, and pages must be designed, coded, usability tested, and code tested.

- Additional pages make your wizard longer, which could be a problem for tabbed designs if additional pages necessitate tab scrolling. Additional wizard pages could also result in the scrolling of table of contents designs. See Chapter 6, "Navigation," for more details.

- For designs that offer two paths through a wizard as a function of the user type, wizard development is complicated because additional coding logic will be necessary.

- The task flow of your wizard may not be as straightforward because users may miss buttons that launch separate expert dialogs.

This section explains three separate design alternatives for wizards that separate expert and novice functions in wizard pages:

- Design alternative 1: Place expert functions in separate windows or dialogs.

- Design alternative 2: Provide additional, optional pages at the end of the wizard for expert functions.

- Design alternative 3: Design two paths through the wizard; one for experts, one for novices.

Design alternative 1: Place expert functions in separate windows or dialogs

Do not display expert functions and controls in your wizard pages, but allow users to access expert functions via buttons that launch separate dialogs. For example, provide an **Advanced** button, which launches a separate dialog or window. This window could provide advanced functionality, the ability to set properties, or the ability to change defaults.

Make sure that the advanced function is optional or has defaults so that novice users can complete the wizard without needing to view these advanced dialogs. Figure 12–3 shows an example of placing expert functions in a separate dialog.

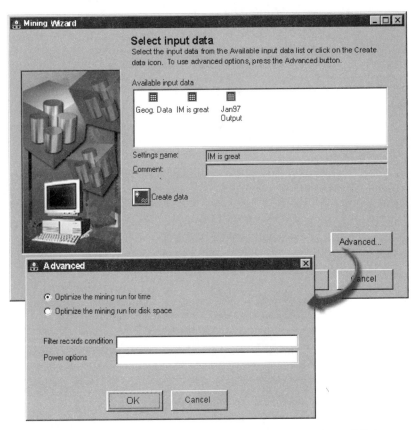

Figure 12–3   *Figure showing an Advanced button launching an Advanced dialog.*

Design alternative 2: Provide additional, optional pages at the end of the wizard for expert functions

You can place the expert functions in separate pages of your wizard. These pages are usually placed at the end of your wizard. Try to make these pages optional; do not require novice users to complete them. However, provide some type of on-line help for novices in case they decide to visit the optional pages. This could be in the form of context-sensitive help or hints and tips. Figure 12–4 shows an example of an optional page containing expert functions.

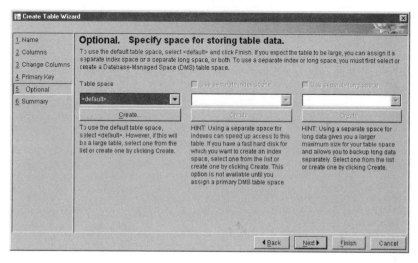

Figure 12–4   Optional page of wizard for placement of expert functions.

Design alternative 3: Design two paths through the wizard; one for experts, one for novices

The first page of your wizard asks the user if he or she is a novice or expert user. Users would then proceed down one of two paths; the choices on the wizard pages would contain controls appropriate for their skill level. For example, if a user selected the novice choice, only novice controls would be displayed in the wizard; if the user selected the expert choice, both expert and novice controls would be displayed on the wizard pages. However, the expert controls would be grouped together. Figure 12–5 shows an example of the first page of a wizard prompting for expert or novice mode and what a later page would look like in expert or novice mode.

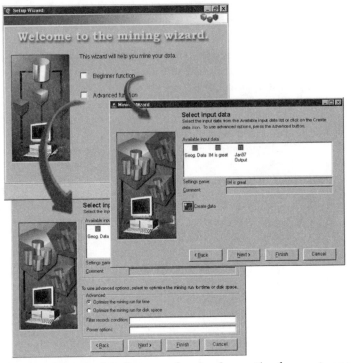

Figure 12–5   *Example of the first page of a wizard prompting for expert or novice mode with later pages containing either novice or novice and expert controls.*

Guidelines for supporting experts

This section explains the following guidelines for paths or pages that support experts:

- Provide access keys and shortcut keys.
- Show expert commands.

Provide access keys and shortcut keys

Provide access keys (also called mnemonics) and shortcut keys (also called accelerator keys) to increase your user's task efficiency. Users may prefer key combinations to a mouse because once learned, key combinations are faster.

Show access keys by underscoring one character (usually the first letter of the first word) in the label of your controls and menus. Some applications require the user to press the Alt key in conjunction with the access key to access the control, while others do not require the Alt key.

Show shortcut keys as Alt+ key or Ctrl+key sequences that are displayed at the right of menu selections. The user types these key sequences to select the menu function. Accelerator keys are usually provided only for the most frequently used menu items.

Show expert commands

Whether you integrate expert functions into your wizard pages or separate these functions, consider allowing your users to view the commands or statements generated by the wizard prior to completing that wizard.

For example, you could provide a **Show Commands** button on the last page of your wizard. This button could launch a window that displays the command or statement the wizard will submit when completed. You might include the programming language that your wizard uses in the name of the button, such as "Show SQL," for a database wizard that creates and executes SQL statements. This method receives high user satisfaction ratings from expert users of our wizards because it helps novices understand what commands the wizard is generating. This method also gives expert users confidence that the wizard is generating the correct options or commands. Figure 12–6 illustrates this design.

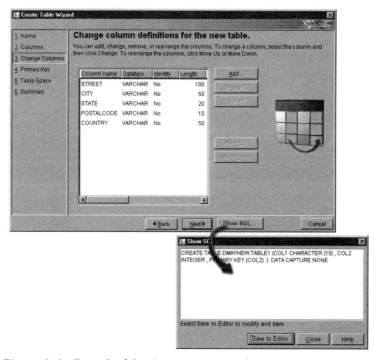

Figure 12–6   *Example of showing expert commands.*

Guidelines for implementing a **Show Commands** function are:

- In the display of the statement, include default parameters as well as those specifically provided by the user.

- Make sure the commands are formatted in a way that allows easy reading. If there are several commands, separate each on a new line.

- If possible, color-code different parts of the command, such as keywords, to enhance readability of the command.

- Allow users to modify the commands generated by the wizard.

- After modifying the commands, decide whether to allow users to return to the wizard. If users are allowed to return to the wizard, then you need to parse the commands to fill in the fields of the wizard. This can cause problems if the user types a command syntax that is incorrect or more complex than the wizard can handle. The simplest solution is to allow users to modify and submit the commands generated by the wizard, but not allow users to re-enter the wizard.

Summary of guidelines discussed in this chapter

❏ Decide whether to integrate expert and novice functions in wizard pages or to separate the functions.

❏ Always provide user assistance.

❏ If you decide to integrate, choose from these design alternatives:

- Provide default values that can be modified.

- Provide expert functions in optional controls or groups of controls.

- Do not separate expert functions at all.

❏ If you decide to separate expert function from novice function in wizard pages, choose from these design alternatives:

- Place expert functions in separate windows or dialogs.

- Provide additional, optional pages at the end of the wizard for expert functions.

- Allow users to choose expert or novice mode on the first page of the wizard. Provide two paths through the wizard: one for novices, one for experts.

❏ Provide access keys and shortcut keys for expert users.

❏ Provide expert users with the ability to see the commands that the wizard will submit via a **Show Commands** button.

Chapter 13

Accessibility

- ▲ Why design for accessibility?
- ▲ Questions to ask before beginning
- ▲ Types of disabilities
- ▲ Understanding users with disabilities
- ▲ Assistive technologies
- ▲ Accessibility guidelines
- ▲ Additional sources for guidelines and information
- ▲ Summary of guidelines discussed in this chapter

S oftware is considered accessible if it is usable and accessible to a wide range of users, including those with disabilities. The National Center for Health Statistics found that over 7.75 million users in the U.S. cannot use a computer unaided by assistive technology. These users may need special tools due to temporary or permanent disabilities, the natural effects of aging, or simply the environment in which they work. The World Health Organization states that more than 750 million people worldwide have a disability and over 54 million are in the U.S. The number of people with disabilities is growing, partly because people are living longer.

This chapter will help you understand the types of disabilities that your users might have, the assistive technologies that currently exist to help disabled users, how to design an accessible wizard, and where to get additional information on accessibility issues.

Why design for accessibility?

Designing your wizard to be more accessible not only allows you access to more users, it improves the usability of your wizard. Reasons to design your wizard for accessibility include:

- **It's the law**. In the U.S., several acts are bringing accessibility issues to the forefront. The United States' Americans with Disabilities Act (ADA) and Telecommunications Act guarantee the rights of disabled employees in the private sector. These rights include access to information required to do their jobs. Section 508 of the Federal Rehabilitation Act bars the government and organizations receiving government funding from purchasing information technology that is not fully accessible. Additionally, several states such as New York, California, and Texas have laws that address accessibility requirements.

- **It ensures compliance with worldwide regulations and standards**. Other countries have also published guidelines and passed regulations to ensure accessible software design. For example, Nordic countries have published their own set of accessibility guidelines. Other countries, such as Canada and Australia, have enacted legislation that makes it a civil right for individuals with disabilities to be able to access certain kinds of information.

- **The potential target audience is greatly increased by including people with disabilities.** Over 7.75 million users in the U.S. cannot use a computer unaided by assistive technology. This is a large target audience. Furthermore, this number is steadily increasing, partly because people are living longer.

- **The potential target audience is greatly increased among those who do not have disabilities.** Designing for accessibility often means that users can use your product with lower-end computers and without needing special hardware. For example, software designed for users who are deaf can also be used by users without sound cards. Another example is the "text-only" option for Web pages, in which textual labels replace Web graphics. This option allows users with slower modems to use the Web page without losing information and may significantly increase your target audience in countries that are not as technologically advanced.

- **Accessible software is often easier for all users to use.** The general population also benefits from the many features of accessible software. For example, many expert users prefer to use the keyboard instead of using the mouse, because it is more efficient. By designing for keyboard access, you provide more user-friendly software for these types of expert users. Elderly users often benefit from features originally implemented for accessibility, such as larger fonts.

Questions to ask before beginning

You may need to design for accessibility if your target audience includes people with disabilities or because of limitations in the users' hardware environment. The user analysis and work environment requirements from Chapter 2, "Gathering requirements," should provide the information to answer the following questions:

- **Does the target audience include users with mental, visual, auditory, or other physical or cognitive disabilities?** If yes, you must ensure that your wizard can be interpreted by assistive technologies.

- **Does the target audience include users in different countries?** Some countries require software that is sold within the country to be accessible for users with disabilities.

- **Are elderly adults a target audience?** Elderly adults often need accessibility features such as larger fonts.

- **Is noise a concern in the target audience's work environment?** Users who work in a noisy environment have needs similar to those of deaf users.

- **What hardware will users be using to view and interact with the wizard?** Special keyboards and other devices use accessibility APIs (application programming interfaces) to interpret software.

- **What display settings do most of your target users use for resolution and number of colors?** The display settings will impact both the design of your graphics and the general layout of the wizard pages.

Types of disabilities

In U.S. adults, disabilities vary in both severity and type. Types of disabilities include: mobility limitations and limited hand use, cognitive disabilities, hearing impairment and deafness, vision impairments, and speech and language disabilities. Figure 13–1 shows the distribution of types of disabilities among U.S. adults who reported disabilities.

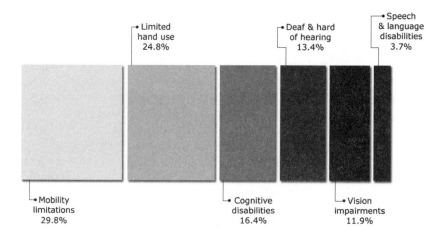

Figure 13–1   *Percentages of types of disabilities in U.S. adults.*

Each of these types of disabilities is described in more detail in this section.

Mobility limitations and limited hand use

Users with mobility limitations have limited (or no) use of their fingers and hands. They may have limited range of movement, slow response speed, low accuracy, low strength, or a combination of all limitations. Some users have movement limitations and cannot press multiple keys simultaneously, such as Ctrl+Alt+Del. Other users have limited accuracy of movement and may accidentally strike several keys while targeting a single key.

These users benefit from access keys and alternative input methods, such as speech input and sticky key functions. Some users must rely on voice input and voice navigation. Others require changing input settings to allow them to enter needed information one keystroke at a time, without timing out the software application.

Cognitive disabilities

Cognitive disabilities include perceptual and memory impairments. Users with cognitive disabilities might need to modify your wizard's interface, such as by customizing dialog boxes or hiding graphics. Similarly, the use of icons and graphics to illustrate choices, such as printing options, helps users with some types of cognitive impairments.

Deaf and hard of hearing

Users who are deaf or hard of hearing cannot hear sounds and warning beeps. These users rely on captions or other mechanisms to communicate content that is otherwise aurally presented.

Users who do not have a sound card, those who have media players that are not compatible for all types of sound files, and those who work in a noisy environment also share the requirements of users who are hard of hearing. All of these users need information to be presented visually rather than aurally.

Vision impairments

Vision impairments range from slightly reduced visual acuity to color-blindness to complete blindness. To accommodate users with reduced visual acuity, allow them to increase the size of text and graphics within your wizard. Users who are blind cannot see graphics or text. Additionally, because mice are hand-eye coordination devices, users who are blind cannot use a mouse to navigate. These users need textual equivalents for graphics and software that are compatible with assistive technologies such as screen/Web readers, Braille output devices, screen magnifiers, and print/optical character readers.

As with visual acuity, users may have various severities of color-blindness. The most common form of color-blindness is red-green color-blindness, where users have problems distinguishing between certain shades of red and green. Howlett (1996) states that about 9% of males have some form of color deficiency or color confusion. The percentage of females is lower, but females may also have problems distinguishing colors. Some people have difficulty distinguishing among dark colors, while others may have problems when the colors are light. Other forms of color-blindness exist, such as blue color perception problems and the inability to see any colors at all, but these forms are rare. Users who do not have color printers or monitors share the requirements of those who are color-blind. These users rely on cues other than color, such as size or pattern.

Speech or language disabilities

Users with attention and language disorders, such as dyslexia, have difficulty reading and writing. Some users have difficulty comprehending and expressing thoughts. These users benefit from reading, writing, comprehension, and prediction aids, such as spell-check utilities and voice input and output technologies. These users may also need more time to respond to software prompts.

Combinations

Users may have a combination of disabilities or limitations. Technologies need to coexist to ensure that users can effectively access their software.

Understanding users with disabilities

Meeting the standards of accessible software requires an awareness of the special needs of users who have disabilities. The following mini-experiments are designed to help you to better understand how users with disabilities may interact with the software products that you use every day.

- **Unplug your mouse and attempt to use your computer for a day without using it**. Those who are blind cannot use a mouse because it is a hand-eye coordination device, so every application must be operable with just the keyboard or voice input. Mobility-impaired users and expert users may also prefer to use alternatives to the mouse.

How easy was it for you to access menu choices? Were you able to edit documents or navigate to Web pages without using the mouse?

- **Use only the mouse to navigate and use a single hand to type**. Users with hand, arm, and other mobility impairments may not be able to use multiple simultaneous keystrokes such as Ctrl+Alt+Del, and therefore, they rely on special keyboard enhancements in the operating system.

  Were you able to successfully use your software applications without using simultaneous keystrokes? Were key equivalents provided to allow you to navigate on-screen?

- **Turn off the sound on your computer**. Deaf users and users without sound cards or certain media players rely on information that is provided visually.

  How easy was it to collect all of the information that you needed without using sound? Did the Web sites you encountered provide transcripts of speaking audio for their animations and movies, or were you at a disadvantage without sound? Did you receive visual confirmation that files completed downloading or textual information when small errors were made?

- **Change your system or browser font to a larger size**. Users with low vision may change their system or browser settings to display larger fonts.

  How well do your various applications handle the larger font? Is any information truncated, or do scroll bars always appear? Are fonts consistent, or do some screen elements have disproportionately large or small fonts?

- **Print Web pages and software dialogs using a black-and-white printer**. Users with low vision and color-blindness have difficulty distinguishing objects that differ along a single dimension such as color, depth, size, location, or font style.

  How easy was it for you to distinguish between visited links and other links? Were graphs and charts easy to interpret, or was color necessary?

Assistive technologies

Assistive technologies include tools such as screen readers, Web page readers, screen magnifiers, speech recognition software, and specialized keyboards. Software accessibility guidelines do *not* require you to provide assistive technologies with your software, but do require that software be compatible with these technologies. Figure 13–2 shows the relationships among assistive technologies, accessibility, and your wizard.

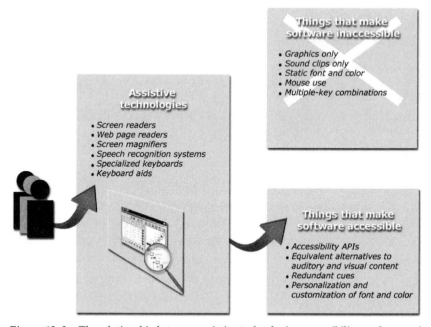

Figure 13–2 *The relationship between assistive technologies, accessibility, and your wizard assistive technology to interact with the software, which is designed to be compatible with the If your wizard contains features that are inaccessible, assistive technologies cannot interpret tent, and users will not be able to interact with the wizard.*

This section describes the different types of assistive technologies that currently exist to help people interact with their computers.

Screen readers and Web page readers

Blind users and users with low-vision often rely on Web page readers and screen readers to read information, controls, buttons, and textual labels. Users with dyslexia may also benefit from these technologies. Screen readers and Web page readers are quite similar, except that screen readers read software applications, while Web page readers read Web pages. Both technologies transform the visual interface into an audio interface by using a speech synthesizer and the computer's sound card to output the content of the computer screen to speakers. Some screen readers also output to Braille displays.

Screen magnifiers

Screen magnifiers are also known as screen enlargers, or large-print programs. These technologies allow users to magnify a portion of their screen. They also keep track of where users are working, and can automatically move the magnified portion to active areas, such as activated menus. Figure 13–3 shows how a tree view would appear when seen through a screen magnifier.

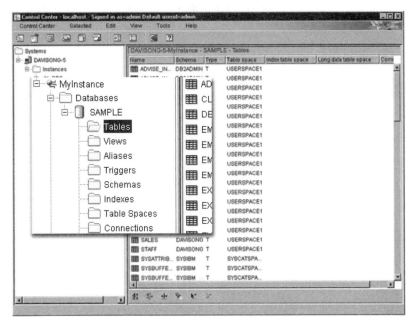

Figure 13–3   *A tree view as seen through a screen magnifier.*

Speech recognition systems

Speech recognition systems are also known as voice-input systems. These technologies allow users to control software with their voices rather than with a keyboard and mouse, and are especially useful for those who are blind or have difficulty typing.

Specialized keyboards and keyboard aids

Some users with physical disabilities cannot use standard keyboards or mice, but can interact with specialized devices such as on-screen keyboards, video camera input devices, and keyboard filters. On-screen keyboards display commands on-screen and allow the user to select them by selecting mechanical switches, which require less precision of movement than standard keyboards. Camera controls allow the user to zoom in, select windows, and scroll by using head movements, such as pointing with one's nose. Keyboard filters attempt to compensate for erratic motions and tremors by filtering out unsuitable keystrokes. The filters can be used in conjunction with standard keyboards. Word prediction and completion functions can also aid users in using keyboards. These functions predict commands or words and complete them, so that the user does not need to type as many letters.

Accessibility guidelines

Many of the design guidelines discussed earlier in the book will help your wizard be accessible. Features such as clear layouts and navigational aids, uncluttered screens, and clear descriptions of the scope of each page help your wizard to be more easily interpreted by assistive technologies. These features will not be discussed at length in this section. However, this section explains what you can do to ensure that you are not creating barriers for users with disabilities. Guidelines include:

- Implement accessibility APIs.

- Provide accessible names and descriptions.

- Support easy keyboard and mouse navigation.

- Provide equivalent alternatives to auditory and visual content.

- Use redundant cues in your display.

- Avoid blinking text and flashing objects.

- Supply orientation and contextual information.

- Allow user personalization and customization.

- Design screens that resize cleanly and support older technologies.

- Provide accessible documentation.

Implement accessibility APIs

The most important step to take to ensure that your wizard is accessible is to use current accessibility APIs when you write your wizard code. APIs are places or hooks in your wizard code that make it easy for assistive technologies to work. Java, Windows, and the Web all have a set of accessibility APIs to allow assistive technologies to interpret software content. These APIs help to ensure compatibility between your software and the accessibility utilities that your users may install.

Provide accessible names and descriptions

Relationships and differences that are obvious to a sighted user may not be easily interpreted by assistive technologies. To ensure that your wizard is properly interpreted:

- Make certain that all wizard controls have names and descriptions that can be interpreted by assistive technologies, even if these names will not appear on the screen. Ensure that the description of each control contains information about its role and state. For example, the description of a check box must include whether it is checked or not.

- Avoid placing more than one object with the same name on the same wizard page or dialog, unless the objects perform the same function.

- Make certain that *all* graphics can be interpreted by assistive technologies.

  - Provide textual descriptions of all images and icons. Ensure that these descriptions include the *relevant* aspects of the image. For example, if the graphic is of a flowchart, the textual description should include the fact that the graphic is a flowchart of the process. If the flowchart is very important, the description should also include details such as what the first step is, what the second step is, and so forth. Similarly, if the image is a graph or chart, you may want to describe the breakdown of the data it represents.

  - Supply text labels for bitmapped text because screen readers cannot read bitmaps.

  - Be sure that *all* aspects of an image, such as a map or chart, are labeled because screen readers will not be able to distinguish among different elements of a single image without the labels.

- Give all dialogs unique and descriptive title bars.

Support easy keyboard and mouse navigation

A good keyboard interface can positively impact users with a wide range of disabilities. You should provide keyboard equivalents for all actions—the user should be able to use the keyboard only; the mouse should *not* be required. Follow these keyboard guidelines:

- **Define shortcut keys (also called accelerator keys) for tasks that are frequently performed.** Shortcut keys are keys or key combinations, such as Ctrl+P for print and Esc for cancel, that provide quick access to an action.

- **Support all accessibility options that are available on the system software.** For example, the Microsoft Windows operating systems provide features such as sticky keys and toggle keys. The sticky keys function allows the user to use the Shift, Control, or Alt key by pressing one key at a time, rather than simultaneously with other keys. The toggle keys function enables the user to hear tones when pressing Caps Lock, Num Lock, and Scroll Lock.

- **Define access keys (also called mnemonics) for all controls.** Mnemonics act as abbreviations for operations, such as menu selections or button clicks, and are represented on dialogs as underlined letters. When users click Alt+ the underlined letter, they are able to access specific menu items without using the mouse.

- **Allow users to navigate on-screen using Tab and Shift+Tab keys.** Provide a logical tab order—left to right, top to bottom for Western languages. Figure 13–4 illustrates such a tab order. Design your wizard so that tabbing to a label navigates the user to the associated control identified by the label rather than to the label itself. If a tab takes a user to a control, the user can interact with the control immediately rather than needing to move the mouse from the label to the control.

- **Provide a visual indicator that moves among interactive objects as the input focus changes.** Supplement keyboard navigation with a visual indicator, such as an insertion bar (or caret), that moves as the user tabs from control to control. Ensure that the assistive technology can interpret the position and contents of the objects that are in focus, so that it can describe, magnify, or manipulate the object for the user. For example, a screen magnifier needs to follow the visual focus as the user tabs around your wizard page.

Figure 13–4 provides an example of how Tab keys would help the user to navigate among the controls. As the user presses the Tab key, keyboard focus moves from control 1 to control 2 and so on until the user tabs to control 10. When the user reaches control 10, the Tab key moves keyboard focus to control 1.

If you must provide a specialized keyboard for your wizard, make sure that it follows the guidelines described above.

Because some users may rely on pointing devices such as mice and camera-based keyboards, you also need to design these interactions well. Make basic functions available via a single click. Reserve the use of drag and drop and multiple clicks as options for advanced functions and users.

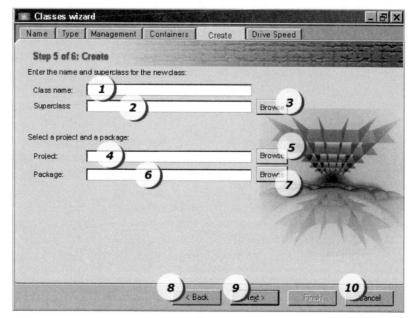

Figure 13–4 *As the user presses the Tab key, keyboard focus moves from control 1 to control 2 and so on.*

Provide equivalent alternatives to auditory and visual content

Do not provide information in a single format; provide textual alternatives for non-textual wizard elements, and conversely, provide non-textual alternatives for textual elements. Because speech synthesizers and Braille displays cannot recognize images, icons, audio, animations, and video, users will not be able to access information provided in these aspects of your wizard unless you provide a textual equivalent. Provide an option to display a visual cue such as an on-screen textual message for all audio alerts. Transcripts of videos (including their visual information) are more effective than audio files because almost all assistive devices can interpret text.

If your wizard is on the Web, ensure that all important graphical Web links have text as well as an image. If images are not important or if they are redundant, assign empty alternative text so that the assistive technology ignores the image. Unlike users who can view the page and automatically ignore irrelevant images, a user who is listening to information read by a screen reader cannot easily ignore the irrelevant text.

Conversely, non-textual information such as pictures and videos can be powerful informational equivalents for non-readers. Be sure to provide non-textual information as an alternative to long textual descriptions and to use non-textual alternatives to emphasize key wizard concepts. This additional information will help non-readers as well as those who learn spatially, rather than verbally.

Use redundant cues in your display

If you rely on color as the only way to convey information, many users will not be able to interpret your graphics. Instead, use visual cues such as font, shape, pattern, or size in conjunction with color to ensure that users with visual disabilities or black-and-white printers will be able to interpret the graphics. Figure 13–5 shows how textual labels can help to clarify color choices within a menu control. The colored square alone would not be enough for users with certain visual impairments to distinguish among or to identify specific choices. These users might need to use specific colors for conference presentations or other purposes.

Figure 13–5   Using redundant cues to clarify menu choices. The colored square alone would be enough for certain users to identify and select specific colors.

Avoid blinking text and flashing objects

Do not use flashing images or blinking text in your wizard. Displays that flicker or flash can cause epileptic seizures in susceptible individuals, especially if the flash has a high intensity and is within certain frequency ranges. When implementing features such as visual focus indicators, ensure the blink frequency or flash rate is *not* between 2Hz and 55Hz.

Blinking text and images can also be problematic for users with either cognitive or visual disabilities. These users may be unable to read moving text quickly enough. Screen readers cannot read moving text, so blind users will miss the information entirely.

Supply orientation and contextual information

Orientation and contextual information is critical for accessibility. Visual cues that are taken for granted by sighted users may not be interpreted or communicated by screen readers. For example, users dependent on screen readers may not be able to take advantage of information provided via proportional scroll bars, such as how much text is left to read.

Your wizard design should not *rely* on features that require your users to understand the spatial relationships between objects. For example, screen readers will not be able to communicate information that is based on the alignment of controls and frames. Users will not "see" that multiple controls are in the same row or column. Screen readers read the controls in order from top to bottom, so users will have some limited information about how controls are ordered on the page.

Furthermore, assistive technologies may hinder the user's ability to grasp contextual information. Unlike sighted users who may quickly scan an entire page or screen to understand its context and narrow in on sections of interest, assistive technologies heavily restrict the amount of information that the user will receive at one time.

To help these users, follow these guidelines:

- **Use layout to clarify some spatial relationships.** For example, always position related objects near each other to ensure that the screen reader will read them one after the other. Because screen readers use proximity to identify labels that are not coded for assistive technologies, place control labels immediately before the control.

- **Do not put a control in the middle of a sentence.** Since screen readers do not "scan" ahead, users may be confused when the reader identifies a control for which only partial information has been read.

- **Place all descriptive text and labels before the controls to which they refer.** For Western languages, place the text and labels immediately to the left or immediately above the control. This ensures that the screen reader reads the relevant text immediately before the user encounters its control.

- **Keep lists and pages short.** Screen readers read only one word at a time and screen magnifiers display only a small portion of the screen at a time.

- **Provide information such as what page of a wizard users are on and what item in a list or table they are in to help users navigate.** For example, you could include text such as "Step X of N" at the top of your wizard pages. If your wizard is on the Web and you have a table with multiple rows and columns, mark each table cell with the header and row that applies to it. This approach helps the user to understand how the information is structured.

Allow user personalization and customization

A personalizable interface accommodates a wide variety of users. Provide several selections for both foreground and background colors, as well as font sizes, to allow users to change the font and colors in your wizard. Ensure that your wizard design works with high-contrast settings such as white on black, yellow on black, and black on white. Additionally, ensure that users can control any time-sensitive content changes. For example, allow users to pause video clips and adjust the interval that the wizard waits for input. Do not automatically hide important messages such as errors, warnings, or confirmation dialogs after a certain time interval; let users dismiss them explicitly. If your wizard contains any audio, allow users to adjust the volume.

Your wizard (or the application that owns your wizard) should check user system defaults for color, font, and accessibility options before loading the wizard and should use these defaults to display the wizard. Do not allow your design to overwrite user settings or interfere with existing accessibility features built into the operating system.

Design screens that resize cleanly and support older technologies

Design wizard screens that resize well to accommodate users who use larger fonts and magnify their screens. Provide scroll bars to allow users access to content that doesn't fit on the screen when the wizard page is resized. Figure 13–6 shows a wizard design that did not transform well when larger fonts were used. You may also want to provide a Zoom command to allow users to scale graphics and other information in your wizard.

Figure 13–6 *An example of a wizard that did not transform well when a larger font setting was selected.*

If your wizard is on the Web, make sure that your tables do not become awkward to use if they are resized and the font is enlarged. Also, test your design with older browser versions because screen reader technologies might be several versions behind the latest browsers. For example, ensure that your screens work without frames or cascading style sheets. Ensure that you provide alternative content for any applets, plug-ins, or scripts that are not accessible.

Provide accessible documentation

The guidelines for documentation are quite similar to those for your wizard:

- Document the accessibility features of your wizard or application.
- Provide documentation formats that work for users who cannot see and those who cannot hear.

- Ensure that on-line documentation is accessible and interpretable by assistive technologies and is not dependent on certain types of hardware.

- If you cannot provide on-line documentation, provide your documentation in multiple, alternative formats such as large print, video or audiotape, Braille, and so on.

- Ensure that paper documentation is bound so that it can lie flat to support users with limited dexterity.

Additional sources for guidelines and information

Several comprehensive guidelines and resources exist to help you ensure that your wizard is accessible. If your wizard is not on the Web, is not written in Java, and is not for the Windows platform, you should research and use guidelines appropriate for your specific wizard design.

You can also use these resources to test the accessibility of your wizard design. The best approach is to include users with disabilities in your design activities; however, you may be able to catch most problems by comparing your design against the guidelines given in this section and by using accessibility evaluation tools, which are software tools that help you to test whether your wizards are accessible.

Additional sources of information include:

- **Cast.** An organization that provides a free tool to help you evaluate the accessibility of your Web site.

- **IBM Accessibility Center.** A general resource for accessibility issues and guidelines for accessible software design. This Web site also includes code samples for several Web site accessibility features.

- **Java Accessibility Guidelines.** A source of guidelines and APIs for wizards written in Java.

- **The Trace Center.** A good general resource for accessibility issues.

- **Windows Accessibility Guidelines.** Guidelines for wizards developed for Windows platforms.

- **WWW Consortium's (W3C) Web Accessibility Initiative (WAI) Web Content Accessibility Guidelines.** The central resource for Web accessibility guidelines.

All of this information can be found on the Web.

Summary of guidelines discussed in this chapter

- ❏ Implement accessibility APIs.
- ❏ Provide accessible names and descriptions.
- ❏ Support easy keyboard and mouse navigation.
- ❏ Provide equivalent alternatives to auditory and visual content.
- ❏ Use redundant cues in your display.
- ❏ Avoid the use of blinking text and flashing objects.
- ❏ Supply orientation and contextual information.
- ❏ Allow user personalization and customization.
- ❏ Design screens that resize cleanly and that support older technologies.
- ❏ Provide accessible documentation.

Chapter 14

Worldwide audiences

- ▲ Why design for a worldwide audience?
- ▲ Questions to ask before beginning
- ▲ Localization versus internationalization
- ▲ Content translation
- ▲ Layout translation
- ▲ Input translation
- ▲ Graphics for worldwide audiences
- ▲ Practical concerns
- ▲ Summary of guidelines discussed in this chapter

By 2010, Nielsen (2000) predicts that the Web will have a billion distributed users, with about 200 million in North America, 200 million in Europe, 500 million in Asia, and 100 million in the rest of the world. Today, if you design your wizard for a single country, you will exclude more than half of your potential users!

Fortunately, if you design for a worldwide audience from the very beginning, you can create designs that can be used in more than one country. With further effort, you can create designs that are optimized for different countries or languages.

Many of the design guidelines discussed earlier in this book will help you design a wizard that can be more easily translated and adapted for other cultures. This chapter explains several guidelines that can help you to further ensure that you are not creating barriers for translation. For the purposes of this chapter, English is assumed to be the primary language for your wizard. However, the guidelines apply regardless of which language is the primary language for your wizard.

This chapter briefly describes two approaches for designing for a worldwide audience: internationalization and localization. This chapter also provides translation guidelines for your wizard content, your wizard layout, and data input and interpretation. This chapter discusses guidelines for creating internationalized graphics. This chapter concludes with a brief discussion of practical concerns, such as schedule impacts, that arise when you attempt to translate your wizard. For more information on differences between cultures, see *Cultures and Organizations: Software of the Mind* by Geert Hofstede.

Why design for a worldwide audience?

If you design for a worldwide audience, your wizard will be usable in many countries, not just the U.S. Benefits of designing for a worldwide audience include:

- **You will sell more copies of your wizard software.** If users from other countries are able to access and understand your wizard, you will sell more copies of the wizard. You will sell even more if your design reflects how users in different countries think and contains examples and graphics that they feel are useful and non-offensive. Most large companies in the U.S., such as IBM, have discovered that they sell more software outside of the U.S. than in the U.S.

- **Users from outside the U.S. will find your Web-based wizard easier to use.** As cited above, over 50% of users on the Web are from outside the U.S. These users will be accessing your wizard, regardless of whether it is designed for their needs. If you do not account for these users, you may encounter problems in data interpretation. For example, if your wizard fails to translate data inputs to match numeric formats used in other countries, users may pay the incorrect amount.

- **If you do not design for a worldwide audience initially, the cost of making your wizard available in other countries later will be much higher.** Translation costs will likely be much higher. Additionally, your wizard code will need to be changed. The time and resources invested in re-learning the code, editing the code, and then testing the code will be significant.

Even if you do not plan to translate your wizard, design your wizard to be as internationally usable as possible. Follow as many of the guidelines listed here as you can, because some flexibility is much better than none. Plus, this approach will make the job of any future translator easier.

Questions to ask before beginning

Your target audience's social and cultural characteristics should dictate the design of your wizard, especially in terms of its look and feel. Cultural background determines what users consider appropriate, how they interpret different symbols and colors, and what they find appealing. The user definition from Chapter 2, "Gathering requirements," should provide you with the information needed to answer the following questions:

- **Are most of your users from the U.S.? What countries or regions are they from?** Your wizard text and graphics must be understandable and non-offensive to your target users. If users are from other countries, it is less likely that your users will be using high-end computers with large monitors and incredibly fast Internet connections.

- **What is your target audience's primary language? Do they speak multiple languages?** Your wizard pages should be designed for your target audience's primary language. If your target audience speaks multiple languages, you might allow them to switch among languages within your wizard.

- **Does your target audience include any users from ethnic groups?** Any wizard graphics that contain images of people should reflect your target audience. Users from different cultures or regions may have different expectations and ascribe different meanings to colors, metaphors, words, and so on.

279

- **What is your users' task?** If you are expanding your wizard to new countries or regions, you must also verify that your task analysis is still valid.

Localization versus internationalization

You can take one of two approaches to designing for a worldwide audience:

- **Localization.** The process of making an adapted version of your wizard for a specific locale. For example, if your target audience lives in three different countries, you would create three different wizards and translate your content accordingly.

- **Internationalization.** The process of creating a single design that can be used worldwide. For example, a wizard that is internationalized for three countries uses simple language that can be understood by non-native speakers.

Figure 14–1 shows the difference between localization and internationalization.

Localization

Internationalization

Figure 14–1   *Localization involves making multiple translated versions of the same wizard. Internationalization is designing a single wizard that can be understood by non-native speakers.*

You should base your decision to localize or internationalize your wizard on cost estimates and your target audience's characteristics. You may also choose to localize for some subset of countries and internationalize for others. If your wizard is on the Web, you probably want to internationalize it rather than localize it because most countries will probably not have enough users to make localization worthwhile.

Content translation

Translation is not a matter of simply using different text on-screen. Other details may also change. For example, translation can also impact mnemonics because the letters in the words used in different languages can be different. Therefore, your wizard code must recognize what language is being displayed to interpret which key combinations refer to which controls. Translation may also result in different punctuation and different metaphors.

This section explains these guidelines for content translation:

- Write text that is easily translatable into other languages.
- Support different word orders across languages.
- Allow the user to select and change the default language for your wizard.
- Ensure that your first wizard page is well-translated.
- Consider providing links to another language version.
- Account for regional differences in the wizard task.

Write text that is easily translatable into other languages

Text that is easily translatable into other languages is also more easily understood by non-native speakers even when it is not translated. Guidelines for making your original text more easily translatable into other languages include:

- **Use simple language and sentence structure.** Writing in active voice and using the present tense make your text easier to understand. Complex verb forms such as past participle and present participle might be ambiguous. For example, the phrase "studying plans might be useful" could be interpreted in a variety of ways.

- **Keep on-screen labels and textual descriptions short.** Limit your sentences to 25 words or less. Shorter text tends to be more precise and allows more room for translation. For example, the word "want" is more precise than the phrase "would like" and is easier to translate.

- **Use complete sentences to avoid ambiguity.** Do not omit prepositions or articles from sentences. Avoid using noun strings, such as "record error," because they may be interpreted in multiple ways. For example, "record error" could mean "there is an error in the record" or "record this error in your notes." In many languages, the spelling of words changes based on their context. Translators might not be able to provide accurate translations for sentence fragments.

- **Limit the number of controls on your page so that you do not run out of letters to use as mnemonics.** Be sure to have fewer controls than letters in the alphabet. You probably do not want to have more than 12 to 15 controls on each wizard page. Remember that the letters used in translated words can be very different than those used in English. For example, if none of your labels begin with the same letter in English, when translated, you may be faced with a situation where multiple labels begin with the same letter. Although you can use letters that do not appear in the on-screen text or even numbers as mnemonics, it is best to use letters that appear in the control label.

- **Avoid using puns and idioms.** These do not translate well and may not even be understood by translators. For example, the phrase "putting one's ducks in a row" means getting everything organized or planned. Because the use of this phrase is very local and culturally specific, it is unlikely that translators and users in other countries would understand it.

- **Avoid using culture-specific standards and names.** For example, do not refer to monarch envelopes, Cowboys blue, or the East Coast.

- **Don't be offensive.** Avoid descriptions and examples that use human body parts, violence or weapons, sexual images, animal symbolism, and gender or racial stereotyping.

Support different word orders across languages

Never put controls in the middle of sentences because word order differs across languages. Figure 14–2 shows an example where the word order is different in English, German, and Russian. Rather than place a control in the middle of a sentence, it is better to treat control text as a label for the choice that follows.

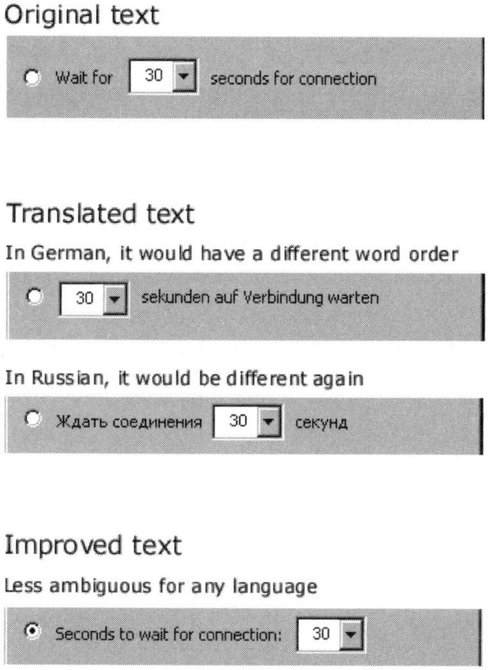

Original text

C Wait for 30 ▼ seconds for connection

Translated text

In German, it would have a different word order

C 30 ▼ sekunden auf Verbindung warten

In Russian, it would be different again

C Ждать соединения 30 ▼ секунд

Improved text

Less ambiguous for any language

⊙ Seconds to wait for connection: 30 ▼

Figure 14–2 *An example of a sentence whose word order differs in English, German, and Russian. To avoid translation problems, phrase control choices so that they act as labels for the control that immediately follows them.*

Bulleted lists are another example where word order can be troublesome. In English, we often use a partial sentence to introduce a list of items. For example, on the first page of your wizard, you might have something like:

This wizard will:

- Create a graph
- Name the graph
- Link the graph to dynamic spreadsheet data

Unfortunately, this page would not translate because sentence construction in other languages differs from English. You can avoid this problem by introducing your lists with full sentences. For example: "This wizard performs three tasks:"

For confirmation dialogs and error message dialogs, support the ability to switch variable order. For example, the message "Copy file 1 to disk 2" may require phrasing such as "Copy to disk 2 from file1."

Allow the user to select and change the default language for your wizard

Always allow users to select the language that they prefer. If your wizard is part of a larger application, be sure that the wizard language matches whatever language choice the user made for the application. You can present the language when the product is installed or on a secondary dialog that is launched in a variety of ways, such as from the application toolbar, from a button on the wizard page, or from a preferences menu option.

If your wizard is the entire application, you must provide a method for users to select their preferred language. The most basic way to present this choice is to provide the language choices on the first page of your wizard.

If your wizard is on the Web:

- Try to have your wizard code check the browser's setting for the user's language or location preference. If this is not possible, make the default language match your target audience's most likely choice. For example, if you know that over 80% of your audience will come from English-speaking countries, you can default your wizard to English.

- Consider allowing users to change the wizard language through a secondary dialog or Web page because not all users may realize that they can change the language through their browser preferences.

- Test your code carefully to ensure that the language of the browser buttons matches the content of the wizard pages.

- Ensure that users can start the wizard only on appropriate pages. Do not allow users to mistakenly enter the wizard on middle pages.

- If you are providing on-line help for your wizard, allow users to view the on-line help in a language different from that of the wizard pages. Also, allow users to bookmark translated pages in the on-line help. For example, your users may want the wizard pages to appear in German because they want the numbers and so forth to match German conventions. However, if the translation quality is poor, the users may want to read the help in its original language version.

When you provide language choices, list each choice using the name of the language as a word, in its respective language, such as "English" or "Español." Do not use flags or other icons to represent language choices. Flags do not always portray a one-to-one mapping to a language. For example, because both French and English are spoken in Canada, it is unclear which language would be selected by clicking on a Canadian flag. Furthermore, some users might be insulted if their language was not the default when they clicked their country's flag.

Consider giving your users the option to reconsider their initial language choice on subsequent pages of your wizard, especially if your wizard is on the Web. Users who are able to read multiple languages might want to change languages if they feel the translation of certain information into their chosen language is difficult to understand. If you allow users to change languages or regions in the middle of your wizard, do *not* re-interpret data that's already been entered. For example, do not automatically perform calculations such as currency conversions. The user may just want to look at a different translation for a certain page and will switch back to the original language again. Also, re-calculations can result in slow-loading pages. However, you can consider asking the users if they want the previous inputs to be re-calculated.

Ensure that your first wizard page is well-translated

Nielsen (2000) underscores the importance of gaining user trust in the first pages. He states that: "It is worth some extra effort to ensure that the instructions on the language choice page are properly translated into each of the appropriate languages. If the first page projects an image of working poorly in one of the languages, then users who prefer that language may never bother entering the site—even if the rest of the site was perfect." Figure 14–3 illustrates an example of a wizard page that is poorly translated. Do you have confidence that the remainder of the wizard is well-designed, well-written, or functions properly?

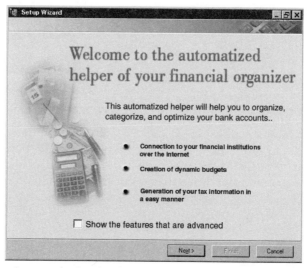

Figure 14–3 An example of a wizard whose first page is poorly translated. A poor job on the first page may decrease user trust that the remainder of the wizard will work properly.

Consider providing links to another language version

If you cannot translate your wizard, your on-line help for the wizard, or all pages of a Web-based wizard into all local languages, provide a link to an English version or another language version that you expect all of your users to have some familiarity with. Figure 14–4 illustrates a wizard that provides a link to an English version. The link is provided on the bottom of the first page; however, you might choose to include it on all pages.

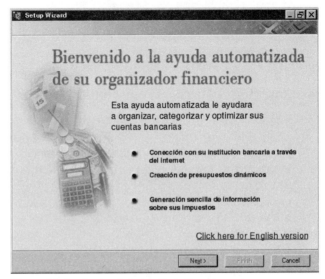

Figure 14–4 *A wizard design that allows users to access an English version, in case they are not familiar with Spanish.*

Account for regional differences in the wizard task

As discussed in Chapter 2, "Gathering requirements," a task analysis should form the basis of your wizard's structure. If you are localizing or internationalizing an existing wizard, be sure to validate your task analysis with users from different countries to ensure that your assumptions about tasks and information flow hold true. Differences in job divisions and roles might impact your wizard's page order or the number of steps. Low-level design differences may also exist. For example, users in some countries use weeks rather than months when scheduling activities—they might plan a meeting for week 20 of the year.

Your wizard should make it clear up-front if different products, prices, warranties, delivery dates, or ordering procedures apply in different countries.

Additionally, warn users if they select a delivery or billing address for which previous choices or information no longer apply. This guideline is especially important in Web-based wizards that are used for on-line purchasing.

Layout translation

Localization from English to most other languages increases the length of text in the interface. It can also affect control layout. Figure 14–5 shows the same wizard page in English, Chinese, and French. The text is longest in French and shortest in Chinese. Vertical character height also varies and is tallest in Chinese.

One quick way to estimate how your layout will look in different languages is to use a website to translate your current text strings. These translations

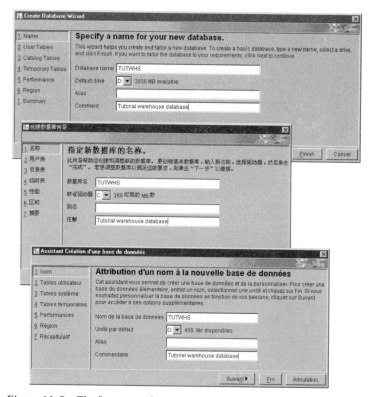

Figure 14–5   *The first page of a Create Database wizard in English (the language it was originally designed for), Chinese, and French. Notice that the text is longest in French and tallest in Chinese.*

should not be used for your final product, but they do provide a good estimate of how much your text may grow in different languages. Some websites that offer this functionality are:

- http://babel.altavista.com/translate.dyn
- http://translate.lycos.com

This section explains these guidelines for layout translation:

- Leave room on the wizard pages for expansion.
- Provide scroll bars and resizable panes.

Leave room on the wizard pages for expansion

A general rule of thumb is to leave 30% white space for text expansion on each wizard page. However, be aware that sometimes more than 30% is needed. To allow for graceful expansion, leave extra space within your control labels and text boxes so that the text can grow without requiring the dialog to resize. Some techniques to support expansion on your wizard pages as well as in secondary dialogs such as error message dialogs are:

- **Place labels above, rather than at the left of, their associated text entry fields.** This placement provides more horizontal space for the label to grow. Figure 14–6 illustrates how a label placed at the left of its text entry field may not work when translated. In the first layout, when the text is translated, the label does not fit on-screen. The second layout is better because it leaves white space between the label and the text entry field. When the text is translated, it fills up the white space, but still fits on-screen without requiring resizing of the original dialog. Also, note that the length of the text grows more than 30% when it is localized to German. The last layout is best; it provides the most real estate for the labels to grow before resizing is required.

- **Do not use long labels for your controls.** Instead, put short labels on the dialog and provide additional information in pop-up help. (See Chapter 11, "On-line help," for more information on pop-up help.) A second approach is to add a sentence or two of text to your wizard page and a short label for the control.

- **Do not size your interface controls, such as buttons, to the exact length of the English phrases.** Make the actual control label or caption longer than the text that appears on-screen. Leave extra lines at the bottom of all text boxes as well as groups of radio buttons and check boxes. This additional space allows the translated label to fit on-screen without requiring controls to be resized. Examples of this approach are shown in Figures 14–7 and 14–8.

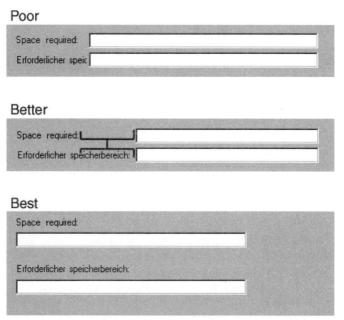

Figure 14–6 *Layouts that place the label above the text field provide the most room for localized text. If you place your label at the left of the text entry field, be sure to leave enough white space to fit the localized text.*

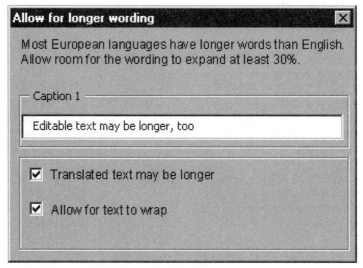

Figure 14–7 *This panel is designed so that each control has enough real estate to grow without requiring code to resize it.*

289

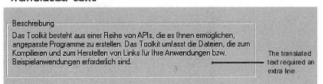

Figure 14–8   *An example where extra space is left in the original text box to allow localized text to fit into it.*

- **If your wizard is on the Web, code it so that it supports scrolling and adapts each page to the user's monitor.** Your wizard should automatically adjust its layout to the space required by each language version if needed. However, you should still attempt to design pages that will not require the user to scroll.

Provide scroll bars and resizable panes

If all wizard content cannot be visible on-screen at a given time, automatically provide scroll bars—horizontal, vertical, or both—to allow users to access hidden information. This scroll bar approach should be used sparingly. It is *always* better to have all content on-screen at once, rather than requiring users to scroll to it. Always allow the user to resize the wizard pages, especially if you use table of contents style navigation. (For more information on table of contents style navigation, see Chapter 6, "Navigation.") Figures 14–9 and 14–10 illustrate two designs for the table of contents control that prevent the need to scroll, even if all the text cannot be visible on-screen at once. In Figure 14–9, the table of contents control and the wizard page can each be resized by moving the bar that separates them. This capability allows users to devote more real estate to either the table of contents control or to the wizard's working area, whichever they deem more important.

In Figure 14–10, the table of contents control can be detached from the wizard pages. This capability also allows users to devote more screen real estate to the working area of the wizard pages. However, it has the negative consequence of requiring users to switch back and forth between the wizard and the table of contents windows to use the table of contents to navigate.

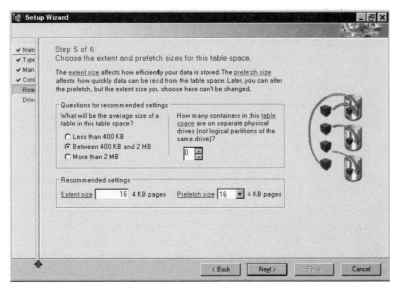

Figure 14–9 *A wizard design in which the user can resize the table of contents control to devote more screen real estate to the working area of the wizard.*

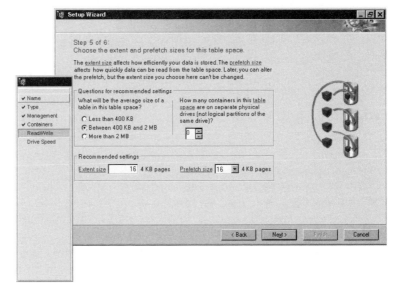

Figure 14–10 *A wizard design that allows the user to remove the table of contents control to devote more screen real estate to the working area of the wizard pages.*

Input translation

Wizards usually require users to answer questions and input information such as names, dates, and numeric values. Unfortunately, user expectations for the formats of these "basic" types of information vary across countries For example, the date 10/11/2001 is interpreted as October eleventh in the U.S., but as November tenth in most of Europe and Latin America. This section identifies potential regional differences between some basic data types that you may want to collect in your wizard and provides tips for dealing with them.

If your wizard requires any of these types of data, use international formats, as defined by organizations such as ISO (International Organization for Standardization), or change controls to local conventions. If you decide to use local conventions, try to follow national standards for the country, such as those set by BSI (the British Standards Institution) and DIN (the German Institute for Standardization). These standards help to ensure that all software represents information in a consistent manner.

This section explains these guidelines to accommodate input translation:

- Take advantage of the operating system's resource base.
- Account for regional differences in names and other words.
- Use unambiguous controls for date and time formats.
- Support flexible formatting for numbers, monetary formats, and currency symbols.
- Account for differences in other data.

Take advantage of the operating system's resource base

Some operating systems store local conventions, such as the proper character sorting sequence and the appropriate date formats, in a central resource base that can be used by any application. If possible, code your wizard so that it communicates with this resource base. This approach is more efficient and effective than having to re-create sorting sequences and other data manipulation routines.

Account for regional differences in names and other words

Some languages include special characters, such as letters with accent marks. Any sorting routines in your wizard must take these characters into account. For example, in some cases, a letter with an accent mark is treated as following the same letter without its accent mark. In other situations, characters are treated as completely different letters.

Name formats and variability also vary from country to country. In the U.S., the family name is considered the last name. In other countries, the family name is actually given first. The U.S. also has a large variability in family names when compared to other countries. Searching and sorting routines in your wizard need to account for these characteristics.

If you are creating your own searching and sorting routine, be aware that Unicode character sets increase the complexity of the calculations needed to transform user-input information to formats used by the actual program code. With Unicode, you cannot simply add 26 to the numeric value to switch from lowercase to uppercase characters. You may want to add additional coding and testing time to account for this increased complexity.

Use unambiguous controls for date and time formats

Many wizards will require the user to input a date or time. For example, an airline reservation wizard would require users to select a departure date and time. Unfortunately, date formats vary quite a bit from country to country. The order of information as well as the punctuation used differs. Some examples of valid formats and a subset of countries where they are used are:

- 15 January 2001 (Netherlands and Portugal)
- 2001.01.15 (the Peoples Republic of China)
- 1/15/2001 (U.S.)
- 15/1/2001 (most of Latin America and Europe)
- 2001-01-15 (Hungary, Japan)

If your wizard requires the user to input a date, do *not* ask the user to type it directly. Instead, provide a calendar control to help avoid ambiguity. When the choice is made, reflect it on-screen by including the month in word form. Figure 14–11 illustrates one way to provide date information. If you do use a calendar control, be aware that not all countries use a Gregorian calendar. Additionally, not all countries that use a Gregorian calendar begin their week with Sunday.

Times of day can also be ambiguous for users for a variety of reasons, including format as well as time zone of reference. Some countries use a 24-hour notation, while others use a 12-hour notation. If you use a 12-hour notation in your wizard, always include AM and PM.

Be sure that your wizard always states which time zone its times refer to. In some cases, your wizard will display a mixture of times. For example, an airline reservation wizard should show departure times in the context of the

Poor

Better

Figure 14–11 *Two options for allowing the user to input a date. The second option is better because the user does not need to worry about what the valid format is for the date.*

country from which the flight is departing. Keep in mind that time zone abbreviations, such as PST (Pacific Standard Time), are not universally understood, so you need to supplement them with an indication of the difference to GMT (Greenwich Mean Time)—such as "PST (GMT – 8)." You may also want to supplement them with an example of a city or country that falls in that time zone such as "GMT: London, England."

Support flexible formatting for numbers, monetary formats, and currency symbols

Different countries use different notations for numbers. Some countries represent a decimal point by using a period, others use a comma. Some countries use special symbols to indicate their currency, such as $ or £, and others use abbreviations, such as DM. Some countries put these symbols and abbreviations before the number, others after. Not all countries use two decimal places in their currencies.

Be sure that your wizard code displays these numerical notations, monetary formats, and currency symbols appropriately. For example, you might create a label before and another label after any input fields that will contain monetary units. After the user selects a region or currency of choice, hide whichever label is not needed. You might also need to vary the length of your input fields and any error-checking procedures to accommodate different numbers of decimal places. Avoid using the word "billion"—it refers to a thousand million in American English, but in British English, it refers to a million.

Account for differences in other data

Other information and data formats also vary from country to country, such as:

- Phone numbers

- Addresses and postal codes

- Measurements (metric system, American system)

- Standard paper and envelope sizes

- Standard keyboards and characters

Ensure that your wizard controls, textual descriptions, and error-checking routines recognize and account for these regional differences.

Graphics for worldwide audiences

Limiting words in favor of graphics and icons is not an easier way to create localized wizards. You need to select all of your images and icons carefully. Many images and colors have different meanings in different countries.

Guidelines for creating wizard graphics that can easily be localized or internationalized include:

- Create graphics that are understandable across cultures.

- Use representative populations.

- Use checkmarks instead of Xs in check boxes.

- Limit the file size and color depth of your graphics.

- Choose colors carefully.

For more detailed information on designing graphics, see Chapter 7, "Visual design," *The Icon Book* by William K. Horton, and ISO 11581.

Create graphics that are understandable across cultures

Making original graphics that are understandable by users who come from different countries is similar to writing text that is easily translatable. To make graphics that are understood by a broad target audience:

- **Use simplified graphics.** Objects often differ in the details across countries. Use abstract versions for your icons. For example, use outline forms of office items such as printers and pieces of paper.

- **Avoid text in graphics.** Do not put words, letters, or numbers into your artwork. Not all languages use the same characters to represent numbers or letters. If you want your wizard graphics to contain text, you will need to create different sets of graphics or text strings to use in the translated versions.

- **Avoid using icons based on plays on words or idioms.** For example, in English, the word "table" is used to refer to a piece of furniture as well as a grid of columns and rows. This association does not exist in all languages.

- **Use internationally recognized symbols.** Natural features (such as the sun for a symbol of day), mathematical symbols, and international signs are the safest options. Refer to the proposed international standard for icons—ISO/IEC IS 11581.

- **Don't be offensive.** For example, avoid graphics that use human body parts, gestures, violence or weapons, sexual images, animal symbolism, and gender or racial stereotyping.

Use representative populations

Design wizard graphics to reflect your target audience, especially if the graphics contain any images of people. For example, a wizard to help African American business owners sign up for a newsgroup should not contain pictures of only Anglo-Saxon people. This guideline also applies to more generic wizards, such as installation wizards. If you hope to sell your product in areas such as Asia and Africa, you should show users of Asian or African descent, not just Caucasians, in your installation wizard graphics.

Use checkmarks instead of Xs in check boxes

If your wizard includes check boxes, be sure to use graphics for the checked state that look like checkmarks, not Xs. An X indicates inclusion (wanted) in some countries and exclusion (not wanted) in others. Additionally, if you represent check boxes in any of your wizard images, be sure that these representations also look like checkmarks, not Xs.

Limit the file size and color depth of your graphics

As stated in Chapter 7, "Visual design," graphics for Web-based wizards should be small to allow for fast download times. The size of the graphics becomes even more critical if your users have slow network connections, as is the case for users from some countries.

The file size and color depth of your wizard graphics can also be critical for wizards that are not on the Web. The average user in many countries is likely to have slower computers and less storage space than the average user in the U.S. Be sure that your wizard can be run on slower machines. For more information on decreasing the color depth and file size of your graphics, see Chapter 7, "Visual design."

Choose colors carefully

Colors have different meanings in different cultures. In the United States, the color blue often represents masculinity and yellow represents cowardice. These meanings are not universal.

When possible, use the color-meaning pairs presented in the following list. This set is used for international signs and symbols.

Red	Prohibitory
Blue	Mandatory
Yellow	Hazard, warning
Green	Safety

Colors can also carry more subtle connotations, such as political association. For example, although red, white, and blue are common patriotic colors in the West, they have powerful connotations of the U.S., and may be offensive for that reason to users in other countries. Red by itself symbolized communism in the former USSR and China. This association is fading, but can still carry a powerful local meaning. Red in Canada can mean Liberal (a political party), and blue can mean Conservative. Greenwood (1993) explains how colors may be interpreted across different cultures.

In addition to the differences in symbolism of particular colors in various cultures, preferences for colors may also differ. You may want to design different wizard packaging for your different target audiences. For example, product packaging targeted for a female market tends to use bright colors in North America as opposed to packaging in the Far East, which uses subtle pastel colors to attract female consumers.

Practical concerns

This section discusses some practical issues to be aware of when designing your wizard for worldwide audiences:

- Installation and packaging
- Schedule
- Changes in task structure
- Sending files for translation

Installation and packaging

Localization can greatly increase the size of your wizard. You might need to provide multiple versions of graphics, on-line help files, and on-line manuals. The code files can also become much longer to account for changing text strings on the wizard pages. This increased size can require changes to your installation disks and setup software.

If your wizard is an entire application and all of your code does not fit on a single CD, you might want to create multiple single-language CDs. Another option is to group several languages that will frequently be used by the same target audience. For example, you may want to create a CD that has French and English for sales in Canada, or one CD with Asian languages and another with European languages. You might also consider including English on all CDs in case users do not like your original translations. The same principle applies to Web-based downloads. You probably do not want to create a single huge file that supports all languages, but instead allow users to choose either an individual language or predefined set of languages for downloading.

Schedule

Translation requires additional development time and resources that you need to consider when you create your schedule. You need to decide if you should release all language versions of your wizard simultaneously or if you will stage them. If you want to release your wizard in all languages simultaneously, you will need to finalize your designs earlier to allow for time for translation as well as time for testing the multiple language versions. The translation process also decreases your flexibility in terms of deliverables. You cannot add useful features at the end of the cycle because they will not be documented in the translated files.

For wizards on the Web, you will probably want to stage the releases. You can select a handful of languages to provide in the first stage and then use statistics about users who visit your site to adjust which languages you provide next. For example, you might decide to add a language if you discover that you are getting large numbers of visitors from a country that you didn't expect. You might also decide to add a language if you discover that you are not reaching users in a particular country that you expected to reach with an English version.

Sending files for translation

You can either translate your wizard in-house or send your files to another company or consultant to do the translation. If you have the skills to do the translation, then you do not need to worry about issues such as security and ownership of files. If you need to hire a consultant or company to do the translation, here are some tips:

- **Choose translators who know your product domain as well as the languages they are translating.** Be sure that translators know the correct technical words and acronyms for your wizard.

- **Choose translators who are natives of the target countries**. For example, English in Britain differs from English in the U.S. and French in Canada differs from French in France. Language taught in classes often varies significantly from how people really speak. Furthermore, language continually evolves and changes. You want to be sure that the translated text does not seem outdated and that common words and phrasing are used.

- **Separate the wizard interface from its back-end code as much as possible.** Rather than storing the on-screen text in each language as part of the procedure calls, store the text strings as separate files in a common location. Your wizard code can then swap language files when different language settings are chosen by the user or when the wizard recognizes that the user is from a specific locale. This separate file approach allows translators to do their job without having to access the source code, leading to more efficient translation and fewer security risks.

- **If possible, retain ownership of the translated files.** It is best to own the final files, in case you need to edit them later.

- **Use software to track changes.** You don't want to re-translate entire files each time you change your wizard. Try to keep most of your content and on-screen text the same across versions for consistency.

- **Provide as much information as possible to the translators**. The more information you provide, the more likely that the translators can choose a translation with the same meaning and underlying connotations. If possible, provide a demo copy or actual copy of your wizard so that the translators can see how it functions. Alternatively, provide printouts of each page with a description of the behavior of each control and the results of user selections.

- **Use industry standards for common interface elements.** Many controls in a wizard, such as the **Back** and **Next** buttons, already exist in other software.

- **Provide a glossary to make sure the same terms are used consistently.** This is especially helpful if the interface and supporting materials are translated by different people.

Summary of guidelines discussed in this chapter

❏ Write text that is easily translatable into other languages.

❏ Support different word orders across languages.

❏ Consider allowing the user to select and change the default language for your wizard, especially if the wizard is on the Web or is the complete application.

❏ Ensure that your first wizard page is well-translated.

❏ If you cannot translate your wizard into all local languages, provide links to another language version, especially if the wizard is on the Web or is the complete application.

❏ Leave room on the wizard pages for expansion.

❏ If all else fails, provide scroll bars and resizable panes to allow users to access localized text and controls that do not fit on the wizard screen.

❏ Rather than write your own code to translate data formats, take advantage of the operating system's resource base to account for local differences in data formats.

❏ Account for regional differences in names and other words.

❏ Use unambiguous controls for date and time formats.

❏ Support flexible formatting for numbers, monetary formats, and currency symbols.

❏ Ensure your wizard accounts for differences in other, miscellaneous data.

❏ If the user changes the language setting, do *not* re-interpret data that's already been entered.

❏ Create graphics that are understandable across cultures.

❏ Use representative populations in your images.

❏ Use checkmarks instead of Xs in check boxes.

❏ Limit the file size of your graphics.

❏ Choose colors carefully.

Chapter 15

Multiple platforms

▲ Why design for multiple platforms?

▲ Questions to ask before beginning

▲ Visual and interface design—Product consistency versus platform consistency

▲ Appearance and behavior differences across platforms

▲ Text across platforms

▲ Summary of guidelines discussed in this chapter

One of the largest challenges to constructing wizards, help systems, and software is platform portability. A product is portable if it can function on more than one platform or in more than one operating environment without being built uniquely for each target platform or environment. If this is a requirement for your wizard, you must approach your wizard design and architecture with platform portability in mind.

Your overall goals should be directed at producing a product whose wizards and help system function at the same level of performance and usability in every target scenario. You will need to find ways to develop your product within the parameters of the least common denominators of each target platform. For example, most platforms support Java, so you might decide to build your wizard with Java to avoid dependencies on the operating system. However, remember that even multi-platform languages like Java will not function exactly the same on each platform.

Consider the following examples of common cross-platform concerns:

- On Windows platforms, product help is often installed in the location of the product, while help documents on UNIX platforms tend to be installed into a central location for all products. Such a difference may affect how your documents use file path information to link to one another.

- Some user environments, like those for x-ray viewing in radiological medicine, use UNIX systems with black-and-white displays to save on equipment costs. Your user interface may depend heavily on color differences instead of contrast to show state changes. Although your design may be technically supported on the target platform, it would fail in this user environment.

- Not all Web browsers are alike. If you plan to create a browser or Web-based wizard as a cross-platform solution, you may need to account for differences in how individual Web browsers function. Also, you will need to ensure that your supported Web browser is available on your target platforms. Internet Explorer and Netscape both contain interface features not supported by one another and implement JavaScript and Java applet security differently. Internet Explorer is not natively available on many UNIX and Linux platforms. Additionally, users may use several different versions of the same Web browser, and there are fundamental differences between versions that you will need to account for.

This chapter will guide you through some of the portability issues you should expect to encounter and provide some examples of how to approach your solutions.

Why design for multiple platforms?

The need to keep a competitive edge in today's industry often forces users to work on several platforms at any one site or operate in completely different environments to perform day-to-day operations. Some users may even have a need for software portable enough to be functional on multiple platforms simultaneously.

A cross-platform solution provides the primary advantage of saving your team resources. Specifically:

- **You design your wizard one time.** Before cross-platform solutions, software had to be designed separately for each target platform and built separately on the target platform.

- **Cross-platform solutions allow you to release your product on multiple platforms simultaneously.** Because of the amount of work and resources required to design and build several versions of a product to support several target platform, releases often had to be staggered.

- **Designing for multiple platforms makes it easier to add additional platforms later.** You might discover a need to port your code or support additional platforms late in your release cycle. If your design and architecture are flexible, supporting additional platforms may be a relatively painless task. You will need to add resources to your testing efforts, but the rest of the project could be unaffected by the addition of several platform requirements.

Questions to ask before beginning

Before you can begin to design for cross-platform portability, you need to understand your users' typical working environment so that you can avoid wasting resources optimizing for rare or insignificant user scenarios. Remember that being all things to all users is an impractical goal, and you will have to focus your efforts on what the majority of your users will use. The user analysis in Chapter 2, "Gathering requirements," should provide the answer to the following question:

- **Does your target audience use Macintosh, UNIX, Microsoft Windows, or another operating system?** Wherever possible, you should focus designs and architecture to work on the most likely platform and adapt for secondary platforms accordingly. Users of different operating systems expect software to behave in different ways. You need to know user expectations so that you can match them in your wizard design.

If your team is not aware of the functional and design differences of the target platforms, you will need to conduct a detailed technical analysis. Despite your best efforts, it is unlikely that every functional or visual feature of your wizard will perform exactly the same on all target platforms. You need to identify your technical requirements and how they are limited on each platform. You need this information to develop solutions or alternative designs to account for the differences or decide which functions not to support.

Visual and interface design—Product consistency versus platform consistency

Many different technologies are available to help you port your wizard from platform to platform. The technical requirements and features of your wizard will help you identify which technology you should exploit. If your wizard is part of a larger product, your developers may favor Java as their cross-platform solution. If your team is using Java or any other off-the-shelf solution, you will have to decide whether the interface design requirements will be met with the interface features provided with the solution or if you will need to build unique design elements. This section explains four options to consider and their advantages and disadvantages with regard to usability and resource requirements.

Option 1: Build a unique design

A purely unique look and feel will work very well on many target platforms. The advantage of a unique design is that it will clearly indicate a distinct functional environment from the target platform, and you have the freedom to develop your own interface paradigms and schemes that your user will identify with your product.

The disadvantage of this approach is that it requires significant resources to implement. Your developers must build an interface API, and your interface designers must research the target platforms to ensure that your design elements do not resemble specific elements on the target platforms that function differently. Failure to do this research may result in usability issues because your users may misinterpret your design intentions.

Option 2: Use the features provided by an off-the-shelf solution

Following the conventions of an off-the-shelf solution provides several advantages. Most off-the-shelf solutions have an established and familiar look and feel distinct from existing platforms. They allow plenty of room for product distinction and branding, yet rarely introduce widgets or controls that users will not intuitively understand. Off-the-shelf solutions come packaged with existing interface APIs so they are less work for your programmers to implement. This also makes it simple to establish a common look and feel across several wizards or products. For example, applications built with Java tend to look similar to users and have familiar interactive functions due to users' experiences with other Java applications.

The disadvantage that you may find with implementing the conventions of a common off-the-shelf solution like Java is that it may be unable to meet all of your interface goals. Although you can deviate from the convention, it should be done carefully because users who recognize the look and feel of the off-the-shelf solution will have expectations of your interface that you may no longer fulfill. Also, off-the-shelf solutions may have additional technical requirements, such as plug-ins for a Web browser, more system resources, installation prerequisites, or changes in system settings.

Option 3: Emulate an existing platform design

Emulating an existing design is a big advantage because it allows an audience of users to work with a familiar environment or platform. There is little visual design work necessary because you are just implementing existing design conventions, not inventing new ones. Usability is less of a concern for the interface because you don't need to educate the user on how to use unfamiliar features.

One disadvantage to emulating existing platform designs is that various functions may differ between the model design and the functional goals of the copy you develop. Also, you need to find ways of accounting for the platform differences that may confuse users. Similar command names can have very different functions. Some functional concepts that exist in the model may not apply to the copy, or vice versa. For example, the security model for an AppleTalk LAN environment is slightly different than that of a Windows NT Server LAN environment. However, those differences affect the level of read, write, and delete access of shared files. Administrators can very easily give AppleTalk users more file access rights than they intended. Consider your audience requirements carefully before pursuing this option because building solutions to account for such differences can take a lot of resources.

Option 4: Work with a Web browser

To achieve portability with a wizard or help system, your team may decide to use a Web browser to render the interface. This option provides several advantages you should consider.

Simple Web interfaces tend to be easy to construct and therefore easy to modify when changes are required. If you are mixing technologies such as custom plug-ins, XML, Java applets, or Dynamic HTML, many inexpensive resources are available to help you integrate them to produce the illusion of one seamless interface for your audience. This approach also allows your wizard or help system to be delivered via a Web server, which will allow your users to access it on various platforms and environments regardless of the client platform.

The major disadvantage of this approach is that your users will expect a help system that looks like a Web page to function like one. They may want to bookmark pages, print pages, use the **Forward** and **Back** buttons, open pages in multiple windows, and exploit other standard browser features. You should expect your users to attempt to use every familiar feature available and account for it.

A common pitfall is maintaining the state in your wizard or help system. The browser's **Back** button can severely disrupt navigation, or it can refresh the page, which resets the state. The **Reload** button may break or stall the application. In such cases, you need to develop a means of disabling disruptive browser function, or you can distinguish your application as a self-contained entity within the browser, which discourages users from breaking your application by using external features. Figure 15–1 shows a self-con-

Figure 15–1 *A self-contained entity within a browser. The Adobe PDF plug-in in the right frame is distinct from the rest of the Web page with its own borders and controls.*

tained entity within a browser. Be aware that users might not appreciate some browser features being disabled. To improve usability, you should consider providing those features for your users in a way that works with your wizard or help system.

Appearance and behavior differences across platforms

The appearance of your wizard can be different across platforms. Figure 15–2 illustrates the differences between a Windows platform and a UNIX platform even though both are built with Java.

The only way to avoid platform conflicts with functionality is to make no assumptions that any features will work natively as designed on foreign platforms. Test as many aspects of your software on the target platforms as possi-

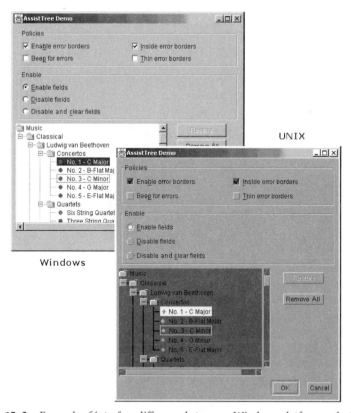

Figure 15–2   *Example of interface difference between a Windows platform and a UNIX platform.*

ble. The sooner you detect a bug, the more likely you will have the resources to repair it or document the bug in your help. This section explains three areas where common problems occur when designing interactive functions:

- Platform and environment nuances
- JavaScript in different browsers and browser versions

Platform and environment nuances

Platforms and user environments have many different methodologies for achieving similar functions or features. As you are building your cross-platform solution, you should identify which differences will affect the function of your product or wizard. Ask the following questions:

- **Do the target platforms detect window position, focus, state, and so on in the same way, and do they allow you the same level of control over them?** For example, some UNIX systems don't allow the ability to detect if the window in focus has no other windows in front of it, while Windows systems tend to put the window in focus in front automatically.

- **Are the file system security models different?** File sharing access rights for the same privilege level allow different abilities on the Macintosh platform than on the Windows platform.

- **Are there differences in how your product or components must be installed on target platforms?** UNIX systems tend to install documentation in one central location, while Windows and Macintosh platforms install documentation in the same directory with the application.

- **Do the target platforms traverse directory structures differently?** UNIX platforms specify the path with a slash, not a backslash like Windows platforms. Interfaces can also vary in appearance.

JavaScript in different browsers and browser versions

If your wizard will be rendered in a Web browser, ask the following questions:

- **Do the enabled/disabled form tag attributes work on target browsers?** In some versions of Netscape, the disable attribute of the form tag is not supported.

- **Are references to X, Y positioning specified with the same commands and units?** With Dynamic HTML, Netscape assumes all units are in pixels, while Internet Explorer places a "px" after numerical units to indicate pixels.

- **Do the conditions that invoke automatic text-wrapping match?** Internet Explorer and Netscape render text of the same font and size with different visual spacing.

- **Are visual effects established through overlapping transparent or semi-transparent images and layers consistent?** Bugs and features in browsers may cause unpredictable variations in color when overlapping transparent GIFs.

- **Do all target browsers support the same image formats and render them the same way?** Not all versions of Internet Explorer and Netscape support PNG file formats.

- **Are different browsers launched the same way on different platforms?** Different platforms may have several methods to launch the default browser; a common system call may not be possible.

- **Are security models in each browser different?** Different versions of Web browsers may be shipped with the same version of Java, and things like "invalid parameter exceptions" require additional class path information to be specified or the use of security certificates to allow proper function.

Text across platforms

The text on wizard pages and help dialogs should use names of components and references to concepts that match the platform of the user.

Follow these guidelines for text for multiple-platform wizards:

- **Use universal references to interface widgets whenever possible.** If there is a universal label for a control on your interface, use it consistently. Users in task failure will not be helped by wizard or help text that refers to controls by names that are unknown to users. For example, do not refer to "check boxes" as "boxes," "selection boxes," "x boxes," or "option boxes."

- **Use consistent action verbs.** Choose the most commonly used verb for each user action and use it consistently. If an action is defined as "clicking," do not use it interchangeably with "selecting," "pressing," "activating," or "engaging." However, be careful to avoid violating conventions unique to a platform or coding language.

- **When possible, customize your help text to the platform on which the product will be run.** If you have the time and resources, make the language and presentation of your help system match each target platform.

311

This can be a maintenance nightmare, but it will affect your users' perception of the quality of your documentation. Although using generalized language is efficient, it limits the detail you can provide and the terminology you can use.

For example, consider these references to commands:

- **Vague reference to an unnamed command:**

  "Bring up the list of files in the directory…"

  This is unspecific and so applies to a similar function that may be found on many platforms.

- **Windows/DOS equivalent command:**

  "Use the dir command…"

  This is direct and clearly indicates what do on the Windows platform.

- **UNIX/Linux equivalent command:**

  "Use the ls –l command…"

  This is direct and clearly indicates what do on the UNIX platform.

Summary of guidelines discussed in this chapter

❏ Test as many aspects of your software on the target platforms as possible. Make no assumptions that any feature will work natively as designed on foreign platforms.

❏ Identify platform differences that affect your product or wizard. For example, be aware of directory structure differences, window focus and position differences, and file system security model differences.

❏ Identify possible browser type and version differences if you plan to render your wizard in a Web browser.

❏ Ensure that the text on your wizard pages and help dialogs uses component names and concept references that match the platform of the user.

Chapter 16

Case study: Installation wizard

▲ Gathering requirements
▲ Design considerations
▲ Iterative design and evaluation

T his case study describes the design and evaluation of an installation wizard for a fictional database product. The installation wizard is for a new version of an existing database product and has the following new design challenges:

- A number of new components are being integrated into the product. Is the previous method of displaying and selecting components still acceptable or does a new method need to be designed? How will the many components be organized?

- A requirement exists to provide installation prerequisites and product information to the user prior to installation.

- Because many new components are being integrated into the database product, users want the installation wizard to be able to create objects or set parameters for some of the components. This would ensure the components were ready to use, or "up and running" once installation was complete.

This chapter follows the design of this fictional installation wizard from the gathering of requirements through iterative design and evaluation. It is organized into three major sections, which follow the chapters of this book:

- **Gathering requirements**. Addresses questions from Chapter 2, "Gathering requirements," that are relevant to this wizard.

- **Design considerations**. Discusses relevant design guidelines from the following chapters:
  - Chapter 5, "General wizard design"
  - Chapter 6, "Navigation"
  - Chapter 8, "Launchpads and linking wizards"
  - Chapter 9, "Interactive feedback"
  - Chapter 10, "Error prevention and recovery"
  - Chapter 11, "On-line help"
  - Chapter 14, "Worldwide audiences"

- **Iterative design and evaluation**. Presents each page in the database installation wizard along with a description of its purpose. In addition, the relevant iterative design and testing guidelines from Chapter 3, "Applying the iterative design process," are discussed as well as issues from Chapter 4, "Evaluating wizard designs."

Gathering requirements

Before designing the installation wizard, the wizard team must answer the most relevant questions from Chapter 2, "Gathering requirements." These questions and the case study answers are listed in the tables in this section. The answers are used to help design the installation wizard.

User definition

The answers to the questions regarding the users' experience are obtained via a focus session of 10 database administrators and system programmers. Some have experience installing database products and some do not. All have some type of experience installing a complex product. Table 16–1 lists the pertinent user characteristics for the database installation wizard.

Table 16–1   Questions to ask about your target audience's experience

Characteristics	Related questions and answers
Job title and job description	**What are your target audience's job titles? What are their job descriptions?** • Job titles are database administrators and system programmers.
Experience with the tasks that your wizard will support	**How well does the target audience understand the task domain that is supported by your software?** • They understand the fundamentals of databases; they may develop and maintain databases. • They have experience installing a complex product. • They can be experts and novices because the wizard should support both types of users.
Experience with previous releases of your product	**How familiar is your target audience with previous releases of your product?** • Some users have previous experience with the product and some do not. For users with previous experience, the wizard should employ similar mnemonics and navigation to avoid frustrating them.
Experience with other software that supports the task	**Does your target audience have experience with products created by your competitors?** • Some users have experience installing competitive products so the team must ensure that wizard actions map to concepts from the competitive product.
Experience with specific operating systems	**Does your target audience use Macintosh, UNIX, Windows NT, or another operating system?** • The target users have experience with all platforms (except Macintosh), so the wizard should match user expectations with these platforms.

Product definition

Before designing the installation wizard, the team gathers the answers to the questions regarding the purpose and scope of the wizard and the tools used to create the wizard. Much of this information is gathered during usability evaluations of the previous release of the database product.

The purpose and scope of the wizard

Table 16–2 provides the answers to questions that help define the purpose and scope of the installation wizard.

Table 16–2   The purpose and scope of the installation wizard

Characteristics	Related questions and answers
Application purpose	**What is the application used for? How does the application work?** • The installation wizard will install the database product. • The wizard will create some initial database objects so the user is "up and running" once installation is complete. • The wizard will also set some defaults and do limited configuration of the database.
Wizard's role	**What is the role of the wizard? Is the wizard the entire application or is it simply part of an application? Are there other ways for users to complete the tasks supported by the wizard?** • The wizard is part of an overall database application. • There are command-line methods to install the product in addition to the wizard method.
Software version	**Is the software a new product or is it a new version of an existing product?** • The wizard is a new version of an existing product. The new version should be consistent with the current product in terms of look and feel.
Measures of success	**What is the key measure for your design? Time to complete the task? Percentage of tasks completed without errors? User ratings of product look and feel?** • The key measures for the installation wizard are successful task completion, errors, and user ratings of satisfaction.

Table 16–2   The purpose and scope of the installation wizard (continued)

Characteristics	Related questions and answers
Translation plans	**Will the wizard and help be translated into multiple languages?** • The wizard will be translated into multiple languages, so design guidelines for internationalization will be followed.
Software prerequisites	**Will the user need to own other software products to be able to use your wizard?** • The software prerequisites are minimal and include a Web browser to display product information and on-line help.

Technology and tools used to create the final wizard

Table 16–3 provides the answers to questions that help define the technology and tools used to create the installation wizard.

Table 16–3   Questions to ask about the technology and tools used to create your wizard

Characteristics	Related questions and answers
Supported platforms	**Will your product run on Macintosh, Windows NT, UNIX, Linux, or something else?** • The installation wizard will run on Windows platforms and all UNIX platforms such as Linux, Sun, and HP.
Coding language	**What language will it be coded in?** • The installation wizard will be coded in Java because it will run on multiple platforms and Java results in a final product that is sharable across different platforms.

Task analysis

The team performs a task analysis to help understand the overall task and subtasks involved in installing a database product. The goal is to determine the structure of the task and what aspects of the task can be simplified. The team asks the database users who participate in the user analysis focus session to also participate in a second session where they are asked to describe the steps they would expect to perform while installing a database product. They are also asked what aspects of the task could be simplified.

What is the underlying structure of the task?

Table 16–4 provides the answers to questions that help define the structure of the task of installing a database product.

Table 16–4   Questions to ask about the underlying structure of the task

Characteristics	Related questions and answers
Number of required steps	**How many steps are required to complete the entire task?** • The number of required steps will vary as a function of what the user decides to install, but the total number should not exceed 10.
Constancy of steps	**Is the number of steps constant or can additional steps be added based on user entries?** • The number of steps in the installation wizard will vary as a function of what components the user selects to install.
Commit points	**Do the tasks or subtasks have multiple commit points?** • The installation wizard has a number of commit points. They are after the Select Installation Type page, Select Components page, and Summary page.

Are there aspects of the task that can be simplified?

Table 16–5 provides the answers to questions that help define what aspects of the installation task can be simplified.

Table 16–5   Questions to ask to determine if there are aspects of the task that can be simplified

Characteristics	Related questions and rationale
Ability to predict defaults	**Can you predict default entries or values for wizard (task) steps or will user entries be needed to complete the steps?** • Default values can be provided for the Create Database page.
Automation possibilities	**Can aspects of the task be automated?** • A default database will be created.
Errors	**What errors can the users make?** • There are many types of errors users can make, but most are at a page level. These include data entry errors and missing data errors.

Table 16–5   Questions to ask to determine if there are aspects of the task that can be simplified (continued)

Characteristics	Related questions and rationale
Error prevention	**How can the errors be prevented?** • Errors will be prevented by providing smartfields for all entry fields, control-level help for controls and fields, mandatory field indications, and controls that allow users to select choices rather than type them.

Design considerations

The guidelines outlined in the chapters of this book should all be considered when designing a wizard. However, for the purposes of this case study, only those chapters and sections within those chapters that are most relevant to the design of an installation wizard are discussed in this section.

The following sections discuss relevant design considerations, which are organized to correspond with the chapters of this book.

General design

The team discusses the design issues and agrees on the following design specifications:

• Keep the length under 10 pages overall, even for the longest path.

• Provide an audible beep when the user exceeds the length of an entry field.

• Make the tab order between the controls on the wizard pages move from top left to bottom right.

• Use **Back**, **Next, Finish**, and **Cancel** buttons in the button area.

• Because the user can complete the wizard only on the Summary page, hide the **Finish** button until the user reaches that page.

• Disable the **Next** button if there are required fields, and enable it only when these fields are filled in.

• Hide the **Next** button on the last page.

• Hide the **Back** button on the first page.

• Place a graphic on most pages, but not on all of them. Do not show a graphic on the License Agreement and Select Components pages due to space restrictions.

Navigation

At first the team considered designing an installation wizard with both button navigation and table of contents-style navigation. The table of contents would allow users to see the total number of steps in the wizard. However, because installation is a sequential task, the team cannot use the table of contents style of navigation.

Launchpads

Usability evaluation feedback from the previous release of the product showed the need for the user to view product, software, and hardware prerequisites before installation. Users also wanted to view the Read Me file before installing the product. A product tutorial exists, which can also be launched prior to installation. And finally, there is the installation itself. Because these tasks are related, the team decides to develop a launchpad to group the tasks (see Figure 16–1).

The launchpad has these specifications:

- There are five tasks, including an **Exit** button.
- All links launch separate processes. Users can view product prerequisites and release notes in a browser or text format. They can also launch the installation wizard at any time. An **Exit** button is provided to make it clear how to exit the launchpad.
- There are no dependencies between tasks; that is, the tasks can be performed in any order.
- There are no progress cues because there are no dependencies between tasks.
- The launchpad is automatically launched when the user inserts the database CD.
- The launchpad is simple in design and does not teach the users how to perform the tasks. As the user "mouses" over the links on the left, the dynamic text description on the right provides a description of what the user would launch if he or she clicked on the link.

Feedback

Feedback is particularly important to the design of an installation wizard. Feedback is provided in these forms:

- **Progress indicator.** While the wizard is installing files, a progress indicator will let the user know what files are being installed, the names of the files, and how much time is remaining (see Figure 16–14).

- **Billboards.** Because installation is a long-running process, billboards display while the code is being installed. Billboards are marketing messages or product information presented in a series of windows that accompany the installation of the code (see Figure 16–16).

- **Confirmation dialog.** A confirmation stating "The setup is complete" is displayed when the installation completes successfully (see Figure 16–17).

- **Between controls within a wizard page.** Within a wizard page, certain controls will not be enabled until the user enters all mandatory information or unless the user makes a certain choice. For example, in the Select Components page, the Subcomponents button will not be enabled unless the user highlights a component that contains subcomponents (see Figure 16–6).

Error prevention and recovery

Error prevention and recovery are important to the design of the installation wizard because of the complexity of the underlying product and the need for correct input and selections to be made. The team decides on the following error prevention and recovery specifications:

- Implement smartfields to monitor entry field input.

- Use drop-down lists with a finite set of selections wherever possible to avoid typing errors.

- Use defaults wherever possible to allow novice users an easier path through the wizard and to reduce typing errors.

Based on the task analysis, the team identifies all possible error points. Two major error points are the existence of a previous release of a product and the lack of mandatory prerequisites. The team designs two warning dialogs to inform users of these error situations.

The first warning dialog informs the user of the lack of mandatory prerequisites. In this case, installation cannot continue without these prerequisites, so the user is not given the choice to continue with the task. Figure 16–2 shows the prerequisites warning message.

The second warning dialog informs the user of the presence of a previous release and gives the user the choice of continuing with the installation and removing the previous release or exiting the installation process. Figure 16–10 shows the warning dialog.

On-line help

One type of help information is chosen for the installation wizard: control-level help. Control-level help allows users quick access to help for a particular control on a wizard page. The team decides to implement the help as pop-up help because all fields and controls can be explained easily in less than 560 characters. Figure 16–5 provides an example of control-level help for the installation wizard.

Worldwide audiences

Because the installation wizard will be translated into several languages, the team tries to implement the following worldwide audience guidelines:

- Use simple language and sentence structure.

- Keep on-screen labels and textual descriptions short.

- Avoid using puns and idioms. These do not translate well and may not even be understood by translators.

- Allow users to select the language they prefer both for the installation and for the language in which the product is being installed. Due to strict development schedules, the team decides to allow the users to select a language, but it must be the same language for both the installation wizard and the product that is installed. See Figure 16–4.

For page layout, the team allows 30% expansion on each wizard page. To allow for graceful expansion, the team leaves extra space within control labels and text boxes so that the text can grow without requiring the dialog to resize. Specifically, the team:

- Places labels above, rather than to the left of, their associated text entry fields.

- Uses short labels for controls.

- Leaves extra lines at the bottom of all text boxes as well as groups of radio buttons and check boxes.

- Is careful not to size the controls to the exact length of the English phrases. They make the actual sizing of the control label or caption longer than the text that appears on-screen.

Finally, translation requires additional development time and resources. The team schedules the design of the installation wizard to be finalized earlier to allow for time for translation as well as time for testing the multiple language versions.

Iterative design and evaluation

Because the installation wizard is a new release of an existing wizard, the team starts the iterative design process with Visual Basic prototypes of the previous version. The team adds new pages to meet the requirements of the new release. Design explorations are first conducted with five database administrators (DBAs). Measures for all evaluations include errors, ratings of satisfaction with the overall wizard's ease of use, and user comments. The team summarizes the results and updates the Visual Basic prototype.

The second usability evaluation is conducted on the updated Visual Basic prototype. Five different DBAs participate in the evaluation. The team summarizes the results, updates the prototype, and begins coding.

When the code is stable enough to evaluate, four DBAs participate in a design validation to ensure that the final product is usable. No new usability problems surface.

Finally, a competitive benchmark is conducted against the closest competitor. Four DBAs participate in the benchmark, and results show the two products to be comparable. Task completion times are also collected, and this measure is comparable for both products.

The following sections discuss the pages and dialogs of the installation wizard. Each section also discusses the usability design issues that arose during the iterative design and evaluation process.

Launchpad: Welcome

Usability evaluation feedback from the previous release of the product showed the need for the user to view product, software, and hardware prerequisites before installing. Users also wanted to view information that is typically found in Read Me files prior to installing. Because these were related tasks, a launchpad was developed to group them together.

Users can view product prerequisites and Read Me files in a browser or text format, and can launch the installation wizard when they want. An **Exit** button makes it clear how to exit the launchpad.

The launchpad is simple in design; the launchpad automatically displays when the user inserts the CD. The text description on the right updates dynamically as the user "mouses" over the links on the left. When the user clicks any button on the left, a separate window or process is launched.

The team performs several iterations of design explorations and evaluations to determine the order and naming of buttons. Ratings of user satisfaction with the launchpad are high. Figure 16–1 shows an example of an installation launchpad.

Figure 16–1   *Installation launchpad.*

Message 1: Missing prerequisites

During a second round of design explorations, several test participants request some type of warning when mandatory prerequisites are missing. The prerequisites are essential to the installation of the database product; in fact, installation cannot continue without them. Users also want to be notified of these prerequisites as early as possible in the installation process.

Figure 16–2 shows the Installation Prerequisites required message, which informs the users of the missing features and allows them to exit the installation

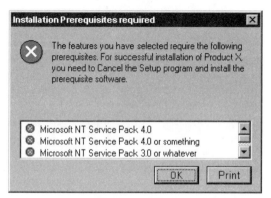

Figure 16–2   *Installation Prerequisites required message in the installation wizard.*

This message tests very well in usability testing. The **Print** button is added in response to user comments from later design evaluations.

Software License Agreement

The second window in the installation sequence is the Software License Agreement window.

Because this is an industry-standard window, the only issue to surface in usability testing is which button is the default when the user presses Enter. During the first round of design explorations, the default is **Decline**. However, because users ordinarily do not read license agreements and automatically press Enter, all are greeted with the "Do you really want to exit installation" pop-up message. This is found to be annoying, so the team changes the default to **Accept**.

When asked if they would rather have the license agreement as part of the installation flow or in hardcopy form, most users state they would rather have it as part of the installation process. Figure 16–3 shows the Software License Agreement window.

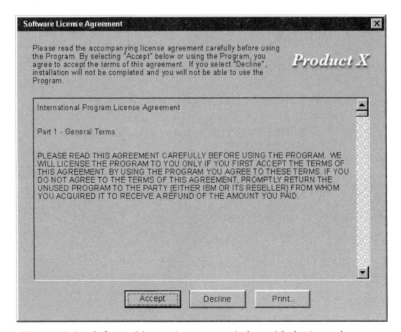

Figure 16–3 *Software License Agreement window with the Accept button as the default.*

Select Installation Language

This window allows users to select the language they would like the product to be installed in. The user clicks on the drop-down list box and chooses from among several languages.

There are no usability issues with this window. Figure 16–4 shows an example of a Select Installation Language window.

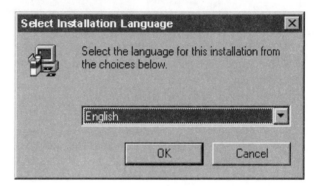

Figure 16–4 *Select Installation Language window.*

Page 1: Select Installation Type

The Select Installation Type page allows users to select a typical, compact, or custom installation.

Because this is also a common page in most installation wizards, the only issue to surface in usability evaluations is what label to provide for the typical installation. Should this be called a "Full" or "Typical" installation? Tied to this issue is the question of what components would be selected in a "Typical" installation. Should a "Typical" installation include all components or only enough to take advantage of most of the common features? Usability testing results are mixed, so the team decides to use the same terminology and meaning as in the previous release of the product, which was "Typical," and would include the most common features.

This page is also a processing point in the wizard. If the user chooses **Typical** or **Compact**, he or she is then presented with the Destination Directory page. If he/she chooses **Custom**, the Select Components page appears.

Figure 16–5 shows an example of a Select Installation Type page.

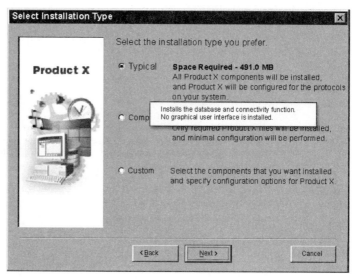

Figure 16–5 Select Installation Type page.

Page 2: Select Components

The Select Components page allows users to select the groups of components they want to install. Each component group consists of a number of subcomponents. Figure 16–6 shows an example of the Select Components page used in the previous release.

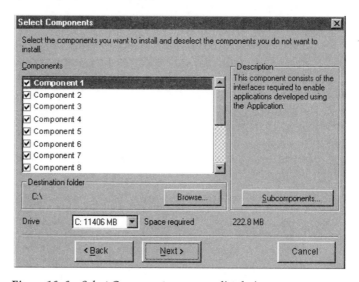

Figure 16–6 Select Components page, one-list design.

329

Users could click on the **Subcomponents** button, which displays the Select Subcomponents page to allow them to view or select the particular subcomponents to install. Figure 16–7 shows an example of the Select Subcomponents window used in the previous release.

The Select Components page and Select Subcomponents window contain the most usability issues of all. Through many design and evaluation iterations, the team resolves the following design issues:

- **What are the component groups and what are the subcomponents contained within each group?** Given the large number of components that could potentially be installed, the team determined the most logical grouping of products and what to call each grouping of components.

- **What should the behavior of the check boxes be?** When the user unchecks a component group check box, all subcomponents are unchecked. When the user checks a component group check box, all subcomponents are checked.

Figure 16–7   Select Subcomponents window.

- **What components should be selected by default?** The components that would be selected in a typical installation are checked by default.

- **Should the destination directory be placed on this page?** Users can select components and determine where to place these components on this page without having to navigate to a different page.

Three designs for selecting components and subcomponents are tested: the "one-list" design, the "two-list" design, and the "tree design."

The one-list design was the design employed in the previous release of the product. This design was in question because of the large number of components being integrated into the product. The team questioned whether there would be too many components to display in a list. Figure 16–6 shows an example of a one-list design.

The two-list design is a new design and allows users to select component groups in the list on the left and simultaneously view and select subcomponents in the list on the right. Figure 16–8 shows an example of this design.

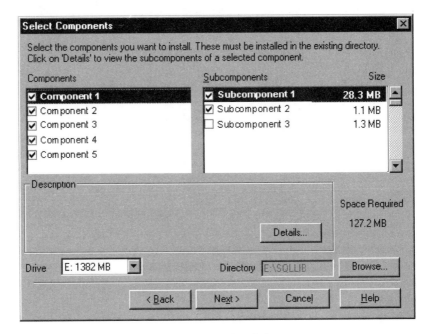

Figure 16–8   *Select Components page, two-list design.*

The tree design is a new design and consists of a tree control with component groupings shown as nodes in the tree. Subcomponents are displayed as "leaves" of the tree when the "twistie" control under a component group is clicked. Figure 16–9 shows an example of a tree design.

Several rounds of usability evaluations show that users prefer the tree design to the other two designs, followed by the two-list design. There are no error differences between designs. Due to resource limitations, however, the team chooses the one-list design because code from the previous release can be used.

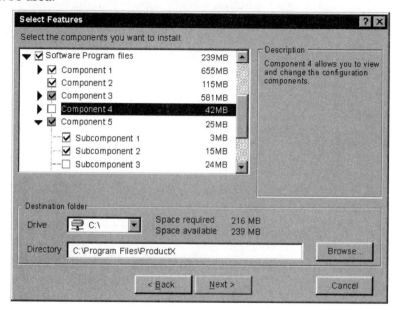

Figure 16–9   *Select Components page, tree design.*

Message 2: Previous version of product detected

This warning message is displayed when the user selects to install the database engine and a previous release of that code exists. The message describes the situation to the user and gives the user a choice of continuing with the installation and deleting the previous release or exiting the installation.

Several iterations of this message are tested to fine-tune the wording and button labels. Early designs contain a **Cancel** button, which surprises users by closing the warning message and exiting the installation process rather than simply closing the message dialog.

Figure 16–10 shows an example of a message indicating the presence of a previous version. The **OK** button closes the message. The **Cancel** button is on the wizard page.

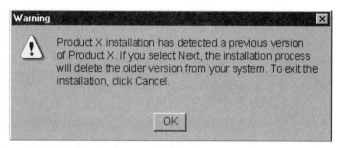

Figure 16–10 *Example of warning dialog for previous product detected.*

Page 3: Choose Destination Location

This page is presented to the users if they select a "Compact" or "Typical" installation in the Select Installation Type page. Figure 16–11 shows an example of the Choose Destination Location page.

There are no usability issues with this page.

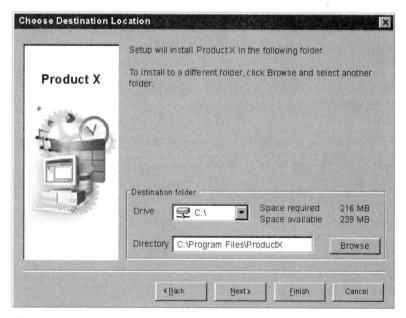

Figure 16–11 *Choose Destination Location page.*

Page 4: "Up and running"

This page allows users to create a default database so they are "up and running" once installation is complete.

During design evaluations, users react very favorably to the concept of "up and running" during a database installation.

Figure 16–12 shows an example of an "up and running" page called "Define a Local Control Database."

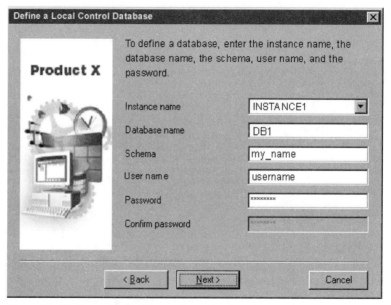

Figure 16–12 Example of an "up and running" page.

Page 5: Summary

This page provides a summary of all user selections and is presented as the final page before the actual installation takes place. The summary is presented in a read-only scrolling list box.

For the new version of the product, a **Create Response File** button is added which saves the user input for this installation for use in other installations. Usability evaluations show the name of this button to be unclear. When the team explains to the users what the button does, the users are happy with the function it performs. Users suggest other button labels, such as "Save responses for other installations…" However, this suggested label is too long for translation, so the original button label is retained. The team must rely on control-level help to provide users with a definition of this label.

In response to additional user testing, the team makes the response file readable.

Figure 16–13 shows an example of the Summary page.

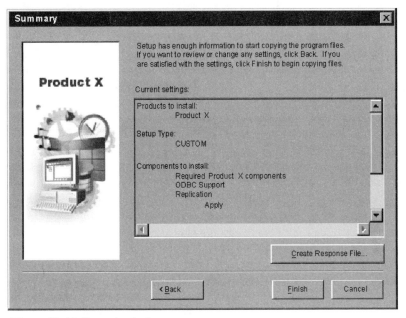

Figure 16–13 Example of a Summary page.

Progress indicator: Installing products

This window provides information about the installation of the database product: the steps of the installation, what files are being installed, and the percentage of installation complete. This window is new for this version. Figure 16–14 shows an example of an installation feedback window.

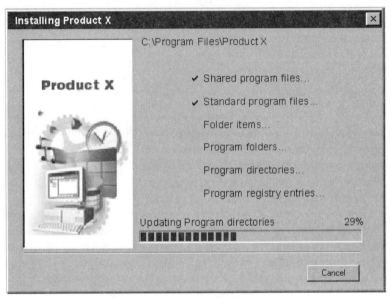

Figure 16–14 Example of an installation feedback window..

Users are presented with this window and with the installation feedback message used in the previous release (see Figure 16–15). Users unanimously favor this new installation feedback window because of the added information it provides.

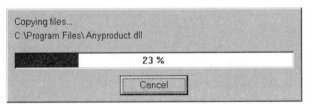

Figure 16–15 Example of the feedback message used in the previous release.

Billboards

Installation billboards are presented during the installation of the product to display marketing messages, "what's new" information, and product features. This type of information is generally presented when there is a long-running process. There are no usability issues with these billboards. Figure 16–16 shows an example of one billboard.

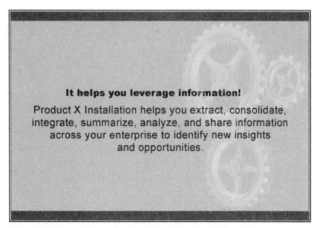

Figure 16–16 *Example of an installation billboard.*

Confirmation window: Setup Complete

This window is displayed when the installation of the database product is complete. It gives users the choice of restarting their computer now or at a later time. There are no usability issues with this window. Figure 16–17 shows an example of a confirmation window.

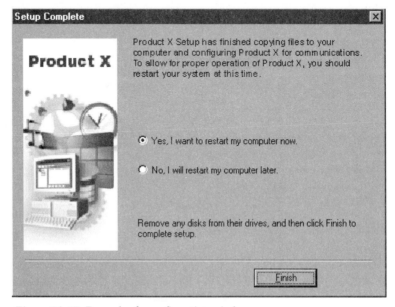

Figure 16–17 *Example of a confirmation window.*

Appendix A

Worksheet for gathering requirements

Tables A-1 through A-5 provide worksheets you can use to collect answers to questions that help define your users, your product, your users' tasks, your users' work environment, and what your competitors are doing. For more information see Chapter 2, "Gathering requirements."

Table A–1   User definition

Characteristics	Related questions	Answer
Age range	Will the product be used by children, adults, or both? Are elderly adults a target audience?	
Gender	Will the product be used by women, men, or both? What proportion of the target audience are women?	
Special needs/ disabilities	Does the target audience include users with mental, visual, auditory, or other physical or cognitive disabilities?	
Educational level	Has the target audience completed college, high school, a specific professional degree? What is its reading level?	

Table A–1   User definition (continued)

Characteristics	Related questions	Answer
Job title and job description	What are your target audience's job titles? What are their job descriptions?	
Experience with computers	How much experience does your audience have with computers in general?	
Experience with the Internet	How much experience does your audience have with the Internet in general? What browsers do they use? What types of Internet applications or Web sites are they familiar with?	
Experience with the tasks that your wizard will support	How well does the target audience understand the task domain that is supported by your software?	
Experience with previous releases of your product	How familiar is your target audience with previous releases of your product?	
Experience with other software that supports the task	Does your target audience have experience with products created by your competitors? How much experience? Is there a particular product that most of your target audience is familiar with?	
Experience with other software products	Does your target audience have experience with specific software products such as Lotus Notes or Microsoft Word?	
Experience with specific operating systems	Does your target audience use Macintosh, UNIX, Microsoft Windows, or another operating system?	
Ethnicity	What ethnic groups does your target audience belong to?	
Languages spoken	Does your target audience speak English? What language is their primary language? Do they speak multiple languages?	
Geographic location (United States, New York State, Italy, and so on)	Are most of your users from the United States? What countries or regions are they from?	

Table A–2   Product definition

Characteristics	Related questions	Answer
Application purpose	What is the application used for? How does the application work?	
Wizard's role	What is the role of the wizard? Is the wizard the entire application, or is it simply part of an application? Are there other ways for users to complete the tasks supported by the wizard?	
Software version	Is the wizard a new product, or is it a new version of an existing wizard or product?	
Integration with other products	Will the wizard integrate with other products or wizards? For example, if your wizard is an airline reservation wizard, will it integrate with a hotel reservation or car rental wizard?	
Tone	What is the tone that you want your wizard to demonstrate or communicate?	
Measures of success	How will you measure the success of your wizard design? Time to complete the task? Percentage of tasks completed without errors? User ratings of product look and feel?	
User tasks supported by the application	What tasks does the user use the application for?	
Prerequisite knowledge	What will the user need to know to use the wizard? What prerequisite knowledge does the target audience need in terms of computers, the task domain, and your software product? Can your wizard provide that information? If so, how?	
Translation plans	Will the wizard and help be translated into multiple languages?	
Software prerequisites	Will the user need to own other software products to be able to use your wizard? For example, if the wizard is on the Web, will a certain level browser be required?	
Structural and architectural issues	What structural or architectural issues may impact the wizard design?	
Supported platforms	Will your product run on Windows NT, UNIX, Linux, or something else?	
Coding language	What language will it be coded in?	

Table A–3   Task characteristics

Characteristics	Related questions	Answer
User tasks	What tasks do the users complete as part of their job? What do they consider the end-to-end set of tasks?	
Supported tasks	What tasks will the wizard support?	
Number of required steps	How many steps are required to complete the entire task?	
Groupings of steps	Do the steps fall into natural groupings (subtasks)?	
Constancy of steps	Is the number of steps constant or can additional steps be added based on user entries?	
Commit points	Do the tasks have multiple commit points?	
Detailed user actions	How do users complete the tasks? What are the detailed actions that users take to complete the tasks? What information do users need to complete the tasks? In what order do users need this information? For example, if the users need to input measurements, what units do they use—inches, feet, meters, or others?	
Constancy of step order	Is the order of the steps static, or might it depend on user entries?	
Dependencies among subtasks	Must the user perform several steps in a sequential order? Can steps be repeated before proceeding to the next step?	
Target users for each subtask	Does the same target user complete all of the subtasks?	
Task frequency	How frequently do users complete the task? Do the users complete the task only a single time, daily, weekly, or other?	
Task importance	How important is the task? Do the users consider the task critical? Is it optional?	
Task difficulty	Do users feel that the task is difficult or easy? If the task is difficult, can it be made significantly easier in a wizard? Are other interventions, such as a product re-architecture or tutorial, needed?	

Table A–3   Task characteristics (continued)

Characteristics	Related questions	Answer
Ability to predict defaults	Can you predict default entries or values for wizard (task) steps, or will user entries be needed to complete the steps?	
Desired defaults	If you can predict default entries, what values will most users want? What percentage of the target audience will agree with these defaults?	
Automation possibilities	Can aspects of the task be automated?	
Errors	What errors might the users make?	
Error prevention	How can the errors be prevented?	

Table A–4   Work environment

Characteristics	Related questions	Answer
General use	Where will the user use the wizard: at home, in the office, other?	
Use during travel	Will users use the wizard while traveling, from hotels, or on the road?	
Ambient light	Will anyone use the wizard outside? Is ambient light an issue?	
Noise	Is noise a concern in the environment where your target audience will use your wizard?	
Hardware	Will the user be using a TV, laptop, computer, palm device, special device (kiosk, car navigation system), or other device to display and interact with your wizard?	
Connection speed	If the wizard is on the Web, what is the lowest speed connection that users can have?	
One-handed use	If the user is accessing the wizard from a portable device, should the design assume one-handed use?	
Assistive technologies	Will the users be using any specialized keyboards, screen readers, or other technologies to access your wizard?	

Table A–4   Work environment (continued)

Characteristics	Related questions	Answer
Monitor size	What monitor (or screen) size can be assumed?	
Display settings	What display settings do most of your target users utilize for resolution and number of colors?	
Computer speed and memory	What computer speed and memory can be assumed?	
Storage space	How much storage space will the users have on their computers?	
Access to software	How will users get the actual software? Do users have CD-ROM drives, diskette drives, or both? Should the wizard be downloadable? What mechanisms will you provide to allow your target audience to get the wizard?	
Training and support	Will the users receive any training or support on your product, the wizard, or both?	
Dedicated computers	Do users share their computers, or does each user have a dedicated machine?	
Interruptability	Will the user be able to devote full attention to the wizard or will he or she be doing other tasks at the same time? How likely is it that the user will be interrupted while completing the wizard?	

Table A–5   Competitive evaluation

Characteristics	Related questions	Answer
Competitor	Who is your competition? What similar products already exist in the marketplace?	
Scope	What is the scope of the competitor's offering? What tasks does your competitor's wizard support? What functions does it provide? What platforms does it support?	
Competitor's strengths	What does your competitor's wizard do well? What are the strengths of your competitor's wizard: ease of use, visual appearance, scalability, speed of completion, integration with other products, or other?	
Competitor's weaknesses	What does your competitor's wizard do poorly? What are the weaknesses of your competitor's wizard: ease of use, visual appearance, scalability, speed of completion, integration with other products, or other?	
Comparison	How do you fare against the competitor?	
Cost	How much does the competitor's product cost?	

Sample design checklist

Table B–1 presents a checklist of usability design considerations we have found useful for designing wizards. Use the following checklist when conducting heuristic evaluations or while designing your wizard interface.

Note that this checklist is just an example. You may want to add your own design considerations or use some of the checklists developed by other authors, for example, *Usability Inspection Methods* by Jakob Nielsen and Robert L. Mack and *Usability Engineering* by Jakob Nielsen.

Table B–1   Checklist of design considerations

Design consideration	Description	Importance
Accessibility features	Implement mnemonics, accelerator keys, and other methods to select within a wizard page.	Accelerator keys and mnemonics are necessary to accommodate expert users or users who are unable to use a mouse.
Defaults	Provide values for entry fields, pre-select a radio button, and provide an initial selection in list boxes.	Providing defaults allows novice users to quickly complete your wizard. For entry fields, defaults also tell the user what type of information is required and what the format of this information will be.

Table B–1   Checklist of design considerations (continued)

Design consideration	Description	Importance
Consistency	Use similar terminology, control placement, and control behavior within your wizard, across your wizards, and between your wizard and your application.	Consistency in an interface helps reduce errors and decreases overall task completion time because the user does not have to relearn new terminology, figure out where controls are, or figure out how they behave from wizard page to wizard page.
Error prevention and recovery	Reduce the chance for users to make errors by providing defaults and controls that allow users to select instead of type. If errors do occur, have your wizard provide immediate feedback telling users what happened and how to correct the error, and provide links to additional sources of help.	Preventing and helping users recover from errors decreases overall task time, increases the likelihood of successful task completion, and increases user satisfaction.
Feedback	Provide validation that the wizard recognizes the user's input. This can be at the wizard page level (for example, highlighting the field the user is interacting with) or when the wizard processes the user's input at the completion of the wizard (for example, by providing status messages and a "successful completion" message).	Users rely on feedback to inform them that the wizard recognized their input and whether their input was correct.
Recognition rather than recall	Provide check boxes, radio buttons, and list boxes when the choices are finite and known. Provide defaults in entry fields.	It is easier to recognize the correct selection than it is to remember it. Providing these types of aids reduces errors, decreases overall task time, and helps ensure successful task completion.
User assistance	Ensure that user assistance is provided. This includes explanatory text on the wizard pages and field and control help.	User assistance helps novice users complete your wizard task. Experts are not always familiar with every aspect of a task and may need some type of user assistance as well.
Simple installation and "out of box" experience (if your wizard is the entire application)	Make installation as simple and quick as possible. Installation should set defaults and create objects so that the wizard is ready to use once installation is complete.	Installation is the first thing a user sees when interacting with a product. A simple installation ensures a positive first impression and the impression that your wizard will be easy to use as well. A simple installation also helps ensure that the wizard or application will be installed successfully.

Appendix C

Sample screener questionnaire

To help Company X design user-friendly products, designers and developers need input from users like you. You can provide input by participating in usability activities such as usability studies, focus group sessions, and Web surveys. If you are interested in participating in future usability activities, please fill out this form and return it to us.

When a usability activity is planned for a product, we will send you a follow-up questionnaire for that product so that we can learn a bit about your experience with the technology. If you meet the criteria, you may be invited to participate in some of these activities. You will get to meet the developers and see and influence what's new in the field. You will also receive an honorarium for participating in these activities.

Company X respects your privacy. In providing information on this form, you are representing yourself as an individual rather than as an employee of your company. Information you provide will be used only to evaluate and obtain participants for such activities; it will not be used to contact you with marketing information or for any other such purpose.

Name:

Home Phone:

Home Address:

Company Name:

Company Location (city and state/province):

Company Web Site:

E-mail:

Work Phone:

Work Address:

Company Industry:

Company Size (check one):

_____ Less than 50 employees

_____ 50-100 employees

_____ 100-1000 employees

_____ More than 1000 employees

Employment Status (check one):

_____ Full time

_____ Contractor/Consultant

_____ Other: _____

Purchasing Decisions (check all that apply):

_____ Evaluation and recommendation of software

_____ Selection and purchase of computer software

_____ Evaluation and recommendation of hardware

_____ Selection and purchase of computer hardware

Job Title (check all that apply):

_____ Database administrator

_____ Data warehouse admin/designer/architect

_____ System programmer

_____ Application programmer/Software developer

_____ Webmaster/Web developer

_____ Server administrator

_____ Business professional

_____ IT professional

_____ Principal/Director/Manager

_____ System operator

_____ Other: _____

Platform Experience (check all that apply):

_____ AIX

_____ BSD

_____ Digital Ultrix

_____ HP-UX

_____ Linux

_____ Mac OS

_____ OS/2

_____ OS/390

_____ OS/400

_____ SGI IRIX

_____ Solaris

_____ UNIX

_____ VMS

_____ Windows 95/98

_____ Windows NT/2000

_____ Other:

_____

Application Development Experience		Programming Language Experience	
Application/Data architect	_____ years	XML	_____ years
Web sites	_____ years	C++	_____ years
Project manager	_____ years	Perl	_____ years
Scripting languages	_____ years	JavaScript	_____ years
Server-side objects (EJB, COM)	_____ years	HTML	_____ years
E-Commerce	_____ years	Java	_____ years
Other (please specify): _____	_____ years	Other (please specify): _____	_____ years

Sample usability participant agreement

Overview

You will be participating in a usability session where you may use Company X's products or prototypes, see demos, and provide feedback on them. We may ask you to answer questions about products you use and tasks you perform in your job. Information from potential users such as you can help us do a better job of developing usable products.

Observers from the development team may be present. We will collect your comments and suggestions. We may also videotape this session to ensure that we capture your comments and suggestions. The information you give us, along with information collected from other participants, will be used to help us evaluate how to make our products more competitive in the market.

In the course of this usability session with Company X, **you agree that you are acting solely as a representative of yourself,** and not your employer or any third party.

Company X Networks

You must not use Company X networks except as explicitly instructed.

License to Information

By signing this form, you hereby irrevocably give your consent to Company X, and to such other persons as Company X may designate, to use your responses, comments, and suggestions for purposes of evaluation and any other lawful purpose. You understand that Company X will not use your identity or any video images that include you for advertising purposes, unless Company X consults with you further and contracts with you separately for that purpose.

Confidentiality Acknowledgement

During this usability session, you may be given information about an unreleased version of a Company X product or other information that is confidential to Company X. By signing this form, you acknowledge that the information you are receiving is Company X Confidential Information. You agree to hold all Company X Confidential Information, including your participation in this usability session, in trust and confidence for Company X and not disclose it in any form to anyone outside of this Company X session. This obligation of confidentiality shall continue for a period of two (2) years from the last date of your participation in this session.

"Company X Confidential Information" shall mean all information disclosed in writing or orally by Company X to you or obtained by you from Company X, that relates to Company X's past, present, or future research, development, or business activities, or that relates to interim work products or deliverables. Company X Confidential Information shall not be deemed to include information that is:

1. publicly available or becomes so in the future without restriction,
2. rightfully received by you from third parties and not accompanied by confidentiality obligations,
3. already in your possession and lawfully received from sources other than Company X,
4. independently developed by you, or
5. approved for release or disclosure without restriction by an authorized Company X representative in writing.

Company X does not wish to receive any information that is confidential or proprietary to you or any third party. Company X shall have no obligation of confidentiality for any information received by you during or in connection with this usability session.

Freedom to Withdraw

Subject to the terms of this agreement, you may withdraw from this study at any time if you do not wish to participate and you may refuse to answer any questions on the questionnaires.

Please acknowledge that you have read and understood this agreement by signing below.

Signature: _____

Date: _____

Name (print): _____

Appendix E

Sample participant instructions

Thank you for participating in the usability evaluation of Wizard X. Feedback from potential users such as you will help us ensure ease of use of the wizard.

You will be performing a number of tasks using a prototype of the wizard user interface. After each task (and sometimes after specific pages), we will ask you some questions about the interface. At the completion of the evaluation, we will ask to you complete a final questionnaire.

Additionally, you will see two wizard designs and we will ask which you prefer after performing tasks with both designs.

We want you to know that we are evaluating our user interface and not your performance. If you have a problem performing a task, we consider that a problem with our user interface, not with your performance.

Because we are interested in what you think of our user interface, we would like you to "talk aloud" as you perform the tasks below. That is, tell us what is going through your head, what you like, what you dislike, and what we could change. Don't worry about hurting our feelings—we want you to be honest!

While you are performing tasks, we will be recording your comments and errors that are made using our product.

Note: Because this is a prototype, not all the functionality will be available.

Sample scenarios for an installation wizard

Your company is interested in Product X and has just purchased the Enterprise Edition for Windows NT, which will allow you to install Product X and other components, such as the sample databases and on-line books.

Your manager has just handed you this package and has asked you to install Product X and the on-line books.

1. Please perform the following tasks:

    - Open up the package and browse the contents.

    - Find the CDs that you will need to install the product and indicate in what order they should be installed. You can use the Information Card to help you with this task.

2.   Please install the product given the following information:

- You want to install the server and client.
- You'd like to install on Drive C.
- You want all components except the documentation.
- The user ID to connect to your server is **new_user,** and the password is **new_password**.
- You want to reboot your computer when finished.

3.   Now that you've installed all the Product X components, create the Component X and Component Y samples only.

Sample post-evaluation questionnaire

1. Overall, how would you rate your satisfaction with the usability of Product X? (Please circle one.)

    1=Very satisfied   **2**=Satisfied   **3**=Neutral   **4**=Dissatisfied   **5**=Very dissatisfied

2. If you used a previous release of Product X, how does the current prototype compare in terms of ease of use? (Please circle one.)

    1=Much easier **2**=Easier **3**=About the same **4**=More difficult **5**=Much more difficult

3. Assume that you are responsible for purchasing a product for your company and the price of Product X is comparable to that of the competition. What is the likelihood that you would purchase Product X? (Please circle one.)

   1= Very Likely   **2**= Likely   **3**= Unsure   **4**=Unlikely   **5**= Very Unlikely

4. What did you like best about Product X?

5. What would you suggest to improve the usability of Product X?

Bibliography

Babbie, Earl. *Survey Research Methods.* Belmont, CA: Wadsworth Publishing Company, 1990.

Beyer, Hugh and Holtzblatt, Karen. *Contextual Design: Defining Customer-Centered Systems.* San Francisco, CA: Morgan Kaufmann Publishers, 1998.

Boggan, Scott, Farkas, David, and Welinske, Joe. *Developing Online Help for Windows 95.* Boston, MA: International Thomson Computer Press, 1996.

Carter, Rob, Day, Ben, and Meggs, Philip. *Typographic Design: Form and Communication.* Second Edition. New York, NY: John Wiley & Sons, Inc., 1993.

Galitz, Wilbert O. *The Essential Guide to User Interface Design: An Introduction to GUI Design Principles and Techniques.* New York, NY: John Wiley & Sons, Inc., 1997.

Gillham, Bill. *Developing a Questionnaire.* New York, NY: Continuum, 2000.

Greenwood, Timothy G. "International Cultural Differences in Software." *Digital Technical Journal*, Vol. 5, no. 3, 1993.

Hackos, JoAnn T. and Redish, Janice C. *User and Task Analysis for Interface Design.* New York, NY: John Wiley & Sons, Inc., 1998.

Hofstede, Geert. *Cultures and Organizations: Software of the Mind.* New York, NY: McGraw-Hill Book Company, 1997.

Horton, William. *Designing and Writing Online Documentation: Help Files to Hypertext.* New York, NY: John Wiley & Sons, Inc., 1994.

Horton, William K. *The Icon Book: Visual Symbols for Computer Systems & Documentation.* New York, NY: John Wiley & Sons, Inc., 1994.

Howlett, Virginia. *Visual Interface Design for Windows: Effective User Interfaces for Win-*

dows 95, Windows NT, and Windows 3.1. New York, NY: John Wiley & Sons, Inc., 1996.

Keppel, Geoffrey and Saufley, William H. Jr. *Introduction to Design and Analysis: A Student's Handbook.* San Francisco, CA: W.H. Freeman and Company, 1980.

Krueger, Richard A. and Casey, Mary Anne. *Focus Groups: A Practical Guide for Applied Research.* Third Edition. Thousand Oaks, CA: Sage Publications, 2000.

McCreight, Tim. *Design Language.* Cape Elizabeth, ME: Brynmorgen Press, Inc., 1996.

Miller, R.B. "Response time in man-computer conversational transactions," *Proceedings of the AFIPS Spring Joint Computer Conference,* (33), 1968, (pp. 267-277).

Nielsen, Jakob. *Designing Web Usability.* Indianapolis, IN: New Riders Publishing, 2000.

Nielsen, Jakob and Mack, Robert L. *Usability Inspection Methods.* New York, NY: John Wiley & Sons, Inc., 1994.

Nielsen, Jakob. *Usability Engineering.* San Diego, CA: Academic Press, 1993.

Norman, Donald A. *The Psychology of Everyday Things.* New York, NY: Basic Books, Inc., 1988.

Nunally, Jum C. *Psychometric Theory.* New York, NY: McGraw-Hill Book Company, 1978.

Oppenheim, Abraham N. *Questionnaire Design, Interviewing and Attitude Measurement.* New York, NY: Pinter Publishers, Ltd., 1992.

Reason, J. *Human error.* Cambridge, England: Cambridge University Press, 1990.

Rockport Staff. *Color Harmony Workbook.* Gloucester, MA: Rockport Publishers, Inc., 1994.

Spool, Jared. *Designing Wizards. Eye For Design.* [Newsletter] Retrieved February 10, 1999 from the World Wide Web: *http://world.std.com/~uieweb/wiz_art.htm,* September/October 1997.

Weinman, Lynda. *Designing Web Graphics.3: How to Prepare Images and Media for the Web.* Third Edition. Indianapolis, IN: New Riders Publishing, 1999.

Index

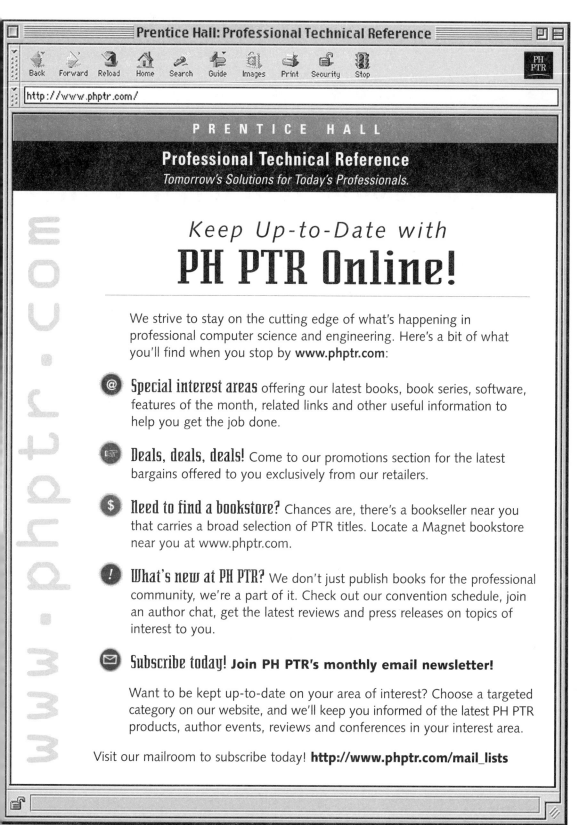

LICENSE AGREEMENT AND LIMITED WARRANTY

READ THE FOLLOWING TERMS AND CONDITIONS CAREFULLY BEFORE OPENING THIS SOFTWARE PACKAGE. THIS LEGAL DOCUMENT IS AN AGREEMENT BETWEEN YOU AND PRENTICE-HALL, INC. (THE "COMPANY"). BY OPENING THIS SEALED SOFTWARE PACKAGE, YOU ARE AGREEING TO BE BOUND BY THESE TERMS AND CONDITIONS. IF YOU DO NOT AGREE WITH THESE TERMS AND CONDITIONS, DO NOT OPEN THE SOFTWARE PACKAGE. PROMPTLY RETURN THE UNOPENED SOFTWARE PACKAGE AND ALL ACCOMPANYING ITEMS TO THE PLACE YOU OBTAINED THEM FOR A FULL REFUND OF ANY SUMS YOU HAVE PAID.

1. **GRANT OF LICENSE:** In consideration of your payment of the license fee, which is part of the price you paid for this product, and your agreement to abide by the terms and conditions of this Agreement, the Company grants to you a nonexclusive right to use and display the copy of the enclosed software program (hereinafter the "software") on a single computer (i.e., with a single CPU) at a single location so long as you comply with the terms of this Agreement. The Company reserves all rights not expressly granted to you under this Agreement.

2. **OWNERSHIP OF SOFTWARE:** You own only the magnetic or physical media (the enclosed software) on which the software is recorded or fixed, but the Company retains all the rights, title, and ownership to the software recorded on the original software copy(ies) and all subsequent copies of the software, regardless of the form or media on which the original or other copies may exist. This license is not a sale of the original software or any copy to you.

3. **COPY RESTRICTIONS:** This software and the accompanying printed materials and user manual (the "Documentation") are the subject of copyright. You may not copy the Documentation or the software, except that you may make a single copy of the software for backup or archival purposes only. You may be held legally responsible for any copying or copyright infringement which is caused or encouraged by your failure to abide by the terms of this restriction.

4. **USE RESTRICTIONS:** You may not network the software or otherwise use it on more than one computer or computer terminal at the same time. You may physically transfer the software from one computer to another provided that the software is used on only one computer at a time. You may not distribute copies of the software or Documentation to others. You may not reverse engineer, disassemble, decompile, modify, adapt, translate, or create derivative works based on the software or the Documentation without the prior written consent of the Company.

5. **TRANSFER RESTRICTIONS:** The enclosed software is licensed only to you and may not be transferred to any one else without the prior written consent of the Company. Any unauthorized transfer of the software shall result in the immediate termination of this Agreement.

6. **TERMINATION:** This license is effective until terminated. This license will terminate automatically without notice from the Company and become null and void if you fail to comply with any provisions or limitations of this license. Upon termination, you shall destroy the Documentation and all copies of the software. All provisions of this Agreement as to warranties, limitation of liability, remedies or damages, and our ownership rights shall survive termination.

7. **MISCELLANEOUS:** This Agreement shall be construed in accordance with the laws of the United States of America and the State of New York and shall benefit the Company, its affiliates, and assignees.

8. **LIMITED WARRANTY AND DISCLAIMER OF WARRANTY:** The Company warrants that the software, when properly used in accordance with the Documentation, will operate in substantial conformity with the description of the software set forth in the Documentation. The Company does not warrant that the software will meet your requirements or that the operation of the software will be uninterrupted or error-free. The Company warrants that the media on which the software is delivered shall be free from defects in materials and workmanship under normal use

for a period of thirty (30) days from the date of your purchase. Your only remedy and the Company's only obligation under these limited warranties is, at the Company's option, return of the warranted item for a refund of any amounts paid by you or replacement of the item. Any replacement of software or media under the warranties shall not extend the original warranty period. The limited warranty set forth above shall not apply to any software which the Company determines in good faith has been subject to misuse, neglect, improper installation, repair, alteration, or damage by you. EXCEPT FOR THE EXPRESSED WARRANTIES SET FORTH ABOVE, THE COMPANY DISCLAIMS ALL WARRANTIES, EXPRESS OR IMPLIED, INCLUDING WITHOUT LIMITATION, THE IMPLIED WARRANTIES OF MERCHANTABILITY AND FITNESS FOR A PARTICULAR PURPOSE. EXCEPT FOR THE EXPRESS WARRANTY SET FORTH ABOVE, THE COMPANY DOES NOT WARRANT, GUARANTEE, OR MAKE ANY REPRESENTATION REGARDING THE USE OR THE RESULTS OF THE USE OF THE SOFTWARE IN TERMS OF ITS CORRECTNESS, ACCURACY, RELIABILITY, CURRENTNESS, OR OTHERWISE.

IN NO EVENT, SHALL THE COMPANY OR ITS EMPLOYEES, AGENTS, SUPPLIERS, OR CONTRACTORS BE LIABLE FOR ANY INCIDENTAL, INDIRECT, SPECIAL, OR CONSEQUENTIAL DAMAGES ARISING OUT OF OR IN CONNECTION WITH THE LICENSE GRANTED UNDER THIS AGREEMENT, OR FOR LOSS OF USE, LOSS OF DATA, LOSS OF INCOME OR PROFIT, OR OTHER LOSSES, SUSTAINED AS A RESULT OF INJURY TO ANY PERSON, OR LOSS OF OR DAMAGE TO PROPERTY, OR CLAIMS OF THIRD PARTIES, EVEN IF THE COMPANY OR AN AUTHORIZED REPRESENTATIVE OF THE COMPANY HAS BEEN ADVISED OF THE POSSIBILITY OF SUCH DAMAGES. IN NO EVENT SHALL LIABILITY OF THE COMPANY FOR DAMAGES WITH RESPECT TO THE SOFTWARE EXCEED THE AMOUNTS ACTUALLY PAID BY YOU, IF ANY, FOR THE SOFTWARE.

SOME JURISDICTIONS DO NOT ALLOW THE LIMITATION OF IMPLIED WARRANTIES OR LIABILITY FOR INCIDENTAL, INDIRECT, SPECIAL, OR CONSEQUENTIAL DAMAGES, SO THE ABOVE LIMITATIONS MAY NOT ALWAYS APPLY. THE WARRANTIES IN THIS AGREEMENT GIVE YOU SPECIFIC LEGAL RIGHTS AND YOU MAY ALSO HAVE OTHER RIGHTS WHICH VARY IN ACCORDANCE WITH LOCAL LAW.

ACKNOWLEDGMENT

YOU ACKNOWLEDGE THAT YOU HAVE READ THIS AGREEMENT, UNDERSTAND IT, AND AGREE TO BE BOUND BY ITS TERMS AND CONDITIONS. YOU ALSO AGREE THAT THIS AGREEMENT IS THE COMPLETE AND EXCLUSIVE STATEMENT OF THE AGREEMENT BETWEEN YOU AND THE COMPANY AND SUPERSEDES ALL PROPOSALS OR PRIOR AGREEMENTS, ORAL, OR WRITTEN, AND ANY OTHER COMMUNICATIONS BETWEEN YOU AND THE COMPANY OR ANY REPRESENTATIVE OF THE COMPANY RELATING TO THE SUBJECT MATTER OF THIS AGREEMENT.

Should you have any questions concerning this Agreement or if you wish to contact the Company for any reason, please contact in writing at the address below.

Robin Short
Prentice Hall PTR
One Lake Street
Upper Saddle River, New Jersey 07458

ABOUT THE CD-ROM

System Requirements

- MS Windows 95/98/NT/2000
- Minimum system—486/60MHz or higher; 64 MB RAM
- Minimum CD-ROM—quad-speed (4X); 600 KB/sec; 450 KB/sec
- Monitor or display settings—minimum 16-bit color (recommended 32-bit color); minimum 800 x 600, (recommended 1024 x 768)
- Disk space: recommended 50 or more megabytes of free hard disk space

Using the CD-ROM

The CD-ROM should launch automatically when you insert it into your CD drive. If it doesn't, start it manually by following these steps: 1. Select Start > Run. 2. In the Run window, type X:\wizbook.exe (where 'X' represents the CD-ROM drive letter). 3. Click OK.

You can navigate through the various features of the CD-ROM from the main window. You can see different navigation options, view the various color palettes in action, see how the different typeface families look on screen, play with various combinations of wizard page layouts, and view the case study pages.

To close the CD-ROM program, you can click the EXIT button in the top right corner of the main window, or you can press the Esc key on your keyboard.

IBM Licensing Information

Licensed Materials—Property of IBM ® Copyright IBM Corp. 2001. All Rights Reserved.

US Government Users Restricted Rights Use. Duplication or disclosure restricted by GSA ADP Schedule Contract with IBM Corp. Licensed Materials—Property of IBM

IBM grants you ("Licensee") a non-exclusive, royalty free, license to use this software in object code form only and only for educational purposes. No title or ownership rights in the software are transferred. You agree not to reverse-compile or disassemble the software. This software is provided as-is and without any warranties, whether express or implied, including any implied warranty of merchantability, fitness for a particular purpose, or non-infringement. IBM and its licensors shall not be liable for any damages suffered by licensee that result from your use of the software. In no event will IBM or its licensors be liable for any lost revenue, profit or data, or for direct, indirect, special, consequential, incidental or punitive damages, however caused and regardless of the theory of liability, arising out of the use of or inability to use software, even if ibm has been advised of the possibility of such damages.

Director ® Copyright 1984-2000 Macromedia Inc.

Prentice Hall PTR Technical Support Statement

Prentice Hall does not offer technical support for any of the programs on the CD-ROM. However, if the CD-ROM is physically damaged, you may obtain a replacement copy by sending an email that describes the problem to: disc_exchange@prenhall.com.

ISBN: 0-13-092377-X

Copyright ® 2002 Prentice Hall PTR, Prentice-Hall, Inc.